THE FATHERS OF THE CHURCH

A NEW TRANSLATION

Founded by
LUDWIG SCHOPP

EDITORIAL BOARD

THE FATHER
OF THE CHUR

A NEW TRANSLATION

VOLUME 15

EARLY CHRISTIAN BIOGRAPHIES

LIVES OF

St. Cyprian, by Pontius; St. Ambrose, by Paulinus; St.
Augustine, by Possidius; St. Anthony, by St. Athanasius;
St. Paul the First Hermit, St. Hilarion, and Malchus, by
St. Jerome; St. Epiphanius, by Ennodius; with a Sermon
on the Life of St. Honoratus, by St. Hilary.

Translated by

Roy J. Deferrari, John A. Lacy, Sister Mary Magdeleine Müller,
O.S.F., Sister Mary Emily Keenan, S.C.N., Sister Marie Liguori
Ewald, I.H.M., and Sister Genevieve Marie Cook, R.S.M.

Edited by

ROY J. DEFERRARI

FATHERS OF THE CHURCH, INC.

BR
1705
.A2
E27
1952

120651

CONTENTS

THE BEGINNINGS OF CHRISTIAN BIOGRAPHY

CHRISTIAN BIOGRAPHY, like most forms of Christian literature, went to the Classical Period of antiquity for its models. On the Latin side, the best from the point of view of modern literary criticism is probably Tacitus' *Life of Agricola,* but even this leaves much to be desired. It resembles the *Lives* of Plutarch in its general plan and in the topics emphasized, showing a weakness for the picturesque and the dramatic and a tendency to moralize. On the Latin side, also, the *Lives* of Suetonius have been popular down the ages to our own time, but they are quite uncritical, seeking to entertain by anecdotes of doubtful authenticity. With such works as models, we probably expect too much when we hold Christian biography up to the strictly scientific interpretation of the term as established by modern literary critics.

Most of the 'Lives' of the early Christian biographers belong to the type of literature known as hagiography,[1] whose primary purpose was religious, specifically, to edify its readers. The beginnings of Christian biography are clearly evident in the 'Acts' of the martyrs. These 'Acts' were compiled

---

1 A document, to be strictly hagiographical, must be of a religious character and have edification as its aim. The term in its general sense refers to every written document inspired by and destined to promote the veneration of the saints. Cf. H. Delehaye, *Legends of the Saints,* p. 2. In this survey, the term is used in a more restricted sense as equivalent to the *passio, vita,* or *encomium* of a saint.

from the official reports of their trials or from the testimonies of eyewitnesses, and were read to the congregations on the anniversaries of the martyrs. St. Augustine tells us[2] that works containing accounts of miracles wrought by the relics of the martyrs were also read.

It was an easy step from such venerations of martyrs to the composing of biographies of other saintly personages who had lived ascetic, heroic, and self-sacrificing lives for the faith. These 'Lives' follow a conventional pattern. The author usually begins by apologizing for the crudeness of his literary style and for the lapses in his grammar, while at the same time protesting a sincere love for his task. He may also give some information on his sources, even declaring that he himself was an eyewitness of many of the events included in his story. Then the hero of the narrative is introduced, with an account of his birth and earliest years and of the prophecies and wonders that accompanied these. The author continues with a description of how the saint devoted himself to the profession of being a real Christian and describes his career with varying detail. Then comes an account of the hero's miracles, visions, combats with demons, and other supernatural experiences, followed by the story of his death and obsequies, the wonders which took place at these, and the miracles wrought at his tomb and through his relics in later years. Details are given according as circumstances permit or suggest. In such 'Lives' there is much borrowing and repetition, depending on the amount of available authentic data. The borrowing is most marked where the extraordinary is concerned. In spite of the author's protestations of sincerity and a desire to tell the truth, he knew that the subject of the biography would suffer in popular esteem if he did not move in the region of the marvelous. The motives which led to

---

2 *De civ. Dei* 22.18.

the creation of this vast hagiographical literature were various. If we may believe the authors, most of them were written at popular demand; some were evidently written to promote or exalt the cult of a saint or martyr; but all were written to edify and instruct in the faith.

The first genuine Christian biography was that of Cyprian written by his deacon, Pontius (259). A deacon at this time was very close to his bishop and had every opportunity that a biographer could desire to observe his subject and to collect information on him. However, although Jerome praises it,[3] it does not satisfy the demands of the modern critic, chiefly because of the extravagance of its panegyric and of its marvelous visions. As to language and style, on the other hand, it should rank high, probably in first place among the representatives of this literary form. It is valuable, also, for certain personal details of Cyprian's life which are not found elsewhere. Following the usual rhetorical practice, Pontius confesses his incompetence for the task of relating the noble deeds of his master in such a way as to give them the greatness in writing that they actually possessed. For the earlier period of Cyprian's life Pontius gives no information, because he refuses to say anything about Cyprian before his new birth in baptism, the real beginning of his Christian life. Pontius followed a definite plan which apparently had been developed before his time. In relating the life of a martyr we usually find first a more or less detailed account of the persecution; the Christians are sought out everywhere; large numbers fall into the hands of the soldiers and among these is the hero of the story, who is arrested and cast into prison; brought before the judge, he confesses his faith and suffers horrible tortures; he dies and his tomb becomes the scene of miracles. Pontius follows this model conscientiously, am-

---

3 *De viris illustribus* 68.

plifying and developing it here and there. The simplicity of
the final act of the tragedy differs from the description of
this part of the narrative as it appears in most accounts of
martyrdom. It would hardly please those who could conceive of no other way of establishing the martyr's heroism
than by making him undergo extended and refined tortures.
Pontius is primarily concerned with showing the supernatural
action of the Holy Spirit in his hero and, secondarily, with
portraying human characteristics.

Pontius' *Life of Cyprian* seems to have had little or no influence on contemporary Latin writers. Christian biography
does not appear again until the fourth century when it forms
an essential part of the ascetical literature of the period. The
Acts of the martyrs had thus far served for the glorification
of Christians who had given their lives for the faith, but
after Diocletian the persecutions had ceased and the Christians could no longer prove their faith by torture and death.
The monk's life of solitude and penance gave this opportunity
and monasticism then extended its influence to the field of
literature.

Athanasius, Bishop of Alexandria, is considered to have
composed the first formal biography of a monk. His *Life
of St. Anthony*, written in Greek, loosed a flood of literature
which followed it directly as a model. Jerome's 'Lives' of
the monks Paul, Hilarion, and Malchus are small master-
pieces in this field. They have delighted readers for cen-
turies and would delight those of our time, were they able
to be content not with the exactitude characteristic of the
modern historical method but rather with the spirit of piety
which guided the author. The most popular example of this
type of biography is that of St. Martin of Tours by Sulpicius
Severus.[4] Its many miracles, including three instances of rais-

---

4 This was published in Volunme 7 of this series, pp. 101-145, translated
   by Bernard M. Peebles.

ing men from the dead, constitute the chief charm for its multitude of readers. The people urged Sulpicius Severus not to omit a single known prodigy from his narrative, and in an effort to satisfy them he produced a biography that has made St. Martin the most widely known man of his time. It is obvious that the glories of many earlier heroes have been gathered here in the *Life of St. Martin*, with the result that his fame is a blending of the legendary and the historic.

Paulinus of Milan, the biographer of St. Ambrose, came under the influence of this literature. His work is marked strongly by both the spirit and the style of Sulpicius Severus. He follows the usual scheme[5] for a biography of a saint who, like St. Ambrose, was not a martyr. There are three main parts: (1) before his birth—nationality, parents, and prophecies of future greatness; (2) his life—childhood, youth, the most important events of his career, his virtues, and miracles; (3) his cult and the miracles after his death.

Paulinus undertook his work at the request of St. Augustine, who at the same time pointed out several biographies celebrated in the Latin Church which he might follow as models: the *Life of St. Anthony* by St. Athanasius, the *Life of St. Paul the Hermit* by St. Jerome, and the *Life of St. Martin of Tours* by Sulpicius, Severus. With such models as sources of inspiration, it is not surprising that Paulinus emphasized miraculous cures, victories over the Devil, and the divine protection extended over St. Ambrose. He also gives considerable space to legends which had already become commonplace by being ascribed to many other great men. Paulinus is evidently overcredulous, but he appears to be recording honestly what he actually believed to be true. As sources for his narrative he had not only his own personal recollections, but also the testimony of Marcellina, St. Am-

---

5 Cf. Delehaye, *op. cit.* 98.

brose's sister, and of others who had known Ambrose intimately. The character of the miracles which are reported on their authority depends on the credence which can be given to these informants.

Judged by modern standards of historical research, Paulinus' *Life of St. Ambrose* falls down miserably. Paulinus disregards chronological details, and only by referring to Ambrose's works or to other writers and documents of the time can we fix the dates of events mentioned by him. Furthermore, he only touches upon the great bishop's activity in civil affairs and he completely overlooks the extent of his influence in all the important affairs of the Empire. We can never gather from Paulinus' narrative that St. Ambrose was one of the greatest men of his time as churchman and statesman and man of letters. While we admit that this biography is something of a disappointment, we cannot agree with Farrar that it is 'nothing better than morbid and monkish fiction.'[6] Paulinus as a biographer does show an inability to organize material; his style is slovenly; and he seems to be unable to distinguish between the important and the trivial. Yet he is a man of integrity, as both St. Ambrose and St. Augustine bear witness. In his narrative he exhibits a conscientious effort a perform his tasks to the best of his ability, and he does give us many interesting details of St. Ambrose's private life which we would never have known from any other source.

The *Life of St. Augustine* by his secretary, Possidius, is quite a different kind of work. No one could have been more competent to tell the life story of Augustine than Possidius. A close intimacy of forty years made him acquainted with those simple domestic incidents which lend such charm to his biography. Possidius considered it his duty to record these

---

6 *Lives of the Fathers* 3.89.

events which St. Augustine himself did not mention in his own works and particularly in the *Confessions*. He writes in a style of his own, quite differently from Augustine and all other writers of his time. The extravagant phraseology so characteristic of the period is missing here. In its place we find throughout a profound love of simplicity and truth. Possidius presents the simple facts and lets them speak for themselves. He assmues that his readers have read the *Confessions,* and he proceeds at once to describe Augustine's repentance and the spiritual friendships formed by him when he returned to Africa as a Christian. Then he proceeds with an account of St. Augustine's priesthood and episcopacy. With the admiration and enthusiasm of a child, Possidius praises the victories which Augustine won over the adversaries of the faith and dwells on the glory which he brought to the African Church.

Strangely enough, Possidius does not once refer to the tragic struggle which was going on in the region about him nor to the complex problems which were taxing the minds of ecclesiastical leaders. He must have realized that the African Church was sinking into its grave. Apparently, his trust in Divine Providence made him confident that the Church in Africa would rise again and that another generation would see the restoration of its desecrated altars.

Possidius was well aware of Augustine's great influence on contemporary thought and doctrines. He realized, also, the great value of the vast output of the great doctor's labors for future generations. Accordingly, he felt it to be his first duty, after completing the *Life of St. Augustine,* to make a study of all the works current under St. Augustine's name and to list them all, eliminating the spurious. He closes the biography with just such a list, telling his readers also of the many letters that had been lost. 'Inspired by the Holy

Spirit,' he writes, 'the holy Bishop Augustine has written for the instruction of human souls, in the form of books, pamphlets, and letters, 1030 works, besides many others not counted, because he himself found it impossible to gather or to remember all of them.' Posterity owes a great debt of gratitude to Possidius and his hermit brethren who assisted him, both for the preservation of Augustine's writings and for eliminating so many problems of authenticity such as have haunted the literary heritage of all ancient writers of high importance.

This type of literature—saints' 'lives,' legends, and monks' biographies, all included under the general term of Christian biography and hagiography—always has been extremely popular. Indeed, the continuations of this type of literature today are various enough and likewise extremely popular. The cults of saints are a phase of religion which springs naturally from the people themselves and is not forced upon them by any authority. In the saints is embodied the Christian ideal of human excellence, and the miracles in their lives prove how God through His supernatural power rewards those who strive to attain perfection. To appreciate Christian biography, then, the reader must understand its spirit, and it is hoped that this introductory sketch will assist the reader in enjoying the translations of its most important early representatives as presented in this volume.

ROY J. DEFERRARI

LIFE OF ST. CYPRIAN
BY PONTIUS

Translated by

SISTER MARY MAGDELEINE MÜLLER, O.S.F., Ph.D.
Cardinal Stritch College

and

ROY J. DEFERRARI, Ph.D.
The Catholic University of America

INTRODUCTION

THE LIFE OF CYPRIAN is the first Christian biography that attained popularity. Although by no means a finished literary product, it is important because of its originality in the field.

This life of Cyprian was written by Pontius soon after the bishop's death. As Cyprian's disciple, the author was deeply convinced of the greatness of his master and anxious to make the world equally conscious of his admirable character.

Apparently, popular acclaim furthered his purpose, for in the opening paragraphs of the *Life* there is a reference to importuning requests of the people for information on Cyprian's life and death. Therefore, the biography actually answers a demand of the day, and Pontius was decidedly not loath to meet it.

With but little definite information at hand, there could not possibly be a purely objective presentation. Undeterred from his purpose, however, the author exerted an abundance of rhetorical skill to attain his end. The facts, from the conversion of Cyprian until his death, are the compass of the work. Because of the elegance of language and multiplicity of verbiage, it is exceedingly difficult to follow any real sequence of events in the biography. Since positive evidence was scarce, Pontius took pains to make up for the deficiency with a variety and extravagance of expression which at times renders it all but impossible to follow the thought.

Doubtless, Pontius' chief aim was to show the unusual

3

sanctity of Cyprian under particularly trying circumstances, as exhibited in his life and martyrdom, but there is an over-straining toward that effect. Of human interest there is little, and the grandiloquence of expression is sometimes overdone, overshadowing the reality. Considering the author's lack of subject matter, however, his flow of words is admirable and his turn of phrase frequently rather remarkable.

The omission of details has been assumed to have arisen from force of circumstances; still, it is possible that Pontius deliberately omitted them. Since the biography was written only a few months after Cyprian's death, contemporaries of the man could easily have filled in the gaps. Because of his remarkable and well-known character, Cyprian and his actions would have been familiar to the people. Moreover, the Acts of the martyr were available to all who were interested, and, again, could supply missing details. Finally, since the principal objective was edification, only enough details to accomplish that end could have been included.

On the whole, the reader is definitely impressed by the richness of phraseology and aptness of metaphor employed. Frequently, a more detailed account would clarify the work and facilitate reading, but there always remains the impression of beauty of language and style, although at times somewhat labored. Perhaps due to the obscurity of fact, the Latin of the *Life* is also sometimes obscure and almost impossible of discernment.

The present translation is based on the edition found in the *CSEL*. There has been a repunctuation of the original, however, in an attempt to clarify the thought and construction. No direct Scriptural citations occur, so all quotations have been rendered directly from the Latin.

THE LIFE OF CECIL CYPRIAN

LTHOUGH CYPRIAN, a devout bishop and God's glorious witness, wrote many works to perpetuate the memory of his worthy name, and although the abundant fruitfulness of his eloquence and God's grace is diffused through the copiousness and richness of his words in such a way that even to the end of the world he probably will never be silent, we have decided to write briefly about him. This privilege is proper to his works and merits, not because such a great man's life may be unknown to anyone, even of the pagans, but so that his incomparable and noble example may attain immortal remembrance among our posterity and that according to his example they, too, may be guided in learning. Our ancestors, in their reverence for martyrdom itself, honored laymen and catechumens who had gained martyrdom so highly that they recorded many details of their sufferings, or, as I almost said, practically all of them, for the instruction of us, also, who were not yet born. Certainly, then, it would be unfortunate to pass over the sufferings of such a priest and martyr. Even without his martydrom he had a lesson to teach, although during his life his accomplishments were not well known. Nevertheless, they are so important, so great, and so admirable that I am frightened by the contemplation of their greatness. Moreover, I confess that I am unequal to the task of using diction in a manner worthy of the honor due his merits and that

I cannot relate such remarkable deeds so that they may seem
as great as they really are. However, the prodigious number
of his deeds is sufficient in itself and requires no other herald.

The difficulty is increased by the fact that you are anxious
to hear much or, if possible, everything about him. With
eager longing and burning desire you wish to know his deeds,
even if his actual words have meanwhile become silent. In
this regard, if I say that the powers of eloquence fail us, I
say too little. Even eloquence is lacking to a degree worthy
of him, and which will satisfy your desires with a full spirit.
So we are sorely pressed on both sides: he burdens us with
his virtues; you importune us with your words.

(2) Where, then, shall I begin? From what point shall
I enter upon a discussion of his virtues if not from the beginning of his faith and from his heavenly birth, since, truly, a
man of God's deeds should be reckoned from no other point
than his birth in God? Although study and the liberal arts
had imbued his devout heart, I omit these, for as yet they
brought him no advantage except in the world. After he had
learned Holy Writ and emerged into the light of spiritual
wisdom by piercing the cloud of the world, I shall relate
whatever I witnessed and whatever I have learned of his
former accomplishments. This indulgence I beg, however,
that whatever I minimize (as I must) be ascribed to my
ignorance rather than to his lack of glory.

Among the first principles of his faith Cyprian believed
that nothing else than the observance of continency was
worthy of God. Then, indeed, the heart and mind could become capable of a full capacity for truth, if by a strong and
wholesome life of sanctity he could crush the concupiscence
of the flesh. Who ever recalls so marvelous a transformation?
His rebirth in faith had not yet enlightened the new man

with all the splendor of divine light, but already he was con-
quering the former old shadows with only preparation for
the light. Then, what is even greater, when as a result of
reading Scripture he had already learned certain facts, not
for the conditioning of his new state but for the hastening
of his faith, he immediately took advantage of what would
be profitable in meriting the Lord. By distributing his goods
to maintain the peace of many needy people and thus dispensing almost all his wealth, he combined two virtues: contempt of worldly ambition, than which nothing is more harmful, and the conferring of mercy. The latter God preferred
even to sacrifices, and he who said that he had observed all
the commandments of the Law did not fulfill it. Thus, by
the very speedy progress of his piety, Cyprian almost began
to be perfect before he had learned how to do so. Who of
the ancients. I ask, did this? Who of the most ancient elders
in the faith, whose minds and ears had been struck by the
divine words for many years, has set forth anything like it?
Moreover, although still unskilled in faith and perhaps not
yet trusted, he surpassed the accomplishments of his elders
by his glorious and marvelous deeds. No one reaps immediately when he has sown; no one presses out vintage from
newly made trenches; no one ever yet sought ripe fruit from
slips that were just planted. In Cyprian, everything happened
in an incredible fashion. Threshing I say, preceded sowing
(if such a thing can be said, for the reality does not admit it),
vintage preceded the vine, and fruit the root.

(3) The Letters of the Apostles say that neophytes should
be excluded [from religious discussions], lest in their unin-
structed new state they commit some offense against God,
should the stupor of paganism still cling to their uncon-
firmed minds. Cyprian was the first and, I think, the only

one to show that more can be accomplished by faith than
by time. Even if in the Acts of the Apostles a eunuch is
described as immediately baptized by Philip because he believed with his whole heart, the comparison is not the same.
The eunuch was a Jew, and because he came from the
Lord's temple was reading the Prophet Isaias and hoping in
Christ, although he did not believe that He had yet come;
Cyprian, coming from ignorant pagans, begins with as mature a faith as that with which few, perhaps, have finished.
Finally, with regard to God's grace there was no delay, no
postponement. I have said too little; he immediately received
the orders of the presbyterate and the priesthood. Indeed,
who would not entrust every degree of honor to such a believing mind? He accomplished much while still a layman,
much when already a presbyter, and thus merited God by
fulfilling the many obligations of religious observance in close
imitation of the examples of the righteous of old. His usual
words on this subject were to the effect that, if he should
read that a certain person had been singled out for giving
praise to God, he would urge an inquiry into the deeds whereby that man had pleased God. Cyprian taught that if Job,
famous by the testimony of some, was called a true worshiper
of God and with whom no one on earth can be compared,
we should do whatever Job did. Thus, while we perform similar actions, we may call forth a similar testimony of God
for ourselves. With little regard for the loss of his property,
he had advanced so far in the exercise of virtue that he did
not feel the temporary losses of affection. Poverty did not
break him, nor pain; his wife's persuasion did not move him,
nor did the dreadful punishment of his own body crush him.
Virtue remained fixed in her abode, and devotion, grounded
with deep roots, did not because of any attack of a tempting

devil cease to bless the Lord with a grateful faith even in the midst of adversity. His house was open to anyone who came; no widow departed with an empty stomach, no blind person was not guided by him as a companion, no lame one was not carried by him as a support, no one devoid of the help of the very powerful was not protected by him as a defender. 'Those who wish to please God should do these things,' he said. And while he thus goes through the evidence of all good men, he always imitated the better. Likewise, he caused himself to be imitated.

(4) Evidently, Cyprian was closely associated with Caecilianus, one of our men of just and laudable memory, who was then a presbyter in age and rank. This man, who had converted Cyprian from worldly error to a knowledge of the true divinity, was the object of his entire love, esteem, and respect, for he regarded him with a gracious reverence, not as his soul's friend of the same age but as the parent of his new life. This man, at first charmed by his attentions, was later greatly moved by the merits of his immense love and, upon departing from this world, with his summons now at hand, he commended his wife and children to his care and made him who was a common partner in his way of life the heir of his devotion.

(5) It would take too long to mention Cyprian's deeds individually; to enumerate all of them is burdensome. I think that this fact alone is sufficient proof of his good works, that by God's judgment and the favor of men he was chosen for the office of the priesthood and the rank of bishop when still a neophyte and considered a novice. Although he was only in the first days of his faith and the rudimentary stage of his spiritual life, so excellent a character shone forth in him that he gave promise of the complete trustworthiness

of his approaching priesthood, even if he was not yet resplendent with the brilliance of his future office. I will not omit this extraordinary incident. When under the Lord's inspiration all the people eagerly demonstrated their love and esteem for him, Cyprian humbly withdrew and gave place to his elders. Thus thinking himself unworthy to claim such an honor, he actually became all the more worthy of it. Indeed, the person who disclaims what he merits becomes more worthy. Because they were excited by this ardor, the people were restless, longing with a spiritual desire, as the event proved, for more than a bishop. In this man whom they were thus demanding with a hidden presage of holiness they wanted not only a priest but a future martyr. Large numbers of his brethren then besieged the portals of his home and an anxious loving care was evident at all the doors. Perhaps that experience of the Apostle might then have happened to him as he desired (namely, to be let down through the window), if then he already had been like the Apostle in the honor of ordination. It was evident that all the rest awaited his coming with an eager and anxious spirit, and upon his arrival received him with exceeding joy. I speak unwillingly, but speak I must. Some there were who resisted him in his efforts. These, however, he kindly indulged with tender patience, and to the astonishment of many he later counted them among his closest and most intimate friends. Indeed, to whom would the forgetfulness of such a receptive mind be anything but a miracle?

(6) Who is qualified to relate how he conducted himself henceforth? What piety and vigor, what great mercy and severity! So much sanctity and grace shone from his face that he confounded the minds of those who looked upon him. His countenance was grave and joyful, neither a gloomy

severity nor excessive affability. Here was mingled a just proportion of both, so that one wondered whether he deserved fear or love, except that he merited to be both feared and loved. Nor was his dress out of harmony with his countenance, being moderately tempered, like himself. Worldly arrogance did not inflate him, but on the other hand neither did affected penury spoil him, for this kind of attire which an' excessive frugality likewise exhibits arises no less from ostentation. Moreover, what might he have done for the poor, the object of his love as a catchumen? The witnesses of his piety might have seen this, both those whom the discipline of the office itself trained to the duty of good works, and those whom the common ties of the sacrament bound to the service of manifesting love. The bishop's chair received Cyprian as he was; it did not mold him.

(7) Immediately, then, he gained the glory of proscription in return for such graces. Indeed, nothing else was more appropriate than that he who in the secret recesses of his conscience abounded in the full honor of religion and faith should also be named publicly on the renowned list of the pagans. In accordance with the rapidity with which he always obtained everything, the merited crown of martyrdom might have hastened to him, especially since by repeated requests he was often demanded for the lion. However, it was first necessary for him to pass through all the ranks of glory and thus come to the highest. Moreover, the impending troublesome times demanded the assistance of a fruitful mind. Imagine him taken away at that time by the honor of martyrdom! Who would have shown the advantage of grace advancing through faith? Who would have held virgins to a becoming life of chastity and a habit worthy of holiness, as though with a bridle of the Lord's choosing? Who would

have taught repentance to the lapsed, truth to the heretics, unity to schismatics, peace and the law of evangelical prayer to the children of God? Who would have overcome the blasphemous pagans by turning against them the charges which they heap upon us? By whom would Christians of rather tender affection or, what is worse, of too little faith be consoled for the loss of their loved ones through hope in the future? Where would we have learned mercy and patience as we did? Who would have restrained the malice arising from envy's envenomed viciousness by the sweetness of the remedy of salvation? Who would have raised up such great martyrs by the exhortation of divine words? Who, finally, with the clarity of a heavenly trumpet, would have spurred on so many confessors to distinguished works, examples of a living martyrdom? Most fortunately, and indeed providentially, it happened at that time that the man who was necessary for so many good purposes was withheld from the crowning glory of martyrdom. Do you wish to know that his withdrawal was not a matter of fear? To offer no other excuses, he himself later underwent sufferings which he certainly would have avoided according to his practice if he had done so before. Fear there was, indeed, but a just one, which dreaded to offend the Lord, preferring to obey God's commands than thus to be crowned. His mind, which was dedicated to God in all things and thus bound by the divine admonitions, believed that, if he had not obeyed the Lord who then ordered retreat, there would be sin even in his suffering.

(8) Finally, I think that something should be said about the usefulness of the delay, although we have already touched upon it in brief. While we are satisfied with what seems subsequently to have occurred, it follows that we should prove

that the withdrawal was not conceived by man's faint-heart-
edness but rather by Divine Providence. The unusual and
fierce rioting of a violent persecution was ravaging the people.
Since the crafty enemy could not ensnare everyone by one
deceit, wherever a careless soldier exposed his vulnerable
side with various forms of madness, Cyprian overthrew them
one by one by different kinds of destruction. There was need
of someone who would do this, who, depending upon the
nature of the wound, would apply the remedy of heavenly
medicine to cut or care for those who were wounded and
attacked by the varied skill of the assailing enemy. Cyprian
was preserved, a man with a nature trained spiritually in
addition to other fields. Amid the resounding waves of conflicting schisms he was able to direct the Church on the
middle path by means of a steady course. Are not these plans
divine, I ask? Could this have happened without God? Let
those who think that such things happen by chance look
to it. The Church answers them, saying in a clear voice: 'I
do not admit, I do not believe, that without God's command
indispensable men are preserved.'

(9) Still, if it seems advisable, let us go through the other
facts. Later in Cyprian's life there broke out a dreadful epi-
demic and the devastation of an abominable disease great
beyond measure. Countless people were seized daily in their
own homes by a sudden attack; one after another the homes
of the trembling crowd were invaded. Everyone shuddered,
fled to avoid contagion, wickedly exposed their dear ones,
as if along with the person who was about to die from the
plague one could also shut out death itself. Meanwhile,
throughout every district of the city there lay no longer the
dead bodies, but many diseased and dying people who asked
the pity of the passers-by. No one regarded anything but

cruel gains; no one trembled at the remembrance of a similar experiences; no one did to another what he wished done
to him. It would be a crime to pass over the actions of Christ
and God's high priest in these circumstances, one who had
surpassed this world's high priests in piety as well as in the
truth of religion. First of all he instructed the assembled
people on the blessings of mercy; by examples from Holy
Writ he taught them how much the offices of charity avail
to merit God. He also added that it was not at all remarkable if we cherish only our own brethren with a proper observance of charity. Indeed, a man would only become perfect
if he did more than the publican or heathen, by overcoming
evil with good and by the exercise of a divine-like clemency,
loving even his enemies, and by further praying for the salvation of his persecutors, as the Lord advises and encourages.
'He continually makes His sun rise and imparts sudden rain
to nourish the seeds, showing all these kindnesses not merely
to His own friends. Should not one who professes to be a
son of God imitate the example of his Father? It is proper
for us to correspond to our birth, and it does not become
those who are clearly reborn in God to be degenerate, but,
as a son, the descendant of a good father should rather prove
the imitation of his goodness.'

(10) There are many other matters, and, indeed, important ones, which the limited scope of this volume does not
permit us to repeat in lengthy discourse. About these it is
enough to have said this much. However, if the pagans could
have heard them on their rostrums, they probably would
have believed at once. Therefore what might not a Christian
do, whose title arises from his faith?

Ministrations were immediately given, then, according to
the nature of the men and their rank. Many who were un-

able to offer wealth for the benefit of the poor manifested more than riches, and by their own labor they made payment dearer than all wealth. Under such a teacher who would not hasten to join in such a service? By it he might please both God the Father and Christ the Judge and, at the moment, the priest. Therefore, through the generosity of superabundant works there was accomplished what is good for all, not merely for those of the household of the faith. Something more was done than has been noted concerning the incomparable devotion of Tobias, who gathered only those of his own race killed or cast out by the king. He would practise forbearance again and again or rightly admit that I have spoken the truth, even if he was before Christ. To His time the fullness of all things is due.

(11) These actions of Cyprian, so good and pious, were succeeded by exile. Impiety always gives this return, the restoration of the worse for the better. Moreover, the reply of God's priest upon questioning by the proconsul is related in the proceedings. Meanwhile, he who had accomplished good for the city was exiled from it—he who had labored that the eyes of the living might not suffer the horror of the infernal dwelling, he, I say, who had been vigilant in the watches of devotion against wickedness. With a goodness that receives no ·recompense he had seen to it that, when everyone was leaving the desolate sight of the city, the deserted state and destitute country should not perceive its many exiles. However, let the world which considers exile a punishment consider it. To the worldly their own country is exceedingly dear, and they have a common name with their parents; but we abhor even our parents themselves if they persuade us against the Lord. To them it is a severe penalty to live outside of their own city; to a Christian this whole world is one home.

Therefore, although he was sent away to a hidden, secret place, he could not regard it as exile, for he was associated with the things of God. Furthermore, when serving God wholeheartedly, he was even a stranger in his own city. While the continency of the Holy Spirit restrains him from carnal desires, pointing out the life of the former man, among his own citizens or, I might almost say, even among his parents, he is foreign to an earthly life. Although this might otherwise seem a punishment, it happens that in circumstances and sentences of this kind which we endure as trials in proof of virtue there is no punishment because it is a glory. However, granted that exile is not a punishment for us, let their conscience as a witness ascribe the gravest charge and worst crime to those who can inflict upon the innocent what they think is a punishment.

At present, I do not wish to describe the charm of the place and for the time being I pass over the description of all its pleasures. But let us imagine that place, sordid in location, squalid in appearance, with unhealthy water, no pleasing verdure, no proximity to the shore, but vast wooded cliffs amid the inhospitable jaws of very deserted solitude, far removed in a pathless part of the world. Could such a place, the destination of God's priest, Cyprian, bear the name of exile if human ministration was not lacking, or birds to minister to Elias or angels to Daniel? Far be it from anyone to believe that anything would be wanting to the least of men as long as they are firm in the confession of His name. So far was God's priest, who always promoted acts of mercy, from needing the assistance of all rewards.

(12) Now, then, as I had decided to tell in the second place, let us recall with thanksgiving that a fitting, sunny dwelling was divinely provided for the soul of so great a

man. In accordance with his wish, he was given a hidden hospice as well as all the comforts promised those as a further reward when seeking the kingdom of God and His justice. Omitting the number of brethren who visited him and the kindness of the citizens who supplied him with all the things of which he seemed to have been deprived, I will not pass over God's wonderful visitation. By this means He wished His priest in exile to be so secure in future suffering that with fuller confidence in his imminent martyrdom Curubis possessed not only an exile but also a martyr. 'Indeed, on that day on which we tarried at the place of banishment' (for the condescension of his love had chosen me among his household companions as a voluntary exile; would that he had included me in his sufferings, too!), 'there appeared to me,' he said, 'when I was not yet enveloped in the quiet of sleep, a youth taller than man's measure. When this person led me, as it were, to the praetorium, I seemed to be moving toward the tribunal of the proconsul who was sitting there. As he looked at me, the latter immediately began to note on his tablet a sentence which I did not know, for he asked me nothing in the usual manner of interrogation. Indeed, however, the young man who was standing behind him very carefully read the notation. Then, because he could not express it in words, he showed by an explanatory nod what were the contents of the writing on that tablet. With his open hand as flat as a blade he imitated the stroke of the customary punishment, thus expressing as clearly as by speech what he wanted understood. I recognized my future sentence of suffering, and therefore began to ask and to beg continuously that a delay of at least one day be granted me to arrange my affairs according to legal decree. When I had repeated my entreaties many times, he began to record some-

thing on his tablet. However, from the serenity of his countenance I perceived that the judge's mind had been moved
by my petition as if it were just. The young man, moreover,
who had already indicated my sufferings by gesture rather
than by word, hastened to signify repeatedly by a secret sign
that the desired delay until the following day had been
granted. This he indicated by twisting his fingers behind each
other. Although the sentence was not yet read, I very gladly
recovered from my joy at the postponement which had been
granted. Moreover, so much did I tremble with fear at the
uncertainty of the interpretation that the remains of my fear
still affect my exultant heart with utter dread.'

(13) What could be more evident than this revelation;
what more fortunate than this consideration? All the subsequent events were foretold to him first; nothing of God's
words was curtailed, nothing of so sacred a promise was
cut short. Finally, recall each detail which I have pointed
out. When his sentence of suffering was under deliberation,
he asked for a postponement until the morrow, begging that
he might arrange his affairs on the day which he had obtained. This one day signified the year he was to live following the vision. To speak more plainly, after the year had ex-
pired, he was crowned on the day revealed to him the previous
year. Although we do not read of a day of the Lord as a
year in Holy Writ, we accept that time as befitting the
promise of future things. Therefore, it is of no concern if
now, under the expression of a day, a single year is indicated, because what is greater should be more abundant.
Moreover, what was explained by a sign and not by words
the utterance of speech reserved for the manifestation of
time. A fact is usually revealed in words as soon as what is
set forth is fulfilled. Truly, indeed, no one knew why this

was indicated, except that he was crowned on the same day
on which he had seen it. In the meantime, however, everyone knew as a certainty of his impending suffering, yet those
same people passed over in silence the exact day of it as if,
indeed, they were ignorant of it. In the Scriptures, too, I
surely find something similar. Because Zachary, the high
priest, did not believe in the son promised him by an angel,
he became speechless. Therefore, he asked by a sign for tablets to write his son's name rather than to pronounce it. Deservedly, here, too, when God's messenger revealed the impending sufferings of His priest rather by sign, he admonished
his faith and strengthened the priest. However, his reason for
requesting the delay arose from the arrangement of his affairs and the disposition of his will. Still, what affairs or what
will did he have to arrange except those of his ecclesiastical
position? The greatest delay was admitted so that he might
arrange whatever needed to be disposed of with regard to
his final decision concerning the care of the poor. I believe,
too, that for no other reason and, indeed, for this reason
alone, indulgence was granted to him even by the very individuals who had expelled him and intended to kill him.
Their aim was that by his presence he might serve the poor
who were present with the final or, to speak more fully, the
entire effort of his last ministration. Therefore, when his affairs were conscientiously arranged and his will thus disposed of, the following day drew near.

(14) A messenger already had come from the city of Xis-
tus, a good and peaceable priest and therefore a most blessed
martyr, saying that the expected executioner was approaching, the man who would strike the faithful neck of his most
holy victim. Such were all his days, lived in the daily expectation of death, so that the crown might be granted to

each one. In the meantime, many eminent people of highly illustrious rank and family came to him, as well as nobles of worldly renown, who repeatedly urged his withdrawal on the grounds of an old friendship with him. No empty persuasion was this, for they even offered places to which he might retire. But Cyprian, with his mind eager for heaven, had already disdained the world and refused consent to their temptihg persuasions. Perhaps even then he would have complied with the request of the faithful, had he been so ordered by a divine command. However, that sublime honor of such a great man must not be passed over without commendation. Now, when the world was swelling with passion and its leaders were breathing out hatred for his name, that man was instructing God's servants, as the opportunity was afforded. With exhortations of the Lord he encouraged them to despise the sufferings of time through a contemplation of the glory to come. Indeed, so great was his love of discourse that he wished the prayers of his sufferings might obtain for him the grace to be put to death in the very act of preaching, while speaking of God.

(15) Such were the daily acts of a priests destined to be a pleasing sacrifice to God. By the proconsul's command, behold, an officer with his soldiers suddenly appeared in the gardens, or, to speak more truly, they thought they came upon him unawares. (In the early days of his faith these gardens had been sold and restored by God's mercy; surely, he would have sold them again for the benefit of the poor, except to avoid ill will from a lawsuit.) How could a mind that was always prepared be taken unawares, as it were, by an unexpected attack? Accordingly, he went forward, certain that what had long been delayed was being accomplished. He proceeded with an eager and resolute mind,

showing cheerfulness on his countenance and courage in his
heart. However, because of the postponement to the following day, he returned to an officer's house from the praetorium.
Suddenly, a rumor which spread throughout Carthage grew,
to the effect that Thascius [Cyprian] had been brought forth.
Everyone knew him, not only because of his fame, which was
celebrated by glorious renown, but also through the remembrance of his very distinguished deeds. From all sides the
people flocked to the scene, a glorious one for us because of
devotion to the faith, but lamentable indeed for the pagans.
A kind guard, however, had charge of him the one night
when he was taken and placed in an officer's house, so that
we, his associates and friends, were in his company as usual.
Meanwhile all the people, anxious lest something should
happen during the night without their knowledge, kept watch
before the officer's door. Divine goodness then granted to
him, so truly worthy, that God's people should even watch
over the sufferings of the priest. Perhaps someone will ask
the reason for his return to the officer's house from the
praetorium? Evidenly, some wished it, asserting that on his
part the proconsul did not want it. Far be it from me to
complain about the proconsul's laziness or aversion in matters divinely effected. Far be it from me to admit this evil
within the conscience of a devout mind, that the caprice of
a man may pass judgment on so blessed a martyr. That morrow, foretold a year before, must truly be the morrow.

(16) Finally, another day dawned—that day marked,
promised, divine, which he could never have succeeded in
deferring, even if the tyrant had been willing. In the mind
of the future martyr that was a happy day, radiant with a
bright sun, although clouds were scattered over the whole
world. He left the officer's house, but the officer of Christ

and God was walled in on all sides by the ranks of a mingled multitude. Thus, moreover, an infinite army kept close to him, as if the band had formed to come and fight death. On the way, the crossing of the stadium caused him some concern. Well constructed it was and, as it were, on purpose, so that Cyprian, upon completion of the contest, when running to the crown of justice, might pass a fitting place of struggle. Still, when he had come to the praetorium, a more secluded place was given him, since the proconsul had not yet appeared. As he sat there after his long journey, bathed in excessive sweat (by chance, the seat was covered with linen, so that even in the moment of suffering he might enjoy the honor of the episcopate), one of the officers, a former Christian, offered him his clothes, as if he might wish to change his garments for drier ones. No doubt, in offering the clothes he sought nothing else than to possess the already bloody sweat of the martyr going his way to God. Cyprian answered him, saying: 'We apply remedies for annoyances which will no longer exist after today.' Is it any wonder that he who mentally despised death despised bodily suffering? Why say any more? Suddenly, he was announced to the proconsul. He was brought forth, led forward, questioned concerning his name; he answered that he was the man. So far, then, the words.

(17) Thereupon, the judge reads from a tablet the sentence which had not been [manifest] recently in the vision. This spiritual sentence, not to be spoken rashly, was worthy of such a bishop and witness, a glorious sentence in which he was called the standard-bearer of his sect and an enemy of the gods. He would be an example to his followers, and, by his blood, discipline would begin to be established. There is nothing more complete or more true than this sentence.

Indeed, although everything was said by a pagan, it is divine. Nor is it any wonder, since bishops usually prophesy their sufferings. Cyprian had been a standard bearer who used to teach about carrying Christ's standard; he was an enemy of the gods and one who commanded the destruction of idols. Moreover, he was an example to his followers, one who, although many were about to follow similarly, was the first in the province to consecrate the firstfruits of his martyrdom. By his blood, discipline also began to be established, as well as by that of the martyrs who emulated their teacher, imitating a similar glory. They themselves have established the discipline of example by shedding their own blood.

(18) When he had left the doors of the praetorium, a crowd of soldiers accompanied him; moreover, centurions and tribunes guarded his side, lest anything be wanting in his passion. The place where he actually suffered is a valley, such that, thick with trees on all sides, affords a noble view. However, because the size of the rather large space shut off the view and the crowd was greatly confused, his friends had climbed into the branches of trees so that the sight might not be denied them. Like Zacchaeus, he would be seen from the trees. Cyprian, when he had bound his own eyes, tried to bring to an end the executioner's delay. The latter, whose duty it was to wield the sword, clasped the sword with difficulty and with faltering hand. With trembling figures he held it until the proper hour of glorification set free the centurion's hand, fortified by strength granted at the last and by help from above to effect the great man's death. O blessed people of the Church, who suffered with their bishop by such sights and feelings, and what is more, by loud prayer; as if they had always listened to his preaching, they were crowned by God their Judge. Although what their common prayers de-

sired could not come to pass, that all the people should suffer a similar glory at once in his company, whoever under
the eyes of the gazing Christ and in the priest's hearing desired with all his heart to suffer, by this fitting testimony of
his desire sent a message to God as an ambassador.

(19) Thus the consummation of his sufferings resulted
so that Cyprian, the exemplar of all good men, likewise was
the first to elevate the sacerdotal crown to martyrdom, for
he was the first after the Apostles. From the time when the
episcopal rank is reckoned at Carthage, none of the good
men, even among the priests, is ever recorded to have come
to suffering. Although, among consecrated men, devotion
rendered to God is always considered martyrdom, Cyprian
attained even to the perfect crown when the Lord commanded it. Thus, in the very city in which he had lived
and had been the first to perform many noble deeds, he
was also the first to decorate the insignia of the heavenly
priesthood with his glorious blood. What shall I do at this
point? My mind is torn in different directions, by joy at his
sufferings and grief at remaining here, so that twofold affections burden a heart that is too confined. Shall I grieve
because I was not his companion? Still, his victory must be
celebrated triumphantly. Shall I celebrate it? I do grieve
that I am not his companion. Nevertheless, I must confess
to you in simplicity something you already know, my sentiment in this sentence. I rejoice exceedingly in his glory, but
I grieve still more because I have been left behind.

LIFE OF ST. AMBROSE
BY PAULINUS

Translated by

JOHN A. LACY, M.A.

The Catholic University of America

INTRODUCTION

HE PRESENT *Life of Saint Ambrose* is one of the few ancient documents dealing with the life of the holy bishop, and this fact alone would suffice to make the work of genuine importance. It was written by Paulinus, who was quite devoted to St. Ambrose, his teacher and friend, and there is every evidence that this friendship was mutual, for he received Paulinus into his presbyterium soon after 375, the date of its establishment in Milan. Here Paulinus received his ecclesiastical training and became a deacon, but there seems some doubt that he attained the priesthood. During the years when he was secretary to the bishop in Milan, he acquired first-hand information as to his life and habits, of which he writes in most glowing terms. Furthermore, the fact that, after the death of St. Ambrose, St. Augustine asked Paulinus to write some memoirs further testifies to the warmth of friendship which must have existed between the bishop and his secretary.

Paulinus also took part in crushing the Pelagian controversy. The only other writing besides that translated here is a letter which he wrote to Pope Zosimus in 416 or 417, relative to Coelestius and this controversy and entitled *Libellus adversus Coelestium Zosimo Papae oblatus*.

Paulinus is rather humble in the estimation of his ability as a writer, but the style seems to reflect his simple straight-

27

forwardness. There can be little doubt as to his integrity, for he was held in high honor and esteem by both Sts. Ambrose and Augustine, and by the two Popes of his time, Innocent I and Zosimus.

The fact that Paulinus, in writing this account, is reflecting upon the life of a departed saint and intimate friend whose gracious magnanimity he knew so well, and the saint's indomitable courage and the Christ-like boldness which made him a tower of strength and a pillar of support to the Church, has a profound influence upon both content and style of this work. Evidently he thought it most important to edify his readers by presenting his saint as he himself would like him to be remembered, one through whom God's Holy Spirit worked to manifest on earth His power and glory. Also, it is likely that Paulinus, handicapped as he was by a too near perspective, did not grasp the full significance of the saint's life, either in the spiritual or in the civic realm, with the result that some events which are now considered very important did not seem so to him at the time.

Although there are a few discrepancies in what he did write, there is not even a hint that this was intentional. On the contrary, there is every evidence that he was most sincere in his statements. Paulinus did not make use of the letters of St. Ambrose, although it is possible that he did not have access to them at the time. He seems to rely on his own personal knowledge of the saint and in some instances on information afforded by those whom he calls most trustworthy witnesses.

The text used for this new translation is the old Benedictine text of the latter part of the seventeenth century. This was improved by Sister Simplicia Kaniecka in her disserta-

tion prepared under the direction of Professor Roy J. Deferrari of The Catholic University of America in 1928. I
have quite consistently accepted this text as established by
Sister Simplicia, and wish to make this acknowledgement.
The Scriptural passages, wherever they could be considered
as quotations, follow the new Confraternity translation. At
times, it seems that Paulinus was using the Greek Septuagint,
or a Latin translation with which we are not familiar. This
accounts for some differences in the rendering, duly indicated
in the footnotes.

CONTENTS

31

THE LIFE OF ST. AMBROSE

Chapter 1

YOU EXHORT, venerable father Augustine, that, as the blessed men Athanasius the bishop and Jerome the priest have adorned by their pen the lives of the saints, Paul and Anthony, who lived in the desert, as, also, Severus the servant of God eulogized the life of the venerable Martin, Bishop of the Church at Tours, that I in like manner adorn by my pen the life of blessed Ambrose, Bishop of the Church at Milan. But, as I realize that I am not the equal in worth of such great men, so also I know that I am inferior to them in speech. However, since I regard it as unreasonable to decline your request, those things which I have learned from the most trustworthy men who were with him before me, and especially from his own venerable sister, Marcellina, or what things I myself saw when I was with him, or what I have learned from those who have related that they had seen him in widely separated provinces after his death, or what things were written to him when his death was still unknown, I, aided by your prayers and by the worth of so great a man, shall write down, even though in simple language, briefly and to the point, so that, even if my writing offend the mind of the reader, its brevity may provoke a reading. Nor shall I envelop the truth with word pictures, for, although a writer may seek pomp and elegance, a reader may miss the awareness of great virtues, since he naturally does not consider the trappings and processions of words more than the virtue of deeds and the grace of the Holy Spirit. For we recognize that wayfarers, when they are thirsty, consider water more pleasing, though it trickles in a tiny brook, than the streams of a gushing fountain whose abundant supply they cannot find at the time of their thirst. So, too, barley bread is sometimes sweet even to those who are accustomed to vomit up the abundance of daily banquets with their hundred-fold succession of dishes. Again, to those who admire the charms of cultivated gardens wild flowers are occasionally attractive.

(2) Therefore, I beseech all of you in whose hands this book will be turned to accept as true the things which we tell. Nor should anyone think that, out of eager devotion, I have related anything which lacks support. How much better it is to say nothing at all than to bring forward something false, since we know that 'we shall render an account of all our words.'[1] I should not doubt that, even if all things are not known by all men, different facts are known by different people, and those things are well known to some which I myself, to a lesser degree, also have been able to hear and see. Therefore, I shall begin my story with the day of his birth, in order that the divine grace which was characteristic of the man from his infancy may be well known.

Chapter 2

(3) Therefore, it came to pass that our Ambrose was born while his father, Ambrose, was administering the prefecture-ship of the Gallic provinces. On one occasion, when the

---

1 Cf. Matt. 12.36.

child had been placed in a cradle in his father's courtyard
and was asleep with his mouth open, a swarm of bees suddenly approached and covered his face, so that they were
continually flying in and out of his mouth. His father, who
was strolling nearby with his wife and daughter, watched
with fatherly affection to see in what way this miracle would
terminate. Meanwhile, he restrained the maid from driving
away the bees, for she had accepted the responsibility of
feeding the child and was anxious lest they harm him. But,
after a while, the bees flew away and rose so high in the air
that they could in no way be seen by human eyes. The father,
terrified by this event, said: 'If this child lives, he will be
something great.' For, even then, the Lord was acting during
the infancy of his servant in order that what was written
might be fulfilled: 'Well-ordered words are as a honey-comb.'[1]
For that swarm of bees was implanting the honey-combs of
his later works, which would proclaim the heavenly gifts
and direct the minds of men from earthly to heavenly things.

(4) Later, indeed, when he had become a young man and
had established himself in the city of Rome with his widowed
mother and his sister (who had made a vow of virginity together with another girl companion, whose sister Candida
is likewise of the same profession and is now an old woman
living in Carthage), upon seeing the hands of bishops being
kissed by someone of the household, his sister or his mother,
he jokingly used to offer his right hand, saying that she
ought to do this for him, also, since he probably would become a bishop. For there was speaking in him the Holy
Spirit who was nurturing him for the episcopacy, but she
used to spurn the proposal, saying he was but a youth and
did not know what he was saying.

(5) After he had been taught in the liberal disciplines, he

---

1 Prov. 16.24.

left the city and began his public career in the court of the praetorian prefect. So well did he plead his cases here that he was chosen by the illustrious Probus, then the praetorian prefect, to be his adviser. After this, he received consular rank so as to govern the province of Liguria and Aemilia. And then he came to Milan.

Chapter 3

(6) About the same time, after the death of Auxentius, a bishop of the Arian heresy who retained possession of the church after Dionysius the Confessor, of blessed memory, was sent into exile, when the people were about to revolt in seeking a bishop, Ambrose had the task of putting down the revolt. So he went to the church. And when he was addressing the people, the voice of a child among the people is said to have called out suddenly: 'Ambrose bishop.' At the sound of this voice, the mouths of all the people joined in the cry: 'Ambrose bishop.' Thus, those who a while before were disagreeing most violently, because both the Arians and the Catholics wished the other side to be defeated and their own candidate to be consecrated bishop, suddenly agreed on this one with miraculous and unbelievable harmony.

(7) And when he realized this, he left the church and had a tribunal prepared for himself—indeed, he mounted higher steps because he would soon become a bishop. Then, contrary to his usual behavior, he ordered tortures to be inflicted on people. Although he did this, the people none the less kept shouting: 'Your sin be upon us.' But these people did not then shout as did the people of the Jews—for the Jews by their words shed the Lord's blood, saying: 'His

blood be upon us,'[1]—but these, knowing that he was a catechumen, were assuring him with a confident voice the re-
mission of all his sins through the divine grace of baptism.
Then, in a disturbed state of mind, he returned home and
wanted to declare himself a philosopher, but he was about
to become a true philosopher of Christ, since, in despising
the pomp of this world, he was about to follow the footsteps
of the fisherman who brought people to Christ not by a show
of words but by simple language and by the reasonableness
of the true doctrine. For they, having been sent without
wallet, without staff,[2] converted even philosophers. But,
when he was restrained from making this profession, he had
public women come to him openly for this one purpose, that,
when the people saw this, they would recall their intention.
The fact was, however, the people kept crying out more
and more: 'Your sin be upon us.'

(8) When he saw that nothing could accomplish his intention, he prepared his flight and left the city at midnight.
Since he intended to make his way to Ticinum, he was discovered the next morning at the gate of the city of Milan
which is called Roman. For God, who was preparing a strong
support for His Catholic Church against His enemies and
a tower of David against the face of Damascus, that is, the
perfidy of the heretics, checked his flight. And when he had
been found and was held in custody by the people, a report
was sent to the most kind emperor, then Valentinian, who
with very great joy realized the fact that the judges he sent
out were being sought for the episcopacy. Probus the prefect
rejoiced similarly, because his word was fulfilled in Ambrose,
for he had said to him as he set out, when his orders were

1 Matt. 27.25.
2 Cf. Matt. 10.9-10.

given to him as is the custom: 'Go, act not as judge, but as a bishop.'

(9) And so, while the result of the report was pending, he again attempted flight and for some time concealed himself on the estate of a certain honorable Leontinus. But, when the answer to the report came, he was handed over by this same Leontinus. For the order had been given to the deputy to insist on carrying out the matter, and, since he wished to fulfill the injunctions, he warned all by a published edict that, if they wished to take counsel for themselves and their property, they should hand over the man. Therefore, when he was handed over and had been taken to Milan and was aware of the will of God concerning himself and that he could no longer resist, he demanded that he should be baptized only by a Catholic bishop. For he was carefully guarding against the heresy of the Arians. Thus, when he was baptized, he is said to have fulfilled all the ecclesiastical offices, so that he was consecrated bishop on the eighth day with the greatest favor and joy on the part of all. Some years after his consecration he went to Rome, to his own estate, and there found the holy maiden mentioned above, to whom he used to offer his hand, in the home with his sister, just as he had left, for now his mother was dead. And when she kissed his hand, he smilingly said to her: 'See, as I used to say to you, you are kissing the hand of a bishop.'

(10) About this same time, when he was invited to the home of a very noble lady across the Tiber that he might offer the Holy Sacrifice in her home, a certain woman caretaker of a bath, who was confined to her couch as a paralytic, on learning that a bishop of the Lord was in the neighborhood, had herself carried in a little seat to the very home to which he had been invited and there touched his garments as he prayed and placed his hands upon her. And

when she fondly kissed them, her health was restored and she began to walk, so that there was fulfilled that saying of the Lord to the Apostle: 'For you shall do greater things than these, believing in my name.'[3] Yet, just as this miraculous cure was wonderful, so, also, it was not hidden; for I learned of it in this very district many years later on the authority of holy men when I was in the city.

(11) When he came to Sirmium to consecrate Anemius bishop, there by the power of Justina, empress at the time, and by an assembled multitude he was about to be driven from the church, so that an Arian bishop might be consecrated in that very church not by him, but by the heretics. But, when he had seated himself on the tribunal, caring nothing for a woman's disturbances, one of the girls of the Arian sect, more impudent than the rest, mounting the tribunal and taking hold of the bishop's vestment, since she wished to drag him to the group of women so that they might beat him and drive him from the church, heard him say, as the bishop himself used to relate: 'Even if I am unworthy of so great a bishopric, it is not fitting that you or your kind lay hands on any bishop of whatever sort. Thus you ought to fear God's judgment, lest something happen to you.' What happened confirmed this warning, for, on another day, he conducted her dead to her grave, repaying insult with kindness. And this deed instilled no light fear in his adversaries and gave great peace to the Catholic Church at the bishop's consecration.

Chapter 4

(12) And so, when he had consecrated a Catholic bishop,

---

3 John 14.12; cf. Acts 4.22.

he returned to Milan and there sustained many plots of a
woman, the above-mentioned Justina. For, by offering offices
and honors, she was stirring up the people against the holy
man. The weak were taken in by these promises, for the
promised tribuneships and divers other positions of rank to
those who would snatch him from his church and take him
into exile. Although many tried to do this, but were not
able, since God was his protector, one more wretched than
the rest, Euthymius by name, was aroused to such fury that
he arranged a house for himself next to the church and
placed a wagon in the same building in order that he might
more easily seize the man, put him in the cart, and carry
him into exile. 'But his iniquity came down upon his own
head,'[1] after a year to the very day on which he planned
to snatch away Ambrose, he himself was placed on the
same cart and sent away into exile from that same house,
doubtless reflecting that this had been turned upon him by
the just judgment of God, namely, that he was being sent
into exile on the very cart which he himself had prepared for
the bishop. And to him the bishop rendered not a very little
consolation, for he gave him expenses and other things which
were necessary.

(13) But this public admission of the man's worth checked
neither the woman's fury nor the madness of the insane
Arians, for, inflamed with greater madness, they tried to
break into the Portian Basilica. Even an army under arms
was ordered to guard the doors of the building, that no one
might dare to enter the Catholic church. But the Lord, who
usually gives triumphs to His Church over its adversaries,
turned the hearts of the soldiers to the defense of His Church,
so that, having turned their shields, they kept watch over the
doors of the church and did not allow the Catholic people to

1 Cf. Ps. 7.17.

leave, but in no way kept them from entering the church. More than this, the soldiers who had been sent were not satisfied with this, but also acclaimed the Catholic faith equally with the congregation. On this occasion, antiphons, hymns, and virgils first began to be practised in the church at Milan, And the devotion to this custom remains even to this very day, not only in the church, but through almost all the provinces of the West.

Chapter 5

(14) About the same time, the holy martyrs Protase and Gervase revealed themselves to the bishop. For they had been placed in the basilica in which there are today the bodies of the martyrs Nabor and Felix. The holy martyrs Nabor and Felix were visited very often, while the names as well as the sepulchres of Gervase and Protase were unknown, and to such an extent that all walked over their sepulchres who wished to approach the grates by which the sepulchres of the holy martyrs Nabor and Felix were protected from harm. But, when the bodies of the holy martyrs were raised and placed on biers, the diseases of many were shown to have been healed. Even a blind man, Severus by name, who even now piously serves in the same basilica which is called the Ambrosian, into which the bodies of the martyrs were taken, when he touched their garments, received his sight immediately. Likewise, bodies possessed by unclean spirits returned to their homes with the greatest gratitude after they had been healed. And as by these beneficent works of the martyrs the faith of the Catholic Church increased, so did the heresy of the Arians decrease.

(15) Finally, after this event, the persecution which was

incited by the fury of Justina, to the end that the bishop be driven from his church, began to abate. Yet, within the palace a great number of Arians who sided with Justina ridiculed such grace of God as the Lord Jesus deigned to confer upon His Catholic Church by the merits of its martyrs. And they claimed that the venerable man Ambrose had by means of money prepared men to state falsely that they were troubled by unclean spirits and to say that they were tortured by him just as by the martyrs. But the Arians said this with a Jewish expression—being, indeed, like them—for the Jews used to say of the Lord that: 'By Beelzebub, the prince of devils, He casts out devils.'[1] But the Arians were speaking of the martyrs and of the bishop of the Lord to the effect that not by the grace of God which was manifested in them were the unclean spirits driven out, but that they received money to declare falsely that they were tortured. For the devils used to say: 'We know that you are martyrs,' but the Arians: 'We do not know that you are martyrs.' For we read this also in the Gospel, where the devils said to the Lord: 'We know you, since you are the Son of God,'[2] and the Jews said: 'But as for this man, we do not know where He is from.'[3] This is not to be taken as the testimony of the devils, but as their confession; and so it is that the Arians and the Jews are more wretched in that they deny what the devils confess.

(16) But God, who usually increases grace for His Church, did not long suffer His saints to be insulted. Thus, one of the number, suddenly possessed by an unclean spirit, began to cry out that those were tortured as he himself was tortured who denied the martyrs or who did not believe the unity of the Trinity as Ambrose was teaching. But they, con-

1 Luke 11.15.
2 Mark 1.24.
3 John 9.29.

fused by this statement, although they ought to have been converted and to have done penance worthy of such confession, killed the man by immersing him in a pond, thus adding murder to heresy; for a fitting urgency led them to this end. Indeed, the holy bishop Ambrose, having become a man of greater humility, preserved the grace given him by the Lord and increased daily in faith and in love before God and man.

(17) About the same time, there was a certain man of the Arian heresy, violent beyond measure as a disputant and harsh and immovable as regards the Catholic faith. This man was in the church one day during a sermon by the bishop. Later, he himself related that he saw an angel there, speaking into the ears of the bishop as he preached, so that the bishop seemed to be proclaiming to the people the words of the angel. By this sight he was converted, and the faith which he formerly attacked he himself now began to defend.

(18) There were also at that time two chamberlains of Gratian, the emperor, who were of the Arian heresy. These two proposed to the bishop a question to be discussed, promising that they would be present the next day at the Portian Basilica to hear it. The question was one concerning the Incarnation of the Lord. But, on the next day, the two miserable men, filled with swollen haughtiness, unmindful of their promises, despising God in the person of His bishop, without any consideration for the injury done the waiting people, and unmindful also of the words of the Lord: 'But whoever causes one of these little ones who believe in me to sin, it were better for him to have a great millstone hung around his neck and to be drowned in the depths of the sea,'[4] mounted a traveling-carriage as if for a drive, and left the city and the waiting bishop and the people in their places in the church, I shudder at this insolence as I relate

---

4 Matt. 18.6.

its end, for they suddenly were thrown headlong from the
carriage and lost their lives. Their bodies were handed
over for burial. But the holy Ambrose, since he did not know
what had happened and since he was not able to hold the
people any longer, ascended the tribunal and began to de-
liver a sermon on the very question which had been proposed, saying: 'Brethren, I wish that my debt be paid, but
I do not find my creditors of yesterday . . . .,' and the other
things which are written in the book entitled, *On the Incarnation of the Lord.*

Chapter 6

(19) Thus, when the Emperor Gratian had been killed,
he undertook a second embassy to Maximus to recover the
body. And whoever wishes to learn how firmly he dealt with
him will discover this by reading the letter of this legation
which was handed to Valentinian the younger. But I have
decided that the insertion of the letter here would constitute
a departure from our promise, lest the prolixity of the letter,
if inserted, bother the reader. Indeed, he restrained Maximus
from receiving Communion, admonishing him to do penance,
worthy of the blood of his master which he had shed, and,
what is more serious, of an innocent man, if he wished to
receive any consideration before God. But, when he refused
with a haughty spirit to do penance, he lost not only future
but present safety as well, and the kingdom which he had
seized after the fashion of a woman he put aside in fear,
and then admitted that he had been the procurator, not
the emperor, of the state.

(20) After the death of Justina, when a certain soothsayer,
Innocent by name, but not in need, was being tormented by
the judge during a trial for his offenses, he began to make con-

fession of something other than was being sought. He exclaimed that he was suffering greater torments from the angel who was protecting Ambrose, because, in the time of Justina, to arouse the hatred of the people against the bishop, he had gone to the very top of the church and had performed sacrifices at midnight. But, the more insistently and unceasingly he carried on his evil practices, the more did the love of the people for the Catholic faith and for the bishop of the Lord increase. He admitted that he had also sent demons to kill him, but that the demons had reported that they not only could in no way approach him; further, they could not even get to the doors of the house in which the bishop was staying, because a fierce fire protected the entire building, so that, although they were a distance away, they were burned. He then terminated the wiles by which he thought he could effect something against the bishop of the Lord. Another had come even to his bedchamber with a sword to slay the bishop, but, having raised his hand with drawn sword, he stood fixed, with his right hand stiffened. And when he acknowledged that he had been sent by Justina, the right arm which had been stiffened when it was raised for the evil deed was restored by the confession.

(21) About the same time, when the illustrious man, Probus, had sent to the bishop his servant, a secretary, who was being troubled by an unclean spirit, the demon went out of the servant as he left the city, for he feared to be brought into the holy man's presence. And it happened that, as long as the boy was in Milan at the bishop's house, no influence of the demon appeared in him, but, when he had set out from Milan and come again toward the city, the same evil spirit which formerly possessed him began to vex him again. And when the evil spirit was asked by the exor-

cists why he had not appeared in the servant while he remained at Milan, he said that he had feared Ambrose and had thus withdrawn for a time, and had waited in that place where he had withdrawn from the servant until he should come back and that upon his return he had re-entered the vessel which he had left.

Chapter 7

(22) When Maximus was executed and Emperor Theodosius was at Milan, and Bishop Ambrose was at Aquileia, in a certain fortified city in a section of the East, a Jewish synagogue and a grove of the Valentinians were destroyed by fire, because the Jews, or certainly the Valentinians, kept scoffing at the Christian monks—for, indeed, the Valentinian heresy worships thirty gods. Now, an Eastern count sent a report of the action to the emperor, who, when he had received the report, straightway ordered that the synagogue be rebuilt by the bishop of the region and that fitting punishment be meted out to the monks. When the tone of this order reached the ears of the holy man, Bishop Ambrose, he directed a letter to the emperor, since he could not at the time go in person. In this letter he requested him to recall this order which he had issued, and to grant him an audience. And he added that, if he were not worthy to be heard by him, neither would he be worthy to be heard by the Lord in his behalf, nor would any one to whom he might entrust his prayers and promises; also, that he was prepared to undergo death for such a cause, lest by his failure in duty he make the emperor an apostate. For the emperor had given such unjust orders against the Church.

(23) Moreover, after he had returned to Milan, he

preached on this very topic in the presence of the people, and the emperor was present in the church at the time. In this sermon he introduced the person of the Lord as speaking to the emperor: 'I made you emperor from the lowest; I handed over to you the army of your enemy; I gave to you the supplies which he had prepared for his own army against you; I reduced your enemy into our power; I established one of your sons on the throne of the empire; I caused you to triumph without difficulty—and do you give triumphs over me to my enemies?' And the emperor said to him as he was descending the pulpit: 'You spoke against us today, Bishop.' But the bishop replied that he had not spoken against him, but for him. Then the emperor: 'Indeed, I issued a stern order against the bishop concerning the rebuilding of the synagogue. Moreover, the monks must be punished.' A like report was given by the counts who were present. But to these the bishop replied: 'I am dealing with the emperor now; with you I must deal later.' And so he secured the recall of those orders which had been issued, but not until he declared that he was unwilling to approach the altar unless the emperor gave assurance that he ought to go on. The bishop said to him: 'Do I act, then, with your promise of compliance?' 'Go on,' said the emperor, 'with my promise.' When this promise had been repeated, the bishop then freely performed the divine mysteries. These facts, moreover, are written in the letter which he wrote to his sister, in which he inserted the sermon which he delivered that same day about the staff of the nut tree which is reported to have been seen by the Prophet Jeremias.

(24) About the same time, because of the city of Thessalonica, much distress came upon the bishop when he had discovered that the city had almost been destroyed. The emperor had promised him that he would grant pardon to the

citizens of the above-mentioned city, but, because of the secret negotiations of the officers with the emperor and without the knowledge of the bishop, the city was put to the sword for more than an hour and very many innocent persons were slain. When the bishop learned that this had been done, he denied the emperor the privilege of entering the church, and he deemed him unworthy of the fellowship of the Church and of partaking of the sacraments, until he should do public penance. But the emperor made the assertion to him that David had committed adultery and homicide as well. To which the bishop replied: 'Since you have followed him in sinning, follow him in making correction.' When the most recipient emperor heard these words, he so took it to heart that he did not shudder at public penance, and the progress of this correction prepared him for a favorable victory.

(25) About the same time, two most powerful and most wise men of the Persians came to Milan to the famous bishop, bringing with them very many questions with which to probe his wisdom. And they discoursed with him from the first hour of the day to the third hour of the night, and then, amazed, took their departure. And to prove that they had not come for any other reason than to gain a better knowledge of the man whom they had known only by report, the next day, bidding farewell to the emperor, they set out for the city of Rome, wishing there to become acquainted with the power of the illustrious man, Probus. And when they had gained this knowledge, they returned to their native land.

Chapter 8

(26 When Theodosius had departed from Italy and was established in Constantinople, a delegation in the name of the Senate was dispatched to Emperor Valentinian in Gaul by Symmachus, at that time prefect of the city, about the restoration of the altar of Victory and the maintenance of the sacred rites. When the bishop learned of this, sending a complaint to the emperor, he demanded that copies of the report be sent to him, adding that he himself would reply to these in behalf of his own position. And when this report was received, he wrote a most remarkable refutation, so that Symmachus, although a very eloquent man, never ventured a reply. After Valentinian, of honored memory, had died in the city of Vienna, which is a city of the Gauls, Eugenius acceded to the imperial power. Not long after the beginning of his rule, at the requests of Flavian, the prefect, and of Count Abrogast, he conceded the restoration of the altar of Victory and the maintenance of its ceremonies, forgetful of his own faith and of the fact that Valentinian, of honored memory, while yet a young man, had denied similar requests.

(27) Now, when the bishop had learned this, he left the city of Milan to which Eugenius was coming in haste and moved on to Bologna, and from there he journeyed on as far as Faventia. When he had spent some days there, at the invitation of the Florentines, he continued his journey to Tuscia, avoiding the sight of the impious man, for he had no fear of the emperor. On the contrary, he sent a letter to him in which he prompted his conscience, and I think that a few of the many remarks from it ought to be inserted here: 'Even though the imperial power is great, consider, Emperor, how great God is: He sees the hearts of all; He

seeks into the inner conscience; He knows all things before
they occur; He knows the hidden thoughts of your heart.
You do not suffer yourself to be deceived, and do you wish
to hide from God? Did nothing suggest itself to your mind?
If they were acting so persistently, was it not your duty,
Emperor, to resist more persistently for the veneration of
the most high, the true, and the living God, and to deny
what was harmful to the holy law? And again: 'Therefore,
since I am bound by my words before God and men, I
thought that I had no other course of action, that no other
was fitting, except that I take thought for myself, since I
was not able to do so for you.'

(28) And so, while he was in the above-mentioned city
of the Florentines, he stayed in the home of the formerly illustrious Decens, for he also was a Christian man. Now,
this man's son, Pansopius by name, though still a mere lad,
was troubled with an unclean spirit. Although he had been
healed by frequent prayers and by the laying-on of the hands
of the bishop himself, yet, some days later, the lad was seized
by a sudden attack and died. As his mother was very devout
and full of faith and the fear of God, she took the child from
the upper to the lower part of the house and placed him
on the bishop's couch—he was absent at the time. When the
bishop returned and found the body on his couch, he had
compassion on the mother. And when he thought upon her
faith, like Eliseus of old he placed himself upon the child's
body and prayed so that him whom he found dead he returned alive to his mother. He also wrote a booklet for this
lad, so that later he might by reading become acquainted with
what he could not know by reason of his tender years. However, he did not mention this good deed in his writings, but
why he declined to do so is not ours to judge.

(29) In the same city he also established a church, in

which he placed the relics of the martyrs Vitalis and Agricola, whose bodies he had raised in the city of Bologna. There, the bodies of the martyrs had been buried among the bodies of the Jews, and this would not have become known had not the holy martyrs revealed themselves to the bishop of that church. And when they were placed under the altar which was in the same basilica, there was great joy and exultation in the hearts of the entire flock, but punishment for the demons as they confessed the merits of the martyrs.

(30) About the same time, Count Abrogast prepared war against his people, the Franks, and in an engagement he routed a considerable force. With the remainder he made peace. But when, at a banquet, he was asked by the princes of his nation whether he knew Ambrose, he replied that he did know him and was loved by him and had frequently dined with him. Then they said to him: 'Thus do you conquer, O Count, because you are loved by that man who says to the sun: Stand, and it stands.'' [1] This fact I have recorded here that those who read may know of what fame the holy man was even among unlettered tribes. For we also know this from the report of a certain youth of Abrogast, who was a devout young man and was present at the time. At the time when these things were spoken, he was also cupbearer.

(31) Then he set out from the district of Tuscia and returned to Milan. For Eugenius already had set out against Theodosius. There he waited the arrival of the Christian emperor, secure in the power of God, knowing that He would not hand over to unjust men the one who believes in Him, nor would He let fall the rod of sinners on the lot of the just, lest the just stretch forth their hands to iniquity. [2]

For Count Abrogast and Flavian the prefect had promised

---

1 Jos. 10.12-13.
2 Cf. Ps. 124.3.

at the time, as they were leaving Milan, that, when they had returned, they would make a stable of the basilica of the church at Milan and would examine the clerics for military service. But men, when they become unduly confident of their demons and 'open their mouths in blasphemy against God,'[3] are to be pitied, for they have deprived themselves of hope of victory. The cause of the disturbance was this. The gifts of the emperor who had taken part in the sacrilege were spurned by the Church and the fellowship of praying with the Church had not been granted him. But the Lord who protects His Church 'cast His judgment from heaven,'[4] and delivered complete victory to the devout emperor, Theodosius. Thus, when Eugenius and his followers were crushed and he received the emperor's letters, Ambrose had no greater care than to intercede for those whom he discovered to be accused. But, first, he made his request to the emperor in writing and sent by a deacon. Then, after John, at that time a tribune and a secretary but now a prefect, had been sent to protect those who fled to the church, he himself went to Aquileia to speak in their behalf. And for them pardon was easily gained, since the Christian emperor testified that he had been saved through his merits and intercessions.

(32) Therefore, he returned from the city of Aquileia, arriving one day before the emperor. And Theodosius, emperor of most gracious memory, did not live long after his sons were received into the Church and entrusted to the bishop. Ambrose survived the emperor almost three years. In this time he raised and transferred to the Basilica of the Apostles, which is at the Roman Gate, the body of St. Nazarius the martyr which had been buried in a garden outside the city. Indeed, we saw in the grave in which the body of

3 Cf. Apoc. 13.6.
4 Cf. Ps. 75.9.

the martyr was lying (but when he suffered we cannot learn
to the present day) the blood of the martyr as fresh as if it
had been poured forth the same day. His head also had been
severed by impious men, yet it was so complete and intact with its hairs and beard that it seemed to us that at
the very time in which it was being raised it had been washed
and placed there in the sepulchre. But, why is this to be
marveled at, when the Lord formerly promised this in the
Gospel: 'Not a hair of their head shall perish'?[5] Moreover,
we were filled with so striking an odor as surpassed the
sweetness of all perfumes.

(33) When the body of the martyr was raised and placed
on a litter, we straightway went with the holy bishop to pray
at the grave of the holy martyr Celsus, who was buried in
the same garden. However, we discovered that he had never
prayed in that place before. And this was the sign of a
newly discovered martyr: if the holy bishop had gone to pray
at a place to which he had not been before. We know, however, from the guardians of the place that it had been handed
down from generation to generation of their people not to
depart from there because great treasures had been buried
in that very place—and truly great treasures, which neither
rust nor moth consume nor do thieves dig through to and
steal, because their guardian is Christ and their dwelling is
the court of heaven, for whom to live was Christ and to die
was gain. Thereupon, the body of the martyr was taken to
the Basilica of the Apostles, where a short time before the
relics of the holy Apostles had been deposited with very
great devotion on the part of all. And on this occasion,
when the bishop was preaching, one of the crowd, who was
filled with an unclean spirit, began to cry out that he was
being tortured by Ambrose. But Ambrose, turning to him

5 Luke 21.18; cf. Matt. 10.30.

said: 'Be silent, demon. Ambrose is not torturing you, but the faith of the saints and your own envy, since you see men ascending to the place whence you were cast down, for Ambrose does not know how to be puffed up.' And when he had said this, the one who was crying out became silent and, prostrate on the ground, no longer made disturbing noise.

(34) About the same time, when the emperor Honorius during his consulship was making a public display of Libyan wild animals in the city of Milan, and while the people were assembling for the show, permission was given the soldiers who had then been sent Count Stilicho at the request of Eusebius the prefect to carry a certain Cresconius from the church by force. But, when he took refuge at the altar of the Lord, the holy bishop with the clerics who were present at the time gathered around to defend him. But the multitude of soldiers, whose leaders were of the Arian heresy, prevailed over the the few and, after snatching Cresconius away, they returned to the amphitheatre in an exultant mood, giving great sorrow to the Church. The bishop, prostrate before the altar of the Lord, long lamented the action. But, just when the soldiers had returned and reported to those who had sent them, the leopards were loosed and sprang with one movement to the very place where those who were celebrating a triumph over the Church were seated, and they left them seriously wounded. When Count Stilicho saw this he was so moved with repentance that for many days he made amends to the bishop and even loosed unharmed the one who had been snatched away. But, because he was guilty of the most serious crimes and could not be corrected otherwise, he sent him into exile, but soon thereafter he was granted pardon.

(35) On one occasion, when he was going to the palace and we were following him out of official duty, it happened

that a certain man lost his footing and fell sprawling to the ground. Theodulus, who was then a secretary, though afterwards he governed the church at Mutina in a most praiseworthy manner, was laughing at the mishap, whereupon the bishop turned and said to him: 'And you who stand, see to it that you do not fall.'[6] When he said this, he who laughed at the fall of another at once lamented his own.

(36) About this time, Frigitil, a certain queen of the Marcomanni, when she heard of the fame of the man from a certain Christian who by chance had come to her from Italy and was conversing with her, believed in Christ. For she recognized him as Christ's servant, and, sending gifts to the Church through her envoys, she asked that she be informed in his own writing as to what she ought to believe. And to her he wrote a most noteworthy letter in the form of a catechism, in which, also, he urged her to persuade her husband to keep peace with the Romans. When she had received the letter, she persuaded her husband to entrust himself, along with his people, to the Romans. When she came to Milan, she grieved very much for the holy bishop whom she had hastened to meet but did not find, for he had already departed this life,

(37) In the time of Gratian, to go back a little, when Ambrose came to the palace of Macedonius, master of the offices at the time, to intercede for a certain man, and had found the doors shut by order of the above-mentioned official and did not succeed in entering, he said: 'And you indeed shall come to the church, and finding the doors closed, you will not find an entrance.' And this happened. For, upon the death of Gratian, Macedonius, fleeing to the church, was unable to find an entrance, although the doors were open.

---

6 Cf. 1 Cor. 10.12.

Chapter 9

(38) Moreover, the venerable bishop himself was a man of much fasting, of many virgils, and of deeds, also, chastising his body by daily denials. It was his habit never to take breakfast except on the day of Sabbath and the Lord's Day, or when the feast days of the most celebrated saints occurred. His zeal in prayer was great night and day, nor did he shun the task of writing books with his own hand, except when his body was afflicted with some infirmity. He also had solicitude for all the Churches, as well as great zeal and constancy in intervening among them. He was equally courageous in discharging Church affairs, to such an extent that the duties which he alone had been accustomed to perform with respect to the catechumens, these same duties five bishops after the time of his death were scarcely able to perform. In like manner he was very solicitous for the poor and for prisoners. At the time when he was consecrated bishop, all the gold and silver which he might have had for himself he gave to the Church and to the poor. Further, the estates which he had, after retaining the portion for his sister, he gave to the Church, having retained for himself nothing which here he might call his own, so that as a lightly clad and unencumbered soldier he might follow Jesus Christ, 'who, being rich became poor for our sakes, that through His poverty we might be rich.'[1]

(39) 'He rejoiced also with those that rejoiced and wept with those that wept.'[2] For, as often as anyone confessed his sins to him to receive a penance, he so wept that he forced the penitent to weep. Thus did he seem to himself to be in a similar state with the penitent. But, cases of crime which

1 Cf. 2 Cor. 8.9.
2 Cf. Rom. 12.15.

used to be confessed to him he spoke of to no one save to the Lord alone, with whom he interceded, leaving a good example for future bishops to be intercessors with God rather than accusers with men. For, also according to the Apostle, with respect to a man of this sort, 'charity is to be confirmed,'[3] because he is his own accuser who, instead of waiting, anticipates his accuser, so as to lighten his own sin by confession, lest he have something which his adversary may accuse. And for this reason, Scripture says: 'The just is first accuser of himself.'[4] For he snatches away the voice of his adversary and, by the confession of his own sins, breaks to pieces, as it were, the teeth prepared for the prey of hostile accusation. In so doing he gives honor to God, to whom all things are naked, and who wishes the life rather than the death of the sinner.[5] Indeed, to the penitent himself confession alone does not suffice, unless correction of the deed follows, with the result that the penitent does not continue to do deeds which demand repentance. He should even humble his soul just as holy David, who, when he heard from the Prophet: 'Your sin is pardoned,'[6] became more humble in the correction of his sin, so that 'he did eat ashes like bread and mingled his drink with weeping.'[7]

(40) He used to weep most bitterly whenever, by chance, announcement was made to him of the death of a holy bishop, and to such an extent that we tried to console him, ignorant though we were of the deep devotion of the man and also ignorant as to why he was so weeping. And to us he used to make such reply, that he was not weeping because the one who had been announced as dead had departed, but because

---

3 Cf. 2 Cor. 2.8.
4 Prov. 18.17.
5 Cf. Heb. 4.13; Ezech. 18.32.
6 Cf. 2 Kings 12.13.
7 Cf. Ps. 101.10.

is was difficult to find a man who was deemed worthy of
the highest dignity of the episcopacy. Moreover, he himself
foretold his own death, saying that he would be with us
until Easter. And this he surely merited by reason of his
praying to the Lord that he might be free to depart hence
earlier.

(41) For he used to lament vehemently when he saw that
avarice, the root of all evils, which cannot be decreased by
abundance or lack, was increasing more and more in men.
Especially was this so in those who had been placed in positions of authority. And to such an extent was this true that
for him the task of putting a stop to it was most trying, for
all things were being upset for gain. At first, this condition
brought upon Italy every kind of evil. Thereafter, there was
a trend to a worse state of affairs. And what shall I add, if
it so works its fury in persons of the sort who usually simu-
late the cases of sons or relatives, 'to make excuses in sins,'[8]
since it actually has taken hold of very many, even of celi-
bates, both priests and deacons, whose portion is God, to
such an extent that even they practice it. And woe to us
wretched ones, for not even at the end of the world are we
so aroused that we wish to be set free from so heavy a yoke
of slavery which descends even to the depths of hell, 'that
we may make for ourselves friends of the mammon of iniquity, that they may receive us into everlasting dwellings.'[9]
Yet, blessed is he who, when he is once converted and has
broken his chains and put off the yoke of such domination,
shall take and dash his little ones against the rock,[10] that is,
he shall dash all his thoughts against Christ, who, according
to the Apostle, is 'the rock'[11] which destroys all who are

8 Ps. 140.4.
9 Cf. Luke 16.9.
10 Cf. Ps. 136.9.
11 Cf. 1 Cor. 10.4.

dashed against it, while it remains intact and does not make him guilty, but rather innocent, who has dashed against it the less desirable intentions of a wicked mind. For, only thus can one say confidently: 'The Lord is my portion.'[12] For, to whom there is nothing in this world, to him in truth is Christ the portion, and, despising these paltry things, he will receive much, and in particular shall possess life everlasting.[13]

(42) A few days before he was confined to his couch, when he was dictating the forty-third psalm, with me carefully taking it down, a fire like a small shield suddenly covered his head, and little by little entered his mouth, just as a person enters his home. After this, his face turned white as snow, but soon regained its usual appearance. When this happened, I was exceedingly scared and was unable to write down what he was saying until the vision itself had passed. At the time, he was speaking of the testimony of the sacred Scriptures which I remembered very well. For he left off writing and dictating that day, since, indeed, he was unable to finish that psalm. I, you may be sure, straightway reported what I had seen to the honorable deacon Castus, under whose care I was then living. But he, filled with the grace of God, pointed out to me from the passage of the Acts of the Apostles that I had seen in the bishop the coming of the Holy Spirit.

(43) Some days before, when Count Stilicho's servant had been troubled with a demon, but, now cured, was staying in the Ambrosian Basilica upon the recommendation of his master, he was reported to be forging letters of the tribunate to such an extent that men who were going to their assignments were detained. And this report was freely believed. But, when Count Stilicho discovered the character of his

---

12 Cf. Ps. 118.57.
13 Cf. Matt. 19.29.

servant, he did not wish to punish him. At the bishop's intervention, he even dismissed the men who had been deceived, but he made complaint to the bishop concerning him. Then the holy man, when he was leaving the Ambrosian Basilica, caused the servant to be sought out and brought to him. And when he had questioned him and had found him to be the author of so great a crime, he said: 'It is fitting that he be handed over to Satan for the destruction of his flesh, in order that no one hereafter may dare become guilty of such deed.' And at the very moment before the bishop completed the statement, the unclean spirit seized upon the man and began to tear him to pieces, so that we were filled with fear and wonderment at the sight, and in no small measure. Indeed, we saw that many in those days were cleansed of the unclean spirits by laying on of his hands and at his word.

(44) About the same time, when Nicentius, one of the tribune and notary class, who was so crippled by pain in his feet that he was rarely seen in public, had approached the altar to receive the sacraments and had cried out when the bishop accidently stepped on his foot, he heard the bishop say: 'Go, and be well henceforth.' And at the time of the bishop's departure from this world, he testified with tears that his feet had pained him no more.

Chapter 10

(45) But after these days, when he had ordained a bishop of the Church at Ticinum, he was taken ill, and, because of this, since he was being kept in bed for very many days, Count Stilicho is reported to have said that, if so great a man should depart this life, ruin would threaten Italy. Ac-

cordingly, having summoned to himself the nobles of the city, whom he knew were loved by the bishop, he threatened them to some extent and then with flattering words persuaded them to go to the holy bishop and induce him to beg of the Lord an extension of life for himself. But, when he heard this from them, he replied: 'I have not so lived among you that I am ashamed to live, nor do I fear to die, because we have a good Lord.'

(46) During this time, when Castus, Polemius, Venerius, and Felix, who were then deacons, were together in the farthest part of the portico in which he was lying and were conversing with one another in a voice so suppressed that they scarcely could hear one another as to who should be ordained bishop after his death, and when they spoke the name of holy Simplicianus, Bishop Ambrose, as if he were taking part in the discussion, although he was lying far from them, exclaimed three times approvingly: 'Old, but good.' For Simplicianus was of mature age. And when they heard this noise they fled, thoroughly frightened. Yet, when he had died, none other succeeded him in the episcopacy except him whom the bishop designated by a triple expression as a good old man. And to this Simplicianus, Venerius, whom I have just mentioned, was successor. Felix, indeed, even to this time governs the church at Bologna. Castus, moreover, and Polemius, having been nourished by Ambrose, good fruits of a good tree, are performing the office of deacon in the church at Milan.

(47) In the same place in which he was lying, as we have learned from a report of St. Bassianus, bishop of the church at Lodi, for he himself had heard it from St. Ambrose, when he was praying with this St. Bassianus, he observed that the Lord Jesus had approached him and was smiling upon him. And not many days later he was taken away from us. On

the very day of his departure to the Lord, he prayed with arms stretched out in the form of a cross, from about the eleventh hour of the day until the hour in which he breathed forth his spirit. We truly saw that his lips were moving, but we did not hear his voice. Honoratius, also, bishop of the church at Vercelli, having composed himself for rest in the upper part of the house, heard the voice of one calling him a third time, saying to him: 'Arise, hasten, for now he is about to depart.' And he went down and offered the holy man the Body of the Lord, which he received, and, as soon as he had swallowed it, he breathed forth his spirit, bearing with him a good Viaticum, so that his soul, more refreshed by this Food, now rejoices in the company of angels according to whose life he lived on earth, and in the company of Elias; for as Elias never feared to speak to kings or to any potentates, so neither did he fear to speak for fear of God.

(48) Thereafter, his body was carried to the greater church the hour before the dawn in which he died and was there the same night on which we kept the vigil of Easter. And a great many baptized infants saw him when they were coming from the font, so that some said they saw him sitting on the throne in the sanctuary, while others indicated with their fingers to their parents that they saw him walking, but they, although they looked, were not able to see him, because they did not have pure eyes. There also were very many who related that they had seen a star over his body. But, as it began to dawn on the Lord's Day, after the divine rites had been performed, when his body was being lifted up to be carried from the church to the Ambrosian Basilica in which it was placed, a crowd of demons there cried out that they were being tortured by him, and so loudly that their wailings could not be endured. And this grace of the bishop re-

mains not only in that place, but even in a great many provinces even to this day. Crowds of men and women also threw their hankerchiefs and sashes so that the body of the holy man might be touched by them in some way. For those taking part in the obsequies formed an innumerable crowd; men, women, and children of every rank and of all ages, not only Christians, but also Jews and pagans. However, the group of those who had been baptized led the procession, because of their greater grace.

(49) On the very day on which he died, as is indicated by the text of the letter which was received by the venerable Simplicianus, his successor, and which was sent from the East to Ambrose himself—the letter being kept even till now in the monastery at Milan—he appeared to certain holy men, praying with them and laying hands on them. And the letter which was sent carries a date, and when we read it, we discovered that it was the day on which he died.

(50) In Tuscia, too, in the district of Florence where the holy man Zenobius is now bishop, Ambrose, because he had promised that he would visit more frequently those seeking him, was seen praying at the altar which is in the Ambrosian Basilica he built. This we learned from the report of the holy Bishop Zenobius himself. In the same house in which he stayed while refusing to see Eugenius, at the time when Rodagaisus was besieging the above-mentioned city, when the citizens had despaired of their safety, he also appeared to a certain man and promised that safety would come to them the following day. When this report was received, the spirits of the citizens were revived. And the next day, upon the arrival of Count Stilicho with an army, victory was gained over the enemy. These facts we know from the report of Pansophia, a devout woman, the mother of the boy, Pansophius.

(51) Holding his staff in his right hand, he also appeared

in a night vision to Mascezel, who was despairing of his own
safety as well as the safety of his army which he was leading
against Gildo. And when Mascezel threw himself at the
holy man's feet, the old man, for in this guise Ambrose appeared to him, striking the ground three times, said: 'Here,
here, here,' signifying the place, and he gave understanding
to Mascezel, for he had adjudged him worthy of the visitation, that he might know that in the very place in which
he had seen the holy bishop of the Lord he would gain a
victory the third day. Therefore, he opened battle with assurance and completed it. We, however, stationed in Milan,
learned this from the report of Mascezel himself. For, in this
province in which we are now stationed and are writing, he
told this very happening to many bishops. But even to these
reports we have thought it safer to add in this book the things
known also to us.

(52) Also at Milan we received with deepest devotion the
remains of the martyrs, Sisinius and Alexander, who in our
time, that is, after the death of Ambrose, gained the crown
of martyrdom in the pagan persecutions in the regions of
Anauni. At this time, there came a certain blind man, who,
by touching the coffin in which the remains of the saints were
being carried, that same day received sight. From his report we learned that in a vision he had seen a ship approaching the shore, in which were a great number of men clothed
in white, when, as they were disembarking he asked one of
the crowd to learn who the men were, he found that they
were Ambrose and his companions. And upon hearing the
name Ambrose, when he was praying that he might receive
his sight, he heard from Ambrose: 'Proceed to Milan and
contact my brothers who are about to go there' (indicating
the day), 'and you will receive sight.' The man was, as he
himself said, from the Dalmatian coast. And he further de-

clared that he had not come to the city before he met with
the remains of the saints on the highway, at which time he
still lacked sight, but upon touching the bier he began to see.

Chapter 11

(53) Thus, having noted these facts, I do not regard it a
serious matter if we exceed a little the bounds of our promise,
in order that we may point out that the word of the Lord
which He has spoken through the mouth of the holy prophets
has been fulfilled: 'The man that sitteth against his brother
and detracteth him in private will I persecute.'[1] And again:
'Love not to detract, lest you be destroyed,'[2] so that who-
soever by chance has been a victim of this habit, when he has
read in what manner vengeance has been taken against those
who dared detract from the holy man, he himself in company
with others may be corrected.

(54) Now, a certain Donatus, an African by race, yet
a presbyter of the church at Milan, was suddenly inflicted
with a serious wound. At the time, he was attending a banquet at which were some military men of devout nature, who
spurned his scurrilous speech and turned from him when he
disparaged the memory of Ambrose. From the very spot in
which the wound struck him down he was raised by unfriendly hands and placed on a couch, and from there was
carried straight to his grave. Again, in the city of Carthage
I went for a meal to the house of the deacon Fortunatus, a
brother of the venerable Bishop Aurelius. Vincentius, Bishop
of Colositanum, Muranus, Bishop of Bolita, as well as other
bishops and deacons were also present. When, on this oc-

---

1 Cf. Ps. 100.5.
2 Paulinus uses the Greek text here; cf. Prov. 20.13.

casion Bishop Muranus was disparaging Ambrose, I mentioned to him the fate of the above-mentioned presbyter, and this story concerning another he confirmed by his own early departure. For, from the very place in which he was lying, when he suddenly had been struck by a huge wound, he was carried to bed by unfriendly hands. And thence, being taken back to the house in which he had been entertained, he brought his last day to a close. Such was the end of those defaming Ambrose, so that those who were present and saw it were struck with awe.

(55) I therefore exhort and implore every man who reads this book to imitate the life of Ambrose, to praise the grace of God and to shun the voices of detractors, if, indeed, he wishes to have fellowship with Ambrose in the resurrection of life rather than to undergo with those detractors a punishment which a wise man avoids.

(56) I ask also your Blessedness, father Augustine, with all the saints who invoke the name of our Lord Jesus Christ in truth, to deign to pray for me, the most lowly and sinful Paulinus, so that, although in gaining grace I am not worthy to have fellowship with so great a man, having gained pardon for my sins, I may have the reward of escaping punishment.

LIFE OF ST. AUGUSTINE
BY BISHOP POSSIDIUS

Translated by
SISTER MARY MAGDELEINE MULLER, O.S.F., Ph.D.
Cardinal Stritch College
and
ROY J. DEFERRARI, Ph.D.
The Catholic University of America

INTRODUCTION

SOME THIRTY YEARS after the death of the renowned
Bishop of Hippo, another member of the episcopal
hierarchy published an account of his co-laborer's
life and merits. Thus, Possidius, Bishop of Calama in Numidia, gave to his contemporaries and followers the graphic
story of the life of St. Augustine. Addressed to the people of his
day, this biography aims at the edification of the faithful
through a consideration of the sanctity of its subject.

Possidius had been a pupil and friend of Augustine. The
influence of his teacher had such a profound effect that the
younger man longed to share his enthusiasm with others.
Keeping this end in view, the author proceeded to write his
panegyric, which contains interesting details on the life and
death of the saint.

Although a comparatively early example of Christian biography, the *Vita Augustini* has considerable merit. Admit-
tedly not a complete picture (Possidius definitely states his intention of omitting all the material included in Augustine's
own *Confessions*), the account clearly portrays an energy
and activity, a zeal for truth and God's glory, which may well
be imitated as well as admired. There is no scarcity of actual
facts, no vague impression of holiness requiring rhetorical
embellishment, but an abundance of Christian social principle
in practice.

The difficult situations which the intrepid defender of the faith encountered are clearly indicated. However, it is not the bare facts alone, but the spirit of the saint permeating them all which attracts attention. Manichaeans, Donatists, Pelagians—each in turn felt the force of his strong personality opposing their heretical teachings. Discourses, sermons, writings—all possible means were employed to further the cause of truth and Christian living.

Many of the facts in the life of Augustine would, perhaps, be lost to the world except for the work of Possidius. Personal details on his inner life, as well as first-hand information on his external activity, last illness, and death are included.

Stylistically, the *Vita* is a good example of early Christian biography, for it combines in pleasing proportion facts from the life of its subject with a eulogistic treatment of it. The author's aim is obviously, but not too obviously, to impress the reader with the merits of the saint; however, this is accomplished by an objective presentation of concrete information rather than by purely laudatory oratory. The Latin is in a good, easy style, without overemphasis on rhetorical effect. Altogether, the work presents a pleasant-reading, instructive, and inspirational history of Augustine's accomplishments.

For the translation, Weiskotten's edition was used. There may be some instances of interpretations similar to those of Weiskotten, but the divergences are probably more conspicuous.

Whenever Possidius quotes Holy Scripture, if his words are an exact rendering of the Vulgate edition, the Douay translation has been followed; otherwise, the Latin version has been translated as it appears.

CONTENTS

THE LIFE OF ST. AUGUSTINE

Preface

UNDER THE INSPIRATION of God, the Creator and Ruler of all things, and mindful of my purpose whereby through the grace of the Saviour I resolved to serve faithfully the omnipotent and divine Trinity, I have striven both formerly in my life as a layman and now in my office of bishop, with whatever talent and eloquence I possess, to help toward the edification of the true and holy Catholic Church of Christ the Lord. For this reason I am by no means disposed to be silent concerning the life and character of the illustrious Bishop Augustine, either as I observed personally in him or as was related by him who was predestined and especially esteemed in his own day. For we have read and observed that this was often done in the past by most devout men of our holy mother, the Catholic Church. Under the guidance of the Holy Spirit, yet using their own language and style, they likewise spoke and wrote accounts for the instruction of those men who wished to be informed. In this way they brought to the notice of the zealous the character and greatness of men who, by the grace of the Lord which is given to all men in this world, merited to live and to persevere until the end of their course.

73

Therefore, by the grace of God I, too, the least of all His stewards, with faith unfeigned as becomes all the righteous and faithful who serve and please the Lord of Lords, have undertaken to unfold the origin, career, and worthy end of the aforementioned venerable man as I have learned from him through many years of close association. But I beseech the Divine Majesty that I may continue and complete this task which I have assumed in such a way that I may not offend the truth of the Father of lights and may seem in no way to deceive the love of good sons of the Church. I shall not attempt to include all the details which the same most blessed Augustine pointed out concerning himself in the books of his *Confessions;* for example, what manner of man he was and what kind of life he led before and after the reception of grace. According to the Apostle, Augustine wished to do this so that no one would believe or think him otherwise than he really was or greater than rumor made him. With this in mind, the holy man certainly did not fail in his practice of humility, since he did not seek his own praise but that of his Lord for his own deliverance and blessings, both those which he had already received and those which he desired to receive through the prayers of his brethren. Therefore, as we read on the authority of an angel: 'It is good to hide the secret of a king: but honorable to reveal and confess the works of God.'

Chapter 1

Augustine was born, then, in the province of Africa, in the city of Tagaste, of honorable parents. He was nourished and fostered by their care and diligence with special training in secular literature, that is, he was instructed in all the disciplines which are called liberal. At first, indeed, he taught grammar in his own city, and afterwards rhetoric in Carthage, the capital of Africa. In later years, he was instructor in the city of Rome and at Milan where the court of the emperor, Valentinian the younger, had then been established. At that time, the episcopacy in this city was being administered by Ambrose, a bishop most pleasing to God and most illustrious among the best of men. As Augustine stood among the people in church, he listened with eager suspense to the frequent discussions of this preacher of the word of God. While still a youth in Carthage, he had been led astray by the error of the Manichaeans, and because of this he attended the sermons with greater anxiety than others, lest something might be said for or against the heresy. Now it happened through the mercy of God the Deliverer, who touched the heart of His bishop, that the questions of the Law relative to that error were solved, and thus Augustine was gradually instructed, so that little by little through divine compassion the heresy was expelled from his soul. Once he was established in the Catholic faith, an eager longing to become proficient in religion was stirred up within him, with the result that at the approaching holy days of Easter he received the waters of salvation. Thus, by extraordinary divine assistance, Augustine received the saving doctrine of the Catholic Church and the divine sacraments through the ministry of the great and illustrious prelate, Ambrose.

Chapter 2

From the bottom of his heart he soon abandoned every hope that he had in the world, with no further desire for wife, children of the flesh, riches, or worldly honors. He

determined, instead, to serve God in company with His
servants, anxious to be in and of that little flock which the
Lord addressed, saying: 'Fear not, little flock, for it hath
pleased your Father to give you a kingdom. Sell what you
possess and give alms. Make to yourselves bags which grow
not old, a treasure in heaven which faileth not,' [1] and so on.
This holy man also desired to fulfill that saying of our Lord
on another occasion: 'If thou wilt be perfect, sell all that thou
hast and give to the poor and thou shalt have treasure in
heaven, and come, follow me.' Therefore he was eager to
build on the foundation of faith, not on wood, hay, and
stubble, but on gold, silver, and precious stones. At this
time he was more than thirty years old. His mother, sole
living relative, clung to him and exulted more over his resolution to serve God than she would have over the hope of
natural offspring. His father had already died sometime
earlier. Then, because of his determination to serve God,
Augustine announced to the pupils whom he taught that
they should look for another teacher of rhetoric.

Chapter 3

After his conversion, Augustine decided that he would return to Africa, to his own home and estate, taking with him
neighbors and friends who, like him, were serving God. Having reached his native land, he lived there for nearly three
years, but then renounced his property and joined those
faithful who, constantly meditating on the law of God, served
Him by fasting, prayers, and good works. By his sermons
and writings he taught his followers the truths which God
had revealed to him during his meditations and prayers. At

---

1 Luke 12.32-33.

about this time it happened that a certain good, God-fearing Christian, established at Hippo—a so-called 'agent in affairs' —heard of Augustine's fine reputation and learning. This man earnestly desired to see him, promising to renounce all the passions and allurements of this world if at some time he might deserve to hear the word of God from the renowned man's lips. When this report reached Augustine on reliable evidence, he immediately departed of his own accord to Hippo, anxious to free that soul from the dangers of this life and from eternal death. Having met the man, Augustine spoke with him frequently and exhorted him to fulfill his vow to God, according to the measure of grace. Day after day the man promised to do so; however, as long as Augustine was present he did not keep his word. The holy man's exhortations, nevertheless, were not vain and useless, for Divine Providence was acting through an instrument cleansed unto honor, profitable to the Lord, and prepared for every good work.

Chapter 4

Now, at this time, holy Valerius was bishop of the Catholic Church at Hippo. Because of the pressing duties of his ecclesiastical office, this man addressed the people of God, encouraging them to provide and ordain a presbyter for the city. Consequently, the Catholics, who already knew about the life and teaching of holy Augustine, laid hands on him. (He was standing among the crowd, in security and ignorance of what was about to happen, for it was his custom as a layman, he has told us, to withhold his presence only from those churches which had no bishops.) Therefore, they seized him and, as is customary in such cases, brought him to the bishop for ordination, since this was what all wished.

Augustine wept freely as they eagerly presented their request
with loud shouting. The cause of his tears, as he himself
told us later, was interpreted by some of the people to be
the result of wounded pride, and therefore by way of consolation they told him that, though he was worthy of a
greater honor, the office of presbyter was close to the bishopric in rank. The man of God, however, as his own words affirm, had a greater understanding of the matter. He grieved
because he anticipated the many imminent dangers which
threatened his life in the rule and government of the Church.
This was the cause of his tears. However, everything was accomplished in accordance with the will of the people.

Chapter 5

Soon after his ordination as presbyter, Augustine founded
a monastery within the Church, and began to live there
among the servants of God according to the rule and custom
established by the holy Apostles. The principal regulation of
that society specified that no one should own anything, but
that all things should be held in common and distributed
according to personal needs. Augustine had formerly done
this when he returned home from across the sea. The holy
Valerius, who had ordained him, being a good, God-fearing
man, rejoiced and gave thanks to God. He said that the
Lord had heard his repeated prayers imploring Divine Providence to send a man of such a character as could edify
the Church of the Lord by the salutary teaching of His word.
Since Valerius was a Greek by birth and less versed in the
Latin language and literature, he realized his limitations in
that respect. Therefore, he gave his presbyter the right to
preach the Gospel in his presence in church and to hold

frequent public discussions—a procedure contrary to that usually practised in African churches. As a consequence, the criticism of some bishops was incurred. The venerable and prudent Valerius, however, fully cognizant of the fact that such was the custom in Eastern churches, and in consideration of the Church's welfare, paid no attention to the tongues of detractors. He was satisfied in knowing that his presbyter was doing what he himself as bishop could not accomplish. Thus this burning and shining light was placed upon a candlestick to enlighten all who were in the house. News of this practice spread quickly, and because of Augustine's good example other presbyters with episcopal authorization began to preach to the people in the presence of their bishops.

Chapter 6

At this time, in the city of Hippo, the false doctrine of the Manichaeans had infected and permeated many people, both natives and foreigners. The cause of this deception and seduction was a certain presbyter of that sect, Fortunatus by name, a permanent resident of the place. Meanwhile, the Christian inhabitants of Hippo, Christians and even Donatists, came to the presbyter Augustine and demanded that he meet this presbyter of the Manichaeans, whom they believed a learned man, and argue with him concerning the law. Augustine in no wise refused to do this. He was, as it is written, ready to give an answer to anyone who might ask a reason for his faith and hope in God, and he was capable of exhorting and refuting his opponents with sound doctrine. Nevertheless, he first endeavored to learn the will of Fortunatus. So the people immediately reported the situation to the Manichaean, asking, exhorting, and even demanding that

he on no account refuse the opportunity. Fortunatus, however, had known Augustine formerly at Carthage, when the
latter was still involved in the same error, so he was afraid
to oppose him. But, when he had been repeatedly urged and
shamed by the insistence of his followers, he finally promised
to meet Augustine face to face and to debate the issue. Whereupon, they met at an appointed time and place. Many people
gathered, some really interested and others merely curious.
The discussion began as soon as the reporter's books were
opened, and ended on the second day. In the debate, the
Manichaean teacher, as the record shows, could not refute
the Catholic argument. He was likewise unable to prove that
the Manichaean sect was founded on the truth. However,
when he failed in his final answer, Fortunatus resolved to
refer to his superiors all the arguments which he had been
unable to refute. If they, too, should not satisfy him, he
would consult the judgment of his own soul. Immediately,
then, all the people who had previously considered him great
and learned, decided that he had accomplished nothing in
the defense of his own sect. Overcome with confusion, he departed from the city of Hippo within a short time, never
again to return. Thus Augustine removed that heresy from
the hearts of all men who knew what had taken place. So,
too, the Catholic faith was expounded and defended as the
true religion.

Chapter 7

Publicly and privately, at home and in church, Augustine
confidently taught and preached the word of salvation. Both
his finished books and his extemporaneous sermons opposed
the African heresies, especially Donatism, Manichaeism, and
paganism. At the same time, the Christians with unspeakable

admiration and praise were not silent about the matter but published it wherever possible. So, by the grace of God, the Catholic Church in Africa began to raise its head. For a long time it had lain prostrate, seduced, oppressed, and over-powered. On the other hand, the heretics gained strength, particularly the rebaptizing Donatist party, which comprised a large number of Africans. Even they gathered together and with the Catholics eagerly listened to Augustine's books and treatises. Through the wonderful grace of God these writings were issued and flowed forth with an abundance of instruction based on reason and with the authority of the Holy Scriptures. At these gatherings, whoever wished and was able to do so brought reporters to take down what was said. In this way the glorious doctrine and the sweet savor of Christ were manifested and spread throughout all Africa. The Church of God across the sea heard about it, too, and like-wise rejoiced. Just as when one member suffers all the other members suffer with it, so when one member is honored all the other members rejoice with it.

Chapter 8

The venerable old man, Valerius, rejoiced more than others and gave thanks to God for the special blessings his church had received. He began to fear, however, for such is human nature, that some other church which lacked a bishop might seek Augustine for the episcopal office and so take him away. Indeed, that would have happened if the bishop himself, upon discovering the plan, had not taken precautions. He arranged that Augustine should go to a secret place and be hidden so that he could not be found by those who were seek-ing him. Nevertheless, the old man continued to fear, realizing his age and extreme infirmity. Consequently, he wrote a secret letter to the Bishop of Carthage, the episcopal primate, stressing the weakness of his body and the burden of his years, and for this reason he petitioned the appointment of Augustine as bishop of the church at Hippo. As such, Augustine would not be his successor, but would be associated with him as coadjutor. Valerius' desire and request were answered by a satisfactory reply. Accordingly, to the astonishment of all, he revealed his plan when Megalius, Bishop of Calama and primate of Numidia, upon request visited the church at Hippo. Those bishops who happened to be present at that time, as well as the clergy of Hippo, and all the people, rejoiced upon hearing this and eagerly shouted for its fulfillment. The presbyter, however, refused to accept the episcopacy, as being contrary to ecclesiastical practice, since his bishop was still alive. Then, everyone tried to convince him that this was common usage by citing examples of its existence in churches across the sea and in Africa, and, although Augustine had not heard of it before, he yielded under compulsion and constraint, consenting to ordination to the higher office. Later, he said and wrote that his ordination to the episcopacy during the lifetime of his bishop should not have taken place, according to the prohibition of the Ecumenical Council. He was unaware of this regulation, however, until after his ordination, but he did not want others to experience what regretfully had happened to him. For that reason he made it his business to have the councils of the bishops decree that consecrating prelates should inform those about to be ordained or already ordained concerning the regulations that govern all priests. Accordingly, this was done.

Chapter 9

As bishop, Augustine preached the word of eternal salvation much more earnestly, fervently, and with greater authority, not only in one church, but wherever he was invited. He was always ready to give an answer to those who asked a reason for his faith and hope in God. The Church of the Lord now flourished and grew rapidly and strongly. Surprisingly enough, the Donatists living in Hippo and the neighboring towns brought his sermons and writings to their bishops. Sometimes, upon hearing them, these men raised objections, which were either refuted by their own followers or referred to the holy Augustine. He studied them slowly and patiently, laboring constantly both day and night. (As we read, he worked out the salvation of men with fear and trembling. He pointed out that the heretics would and could refute nothing, so true and manifest is the doctrine which the Church of God believes and teaches.) Augustine even wrote private letters to some of the prominent bishops and laymen of this heresy. Through the arguments which he presented he urged and exhorted them either to abandon the error or at least to come and discus it with him. In their distrust, however, the heretics were unwilling to reply by written word, but in their resentment they furiously denounced Augustine, both publicly and privately, as a seducer and deceiver of souls. They preached that, in order to defend their flock, the wolf had to be killed. Neither fear of God nor shame before men troubled them as they taught the people to believe that whoever would successfully accomplish this would undoubtedly have all his sins forgiven. Augustine, meanwhile, tried to show them their lack of faith in their own cause. When they met in public conferences, no one dared to debate with him.

Chapter 10

Now, these Donatists had in almost all their churches a strange group of men, perverse and violent, who professed continency and were called Circumcellions. They were very numerous and were organized in bands throughout almost all the regions of Africa. Inspired by evil teachers of insolent boldnes and lawless temerity, they spared neither their own people nor strangers, but, contrary to right and justice, deprived men of their civil rights. Those who refused to submit to them were visited with the severest losses and injuries, as the Circumcellions, armed with various kinds of weapons, madly overran farms and estates and did not even fear to resort to bloodshed. Moreover, when the word of God was diligently preached and a plan for peace was suggested, they who hated peace freely assailed the person who proposed it. Those Circumcellions who wished and were able broke away or secretly withdrew from their sect, when, in the face of their teachings, the truth became known. They then came back to the peace and unity of the Church, with as many of their own group as they could take with them. Consequently, when the remaining Circumcellions saw that the congregations of their sect were growing smaller, they became envious of the Church's growth. Inflamed with intense anger, they carried out intolerable persecutions against the unity of the Church, with the help of confederates. By day as well as by night, Catholic priests and ministers were attacked; they were robbed of all their possessions; many servants of God were even crippled by torture. Some had lime mixed with vinegar thrown in their eyes, and others were killed. As a result, these rebaptizing Donatists came to be hated even by their own people.

Chapter 11

As the divine teachings prospered, the clerics of the church at Hippo, who had served God in the monastery with holy Augustine, began to be ordained. Consequently, the truths taught by the Catholic Church, as well as the manner of life practised by the holy servants of God, especially their continence and extreme poverty, became more celebrated day by day. To insure peace and unity, the Church eagerly began to demand bishops and priests from the monastery that had been founded and strengthened by the zealous Augustine. Later, the request was fulfilled. The most blessed founder gave about ten men, holy and venerable, chaste, and learned, to various churches, some of them being quite prominent. Like him, those holy men who came from that community increased the churches of the Lord and also established monasteries. As their zeal for spreading God's word increased, they in turn supplied other churches with brethren who had been elevated to the priesthood. And thus, because of their number, the teaching of the Church's salutary faith, hope, and charity became known to many people. This was true not only throughout all parts of Africa but even across the sea, by means of Greek editions and translations. So, too, as we read, 'the wicked saw it and was angry,' gnashing with his teeth and fainting away. Thy servants, however, as we read again, were peaceable toward those who hated peace, and acceded willingly to any discussion.

Chapter 12

These armed Circumcellions frequently blocked the roads
even against the servant of God, Augustine, when, upon request, he chanced to visit the Catholics whom he frequently
instructed and exhorted. It once happened that, although the
heretics were out in full force, they still failed to capture
him. Through his guide's mistake, but actually by the providence of God, the bishop happened to arrive at his destination
by a different road. He learned later that, because of this
error, he had escaped impious hands. Thereupon, together
with his companions, he gave thanks to God, his Deliverer.
However, as the public records show, the heretics, adhering
to their old practice spared neither the clergy nor the laity.

In this connection we must not fail to mention what the
illustrious Augustine accomplished for the glory of God
against the above-mentioned rebaptizing Donatist, through
his ardor and zeal for the house of God. On one occasion,
one of the bishops whom he had given to the Church from
the clergy of his monastery, together with several priests,
visited the church at Calama. This diocese was under his
care, and in the interest of the Church's peace the bishop
had used all his knowledge in preaching against the heresy.
Accordingly, in the middle of his journey, he fell into an am-
buscade. Although he escaped with all his companions, their
animals and baggage were stolen. The bishop himself was
left seriously injured and wounded. Therefore, in order that
the progress of the Church's peace might not be further im-
peded, this defender of the Church did not remain silent
before the law. A warning was consequently issued to Crispinus, the Donatist bishop in the city and region of Calama,
who long had been recognized as a learned man. According
to the civil laws which were directed against the heretics,

he became liable to a fine of gold. When he protested against the regulations, Crispinus was brought before the consul, where he denied that he was a heretic. It then became necessary that the defender of the Church withdraw and as a Catholic bishop oppose and convict Crispinus of being a heretic. For, if the heretic had succeeded in his dissimulation, ignorant people might have considered him a Catholic bishop. Thus, due to neglect, an obstacle might have arisen in the path of weak people. Upon the firm insistence of the illustrious Bishop Augustine, however, both bishops of Calama met for a debate. Consequently, for the third time they came together in conflict concerning their different communions, while a great multitude of Christian people in Carthage and throughout all Afrca awaited the outcome of the case. The result was the Crispinus was pronounced a heretic by written proconsular sentence. However, the Catholic bishop interceded with the judge in Crispinus' behalf. He asked that the fine of gold be withdrawn, and his request was granted. Then Crispinus ungratefully appealed to higher authority, to the most clement prince. His appeal required a decisive answer from the emperor. Therefore, he ordered that the Donatists should have no rights anywhere and should be held to the binding force of all laws enacted against heretics. By the same order the judge and the officers of his court and Crispinus himself, although he had not previously been forced to pay, were ordered to contribute ten pounds of gold into the treasury. Immediately, however, the Catholics bishops, and especially Augustine of blessed memory, attempted to have the general sentence withdrawn through the indulgence of the emperor. With the Lord's help, this was accomplished. Because of this vigilance and holy zeal, the Church increased greatly.

Chapter 13

Because of all these efforts for the Church's peace, the
Lord gave the palm to Augustine in this life, and reserved
the crown of righteousnes for him in the life with Himself.
With Christ's help, the unity of peace, that is, the brother-
hood of God's church, grew and multiplied more and more
from day to day. This was especially true after the conference which was held a little later at Carthage. All the
Catholic together with the Donatist bishops met at the command of the most glorious and devout emperor, Honorius,
who, to accomplish his purpose, had sent the tribune and
notary, Marcellinus, from his own court to Africa to act as
judge. In the controversy the heretics were completely silenced, and, after they had been convicted of error by the
Catholics, were reprimanded by sentence of the judge. In
answer to their appeal, these unrighteous men were condemned as heretics by a rescript of the most clement ruler.
For this reason their bishops, together with their clergy and
people, surprisingly returned to our fold. However, to maintain the Catholic peace they endured many presecutions, even
to the extent of losing life and limb. All this good work, as
I have said, was begun and carried to completion by the holy
Augustine. At the same time his fellow bishops acquiesced
and were equally pleased.

Chapter 14

However, after the aforementioned conference with the
Donatists, there were those who stated that the heretical
bishops had not been permitted to speak fully in defense of
their sect. Moreover, the magistrate who heard the case in

the position of judge belonged to the Catholic faith and thus favored his own Church. Still, it was only after failure and defeat that this objection was raised, while the heretics were aware of his Catholic allegiance even before the controversy. When summoned by him to the public proceedings for a discussion, they had agreed to come. Surely, if they had been suspicious of him, they could have refused to attend. Nevertheless, the help of Almighty God was evident when, somewhat later, Augustine of venerable memory stopped in Mauretania at the city of Caesarea. He was told to go there with other fellow bishops by letter from the Apostolic See, evidently to settle further Church difficulties. On that occasion he happened to see Emeritus, the Donatist bishop of that place, whom the members of his sect had regarded as their chief defender at the conference. In church, Augustine publicly debated with him in the presence of people of different communions, challenging him with the ecclesiastical records. His purpose was that, if, perchance, as his followers alleged, Emeritus had not been permitted to speak openly in the conference, he might now not hesitate to do so safely, without the prohibition or restraint of any magistrate. Besides, he should not refuse to confidently defend his own communion, in his own city and in the presence of all his townsmen. However, in spite of the urgent and insistent entreaty of his parents and fellow citizens, Emeritus was unwilling to do so. Even at the risk of their property and temporal welfare they had promised to return to his communion, if only he would overthrow the Catholic argument. Nevertheless, he was neither willing nor able to say anything further than the records contained, except the following statement: 'Those records of the proceedings of the bishops at Carthage contain proof of whether we were victors or vanquished.' Later, urged by a reporter, he defended his stand at another time. Then, when he again became silent, his lack of confidence betrayed his true position. At the same time, the growth and strength of the Church were revealed. Therefore, let whoever wishes to know more about the diligence and work of Augustine of most blessed memory foɪ the welfare of God's Church peruse the records. He will discover the kind of arguments that were proposed to provoke and encourage that learned, eloquent, and illustrious man to state whatever he wished in defense of his sect. He will learn that Emeritus was defeated.

Chapter 15

I remember, and so do my brethren and fellow servants who at that time were living with the holy man at Hippo, that when we were seated at table Augustine remarked: 'In church today did you notice that the beginning and end of my sermon were contrary to my usual method? I did not fully explain the subject I introduced, but left it unfinished.' Thereupon, we replied: 'Yes, we know it and we recall our surprise at the time.' To which Augustine answered: 'I believe that the Lord perhaps wished some erring person to be taught and healed by our forgetfulness and error on that occasion, for both we and our sermons are in the Lord's hands. As I was still considering the introduction of my proposed topic, I digressed and changed to another subject. Thus, without concluding and fully explaining the original question which I had started out to prove, I closed my sermon with an argument against the error of the Manichaeans, about which I had intended to say nothing.' On the next day or the day following, if I am not mistaken, a certain merchant, Firmus by name, came to the holy Augustine as he was sitting with us in the monastery. The stranger fell upon his knees and prostrated himself at the feet of Augustine, shedding tears and begging the priest and his holy companions to intercede with the Lord for his sins. He confessed that he had followed the Manichaean sect, living in it for many years, and that, therefore, to his sorrow, he had contributed much money to the Manichaeans, or rather to their so-called Elect. Recently, however, by the mercy of God, he had been present in church, was converted and became a Catholic through Augustine's words. Thereupon, when the venerable Augustine himself and those of us who were present at the time diligently inquired what had particularly struck him in that sermon, he told us, and we recalled the trend of Augustine's discourse. In wonder and admiration at God's profound plan for the salvation of souls, we glorified and blessed His holy name. For He effects their salvation when and how He wishes through His own instruments, whether they are aware of it or not. From that time on, then, Firmus adhered to the manner of life of God's servants, abandoning his career as a merchant. Later, he became conspicuous by his activity among the members of the Church and, having been called and constrained by God's will, entered upon the office of presbyter in another region. In this position he constantly maintained the sanctity of his way of life, and perhaps across the sea he is still living an active life in the world.

Chapter 16

At Carthage, also, a certain Catholic procurator of the royal house, Ursus by name, visited a gathering of Manichaeans who were called the Elect. This group, comprising both men and women, was brought to church by Ursus, where they were examined by the bishops and given a hearing which was entered on formal records. Among the bishops was Augustine of holy memory, who knew this accursed sect better than others. With arguments taken from the books accepted by the Manichaeans he exposed their damnable blasphemies and even brought them to confess them. The unworthy and base acts which they practiced to their own great harm were revealed in the ecclesistical records, disclosed by those women, supposedly the Elect. Thus, through the diligence of its shepherds, the Lord's flock was increased and an efficient defense provided against thieves and robbers.

In the church at Hippo where reporters recorded the proceedings, Augustine, in the presence of the people, publicly debated with a certain Felix, one of those whom the Manichaeans call Elect. After the second or third discussion, when the emptiness and error of his sect were exposed, Ursus was converted to our faith, as the records will show if consulted.

Chapter 17

There was also a certain Pascentius, an Arian, a count of the royal house, and a most energetic tax collector. By reason of his important position he was able the more violently and persistently to attack the Catholic faith. Through raillery and authority he tormented and disturbed many of the more simple priests of God who were living by faith. Challenged by him, Augustine met the heretic at Carthage, in the presence of a number of honored and noble men. Both before and during the meeting he urgently advised that tablets and pen be at hand, but Pascentius utterly refused on the grounds that, through fear of the public laws, he was unwilling to be endangered by such records. He had even appealed to the bystanders to support him. Bishop Augustine nevertheless took up the discussion, upon the advice of his fellow bishops who urged him to debate privately even without a record being taken. Augustine then predicted what later actually happened, that, without a written record, anyone who wished could claim after the meeting was ended to have said what he did not or to deny what he did say. However, Augustine joined in debate with Pascentius, stating his beliefs and listening to the arguments of his opponent. Moreover, by true reasoning and by stating the authority of the Scriptures, he explained and proved the foundations of our faith. Then, since the claims of Pascentius were supported neither by truth nor by the authority of Holy Scripture, Augustine explained and refuted them. Later, as the parties separated, Pascentius, becoming more and more angry and furious, uttered many lies in defense of his false position, proclaiming that Augustine, although praised by many, had really been defeated. Because the truth could not be kept from public notice, Augustine was forced to write to Pascentius himself, omitting through fear the names of those attending the conference. In these letters he faithfully revealed what had been said and done by both parties. To prove the facts, in case of denial, he had a large number of witnesses, very famous and honorable men, who had been present on the occasion. Pascentius, however, in answer to two letters addressed to him, sent back a single meager reply, in which he could only offer insults rather than declare the arguments of his sect. This is attested by those who are willing and able to read the facts.

Augustine also held a conference at Hippo with a bishop of these same Arians, a certain Maximinus, who came to Africa with the Goths. This was in accordance with the desire of many illustrious men who requested it and were

present for the discussion. There is, moreover, a written report of each party's assertions. If the studious will take the
trouble to read that report carefully, they will surely discover what this crafty and unreasonable heresy professes in
order to seduce and deceive, as well as what the Catholic
Church maintains and teaches concerning the divine Trinity.
When Maximinus returned from Hippo to Carthage, because of his great loquacity in the conference he boasted that
he had returned victorious from the debate. Since he lied thus
(and, of course, he could not easily be examined and judged
by persons ignorant of divine Law), the venerable Augustine
sometime later wrote a recapitulation of the separate charges
and rebuttals of the entire conference. Although Maximinus
could not answer the charges, he nevertheless added supplementary details to clarify matters which could not be introduced and written in the short time of the conference, for
his craftiness led him to occupy the rest of the day with his
last, and by far longest, speech.

Chapter 18

For almost ten years Augustine labored against the Pelagians, new heretics in our day and skillful debaters. They
wrote with an even more subtle and noxious art, while they
spoke both in public places and in private homes. Augustine
wrote and published many books against them, and frequently
debated that heresy in church. When, through flattery, these
perverse men tried to persuade even the Apostolic See with
their false doctrine, decisive action was taken by the African
councils. First, the holy bishop tried to convince the venerable Innocent, the holy Pope of the city, and later his successor, holy Zosimus, that this sect should be abhorred and

condemned by the Catholic faith. At various times, the bishops of that great See censured them and cut them off from the membership of the Church. Moreover, letters were sent to the African Churches of the East and West, stating that heretics should be anathematized and shunned by all Catholics. Furthermore, the most pious Emperor Honorius, hearing about the sentence passed by the Catholic Church of God, followed with another decree that they should be condemned by his laws and regarded as heretics. Consequently, some of the heretics returned to the bosom of Holy Mother Church, which they had left; others are still returning, as the truth of the right faith shines forth and prevails against that detestable error.

The memorable Augustine, a noble member of the Lord's body, was always solicitous and viligant concerning the welfare of the universal Church. To him was granted the divine gift of enjoying even in this life the fruits of his labors. While peace and unity were established in the part of the Church around Hippo over which he had special jurisdiction, and later in other parts of Africa, he saw the Lord's Church increase and multiply. All this was accomplished either personally by him or by others, including priests whom he had prepared. He experienced further joy at the sight of Manichaeans, Donatists, Pelagians, and pagans, who were diminishing in number and were uniting with the Church of God. He also took pleasure in the pursuit of study, rejoicing in all good. Although piously and devoutly tolerant of his brethren's shortcomings, he grieved because of the iniquities of the wicked, whether within or without the Church. Thus, he always rejoiced, as I said, in the Lord's gains, and sorrowed over His losses.

So many articles were dictated and published by him, and so many topics discussed in church, written down and

amended, either against various heretics or expounded from
the canonical books for the edification of the Church's holy
sons, that scarcely any student could read and know them
all. However, lest we seem in any way to cheat those who
are eager for the truth of his word, I have decided, with
God's help, to add an *indiculus* of these books, homilies, and
epistles, at the end of this little work. When those who love
God's truth more than temporal riches read this, each one
may choose for himself what he wishes to read. Let him
look for the work in the library of the church at Hippo, where
more perfect copies can probably be found, or let him search
wherever possible. If, perchance, he has found the work, let
him copy and preserve it and may he generously lend it to
anyone else who desires it.

Chapter 19

According to the teaching of the Apostle, who said: 'Dare
any of you, having a matter against another, go to law before the unjust and not before the saints? Know you not that
the saints shall judge this world? And if the world is judged
by you, are you unworthy to judge the smallest matters?
Know you not that we shall judge angels? how much more
the things of this world! If, therefore, you have judgments
of affairs pertaining to this world, set them to judge, who
are the most despised in the church. I speak to your shame.
Is it so that there is not among you any one wise man, that
is able to judge between his brethren? But brother goeth to
law with brother, and that before unbelievers,'[1]—Accordingly, Augustine, when called upon by Christians or by men
of any sect, carefully and dutifully heard their cases, having

---

1 Cf. 1 Cor. 6.1-8.

constantly before his eyes the remark of someone who said he preferred to hear cases between strangers rather than between friends, for he could win a friend in the stranger in whose favor the case was justly decided, whereas he would lose the friend against whom the judgment was passed. Although he was sometimes detained until mealtime and sometimes even had to fast all day, he always examined and judged these cases with paticular attention to the value of Christian souls, noting especially the degree of increase or decrease in faith and in good works. Whenever the opportunity was favorable, he taught both parties the truth of divine Law. He stressed its importance, and suggested means of obtaining eternal life. No recompense was asked of those to whom he thus devoted his time, except the Christian obedience and devotion which are due to God and men. Moreover, sinners were rebuked in the presence of all to inspire fear in the hearts of others. He did this as one whom the Lord made 'a watchman to the house of Israel,' preaching the word, instant in season, out of season: reproving, entreating, exhorting, rebuking, in all patience and doctrine. Special effort was made to instruct those who could in turn teach others. When requested, he also wrote letters to some concerning their temporal welfare. This work, which, however, took him away from better things, he regarded as an obligation. His greatest pleasure was always found in the things of God, or in the exhortation or conversation of intimate brotherly friendship.

Chapter 20

We know also that Augustine did not grant the request of his dearest friends when they asked him for letters of intercession to the evil authorities. He said that it was wise for a prudent man to observe that rule and out of concern for

his reputation not be responsible for his friends. Approving
of the policy, Augustine further added a personal comment,
stating that, often, the authority petitioned later becomes oppressive. Nevertheless, if, when requested, he saw a need for
intercession, he acted with such forthrightness and tact that
he did not seem irritating and annoying, but rather admirable. Indeed, when one of these cases arose and Augustine
as usual interceded by letter with Macedonius, a vicar of
Africa, on behalf of a suppliant, Macedonius granted the
request and wrote as follows: 'I am amazed at your wisdom,
both in your published works and in this letter which you
have not found too great a burden to send, interceding for
those in distress. The former writings, my venerable and esteemed father, possess such discernment, knowledge, and holiness as leave nothing further to be desired; the latter possess
such modesty that, if I failed to fulfill your request, I could
not consider myself free from blame in this matter. For you
do not insist, as do most men in your position, upon extort-
ing everything that the suppliant requests. Instead, with a
humble modesty which is most efficacious in settling difficulties between good men, you advise whatever seems to you a
reasonable request to ask of a judge who is occupied with
so many cares. Therefore, as you have reason to expect, I
have not hesitated to grant the request you have recom-
mended.'

Chapter 21

Whenever he could, Augustine attended the councils of
the holy priests in the various provinces, 'seeking in them not
his own, but the things of Jesus Christ.' His desire was that
the faith of the holy Catholic Church might remain inviolate

and that some of the priests and clerics who had been excommunicated, either justly or unjustly, might be absolved or expelled. Augustine moreover believed that, in the ordination of priests and clerics, Church custom as well as the approval of the majority of Christians should be observed.

Chapter 22

His clothing and footwear, and even Augustine's house furnishings were modest yet adequate—neither luxurious nor too plain. In such matters, men have the habit either of arrogantly displaying or of degrading themselves; in either case 'seeking not the things which are of Jesus Christ, but their own.' Augustine, however, as I have said, held the middle course, deviating neither to the right nor to the left. His table was frugal and sparing, although, indeed, it sometimes included meats, herbs, and vegetables, out of consideration for guests or the sick. Moreover, he always had wine, because he knew and taught, as the Apostle says, 'every creature of God is good, and nothing is to be rejected that is received with thanksgiving; for it is sanctified by the word of God and prayer.' As holy Augustine himself has written in the books of his *Confessions*: 'I fear not the uncleanness of meat, but the uncleanness of lust. I know that Noe was permitted to eat every kind of flesh which was useful for food; that Elias was reinvigorated by eating flesh; that John, who was gifted with marvelous abstinence, was not defiled by the creatures, that is, the locusts, which became his food. I know, too, that Esau was deceived by his craving for a pottage of lentils, and that David rebuked himself for his longing after water, and, finally, that our King was tempted, not with meat, but with bread. Likewise, the people in the desert deserved to be condemned, not because they desired meat, but because in their desire for food they murmured against God.' With regard to the use of wine, there is the Apostle's injunction when he wrote to Timothy: 'No longer drink water, but use a little wine for thy stomach's sake, and thy frequent infirmities.'[1] Only his spoons were of silver, but the vessels in which food was served were earthen, wooden, or marble; this was not by force of necessity, but from Augustine's own choice. Moreover, he always showed hospitality. At the table itself he preferred reading and discussion to mere eating and drinking, and against the pest of human nature he had the following inscription carved on his table:

'Who slanders the name of an absent friend
May not as guest at this table attend.'

Thus he warned every guest to refrain from unnecessary and harmful tales. When, on one occasion, some of his closest fellow bishops forgot that warning and spoke heedlessly, Augustine became exasperated and sharply rebuked them, declaring that either those verses should be removed from the table or he would leave in the midst of the meal and go to his room. Both I and others who were at the table experienced this.

Chapter 23

Ever mindful of his fellow poor, Augustine supplied their needs from the same funds he used for himself and all who lived with them, the revenues being derived from church property or from the offerings of the faithful. When, perchance, as frequently happened, jealousy arose among the

---

1 Cf. 1 Tim. 5.23.

clergy concerning these possessions, Augustine called a con-
vocation of the people of God. He stated that he preferred
to live on the contributions of God's people rather than to
be burdened with the use and administration of them. Moreover, he was ready to renounce them in order that all the
servants and ministers of God might live according to the
practice of the Old Testament, partaking of the same altar
which they served. This proposal, however, the laity were
never willing to accept.

Chapter 24

The care of the church building and all its property Augustine assigned and entrusted in turn to more capable clerics,
for he never held the key nor wore a ring, but all receipts
and expenditures were recorded by these household overseers.
At the end of the year, the accounts were read to him so that
he might know how much was received and how much spent,
and also what balance remained. In many cases, he took the
word of the overseer rather than investigate its veracity by
actual proof. He never wished to buy a house, land, or a
farm; however, if anything of the kind was donated, perchance, or left as a legacy, he did not refuse it, but insisted
that the gift be accepted. Still, we know that he did refuse
some legacies, not because they could not be used for the
poor, but because it seemed right and just that the children,
parents, or relatives of the deceased should own them, even
though that was not the will of the deceased. In fact, one of
the chief men of Hippo who was living at Carthage wanted
to donate his property to the church at Hippo. Retaining only
the interest for himself, this man of his own accord sent the
certified papers to Augustine of holy memory. The latter

gladly accepted the offering, and congratulated the donor as being mindful of his eternal salvation. However, several years later, when we happened to be living in Augustine's house, behold, the benefactor sent a letter by his son, asking that the deeds of donation be given to him, but also requesting that one hundred pieces of gold be given to the poor. The holy man groaned at the news because the man had either feigned the donation or repented of his good work. In grief of soul at this perversity, he admonished and reproved the man, at God's prompting, and immediately returned the papers which had been voluntarily donated. The gift of money, however, he rejected. Moreover, as though in duty bound, he censured and reproved the man in writing, warning him to make his peace with God in humble repentance for his hypocrisy and sin, that he might not die in the state of so serous a fault.

Quite frequently, Augustine also pointed out that the Church might with greater security and safety accept legacies left by the dead rather than gifts which might cause anxiety and loss. Furthermore, he indicated that legacies should be offered rather than solicited. He accepted nothing which was given in trust, but did not forbid his cleargy to accept such gifts if they so wished. Moreover, he was not fondly devoted to nor entangled in property which the Church held in possession, yet, though most intent and eager for greater, spiritual concerns, he sometimes relaxed from the thought of eternal things and turned to temporal affairs. As soon as the latter were arranged in order, then his soul, as if freed from consuming and annoying cares, returned to the higher, more intimate pursuits of the mind. Thereupon, he either thought about discovering divine truth or he dictated some of the things already discovered, or he corrected points of works which had been previously dictated and transcribed. This

Augustine accomplished by working all day and toiling by lamplight at night. Thus he portrayed a type of the Church on high, like that most glorious Mary, of whom we read that she sat at the feet of our Lord and listened intently to His words; and when her sister, busy with much serving, complained that she received no help, she heard: 'Martha, Martha, Mary has chosen the better part, which shall not be taken away from her.'[1]

New buildings Augustine never desired, avoiding entanglement of his soul in them, because he wanted it always free from all temporal annoyance. Nevertheless, he did not prohibit those who wanted to build them, unless their plans were too extravagant. Meanwhile, if his church needed money he told the Christian people that he had nothing to give to the poor. For the benefit of captives and the large number of needy he ordered the holy vessels to be broken and melted down for distribution among the poor. I would not have mentioned this fact if I did not see clearly that this was done contrary to the carnal judgment of some men. Ambrose of venerable memory, both in speaking and in writing, ordered the same procedure without any hesitation in such extreme cases. Sometimes, too, when the faithful neglected the treasury and consistory, from which were supplied necessary articles for the altar, Augustine admonished the people in church, just as he told us most blessed Ambrose had handled the situation when he was present.

---

1 Cf. Luke 10.41-42.

Chapter 25

At the same house and table with him the clergy were always fed and clothed at the common expense. Now, lest anyone by careless swearing should fall into perjury, he preached to the people in church and instructed the members of his household that no one should utter an oath, not even at table. According to the rule, if anyone failed in this matter he lost one drink, for the number of cups granted each one who lived and ate with him was determined beforehand. Faults of omission and commission in this regard Augustine strictly and properly rebuked or tolerated as far as was fitting and necessary, in such cases teaching especially that no one should turn his heart to evil words or offer excuses for his sins. Moreover, if anyone offered a gift at the altar and there remembered that his brother had anything against him, the gift had to be left there and reconciliation first effected; then the person might come and make his offering. However, if he had anything against his brother, he should rebuke him privately; if his brother listened, he gained him; if not, one or two other men should be summoned. If they, too, should be despised, the Church should be called in.[1] If the man should not even obey her, he should be regarded as a heathen and publican. This, too, he added, that if a brother offends and asks pardon he could be forgiven, not seven times, but seventy times seven times.[2] just as each one daily asks the Lord for the forgiveness of his sins.

---

1 Cf. Matt. 18.15-17.
2 Cf. Matt. 18.21-22.

Chapter 26

No woman ever lived or stayed within Augustine's household, not even his own widowed sister, although she had long served God and lived as superior of His handmaids until the day of her death. He also refused his brother's daughters who were also serving God, although they were considered exceptions to this law by the councils of bishops. However, Augustine used to say that, even if no evil suspicion could arise from the fact that his sister and nieces lived with him, they could not exist without other servants and women being with them, and that still others would enter from outside to visit them. From these, in turn, a stumbling block or scandal might arise for the weak. He added that those men who happened to be staying with the bishop might perish by human temptation, resulting from all those women living together or coming there, or at least be most disgracefully maligned by the evil suspicions of men. For this reason, then, Augustine stated that women should never live in the same house with God's servants, even the most chaste, lest by such an example (as we read) some scandal or stumbling block be placed before the weak. Moreover, if some women asked to see or greet him, they never came to him except with some of the clerics as witnesses, and he never spoke to them alone, even if it was a matter of secrecy.

Chapter 27

In the matter of visitations, Augustine adhered to the rule established by the Apostle, and visited only widows and orphans who suffered tribulation.[1] However, if, perchance,

1 Cf 1 Tim. 5.10.

the sick asked him to come in person to pray to the Lord for
them and lay his hand upon them, he went without delay.
Monasteries of women, nevertheless, he did not visit except
in cases of urgent necessity. He said that in the life of one
of God's servants the rule should be observed which he had
learned from St. Ambrose of holy memory's teaching, namely,
never to seek a wife for another man, nor to encourage anyone who wished to go to war, nor to attend a feast in one's
own civic community. His reasons for each of these points he
clearly explained. In the first case, if the husband and wife
should quarrel, they might blame the one who was instru-
mental in their meeting; but, if they first agree to marry,
the priest should certainly help them so that what was agreed
upon to their satisfaction may be confirmed and blessed.
Secondly, he did not want the man who had been urged to
enter military service to blame the one who had encouraged
him if through his own fault he suffered injury. Thirdly, he
feared that the bounds of temperance might be exceeded in
the customs proper to feasts.

He likewise stated that he had heard the very wise and
pious answer of the above-mentioned man of blessed memory
at the end of his life. This statement Augustine extolled and
preached. When the venerable old man lay in his last illness,
the foremost members of the faithful kept virgil at his bedside when he was about to leave this world for the presence
of God. They grieved that the Church should be deprived
of such a great prelate's ministry of God's word and sacrament, and they begged him with tears to ask the Lord for
a prolongation of his life. Ambrose replied: 'My life has not
been such that I should be ashamed to live among you: but
I am not afraid to die, for we have a kind Lord.'[2] These
well-chosen, well-weighed words Augustine used to admire

2 Cf. above, p. 61.

and praise later in his old age. He said that we must understand that Ambrose added 'and I am not afraid to die, for we have a kind Lord,' lest anyone think that through too great confidence in the perfect purity of his life he said first, 'my life has not been such that I should be ashamed to live among you.' This he had stated concerning what men can know about their fellow men, but, as for the test of divine justice, he preferred to trust the kind Lord to whom he daily prayed: 'Forgive us our trespasses.'

In this connection, moreover, Augustine very frequently toward the end of his life repeated the words of a certain fellow bishop, his very intimate friend. When Augustine had visited him as he was approaching death, the man indicated by a gesture of his hand that he was soon to leave this world. Augustine, however, replied that his life was still necessary for the welfare of the Church, but the other answered, lest he be thought captivated by a desire for this life: 'If I should never die, very well; but if at some time, why not now?' This sentiment Augustine admired and praised as coming from a God-fearing man who had been born and raised on a farm but was not very learned in reading knowledge. On the other hand, we have the sentiment of an ailing bishop concerning whom the holy martyr Cyprian wrote in his letter on mortality, when he said: 'When one of our colleagues and fellow priests who was weary with infirmity and anxious at the approach of death prayed for a prolongation of life, there stood at his side as he prayed in the throes of death a youth, venerable in glory and majesty, tall of stature and radiant in countenance. As he stood there, the human vision of mortal eyes could scarcely look upon him and, except for the fact that the one was about to die, he would not have been able to behold such a creature. Thereupon, the youth rebuked him with a certain indignation of soul and voice, saying: "You are afraid to suffer, unwilling to die; what am I to do for you?" '

Chapter 28

A short time before his death, Augustine revised the books which he had dictated and edited, both those which he had written as a layman in the early days of his conversion and those from his days as priest and bishop. In them he censured and corrected everything contrary to ecclesiastical usage, for he recognized them as compiled when he still knew and understood very little about such matters. Thus, he wrote two volumes entitled *De recensione librorum* (*On the Revision of Books*). He complained, however, that some of his brethren had carried off certain books before he could carefully correct them. Later, however he did correct them, although death came by surprise and caused him to leave some books unfinished. Moreover, desiring to be of service to everyone, both those who could read many books and those who could not, he made selections from both the Old and the New Testament of the divine commands and prohibitions which pertain to the conduct of lfe. A preface was added and the whole composed in one volume. Anyone who desires may read it and learn therein how obedient or disobedient he is to God. This work he wished called *Speculum* (*The Mirror*).

It happened soon after, in accordance with the divine will and power, that a great host of men, armed and trained for war, came in ships from the land of Spain across the sea and rushed into Africa. They were a mixed group of savage Vandals and Alans, together with a Gothic tribe and people of different races. Everywhere throughout the regions of Mauretania, and even crossing to other provinces and lands, they gave vent to their rage by every kind of atrocity and cruelty, devastating everything they possibly could by pillage, murder, various tortures, fires, and other countless indescribable evil deeds. No sex or age was spared, not even God's priests and ministers, neither church ornaments and vessels nor the very buildings. Now, the man of God did not feel and think as others did concerning the enemy's fierce assault and devastation, but he considered them more deeply and profoundly. Most of all, he perceived in them the dangers and even death of souls, so that more than ever (since, as we read, 'He that addeth knowledge, addeth also sorrow,' and, 'an understanding heart is a worm in the bones') tears were his bread both day and night. Thus he spent those days, almost the last of his life, and endured them as most bitter and sad in comparison with the rest of his old age. He saw cities completely destroyed, and farmers together with their buildings either annihilated by the enemy's slaughter or put to flight and scattered. Churches were deprived of their priests and ministers; consecrated virgins and monks, dispersed in all directions. In one place some died from torture, others were killed by the sword; still others, in captivity, lost their chastity and faith in soul and body, serving the enemy under vile, harsh treatment. Hymns and praises of God disappeared from churches, church buildings in many places were burned down, while the regular offerings due to God in their usual places were cut off. The divine sacraments were no longer sought, or if they were, it was difficult to find someone to administer them. Moreover, when the people fled together to mountain forests or rocky caves and caverns or any kind of shelter, some were captured and killed while others were robbed and deprived of necessary nourishment to such an extent that they perished from hunger. Augustine likewise saw bishops of the churches and clergy who, perchance, through God's kindness, did not meet the enemy or who escaped if they did, despoiled and stripped of everything, forced to beg in dire poverty, and they could not all be supplied with enough to live. Of the countless churches scarcely three survive—at Carthage, Hippo, and Cirta. It was through God's kindness that these were not destroyed. These cities likewise remain, supported by divine and human protection, although after Augustine's death the enemy burned the city of Hippo, which had been abandoned by its inhabitants. Amid these disasters Augustine was consoled by the sentiment of a certain wise man who said: 'He is not great who thinks it wonderful that wood and stones fall and mortals die.'

Because of his profound wisdom, Augustine daily and copiously lamented all these occurrences. His grief and sorrow were intensified by the fact that the enemy came also to besiege the city of the Hippo-Regians, which so far had maintained its position. At this time the defense of the city was in charge of the former Count Boniface and an army of allied Goths. For almost fourteen months the enemy blockaded and besieged the city, cutting off even its seacost with their blockade. We and other fellow bishops from the neighborhood had taken refuge there, and were present during the entire siege. Therefore, we frequently conversed with each other and considered the dreadful judgments of God which were placed before our eyes, saying: 'Thou are just, O Lord, and thy judgment is right.' In our common grief, with groans and tears we prayed the Father of mercies and the Lord of all consolation to deign to help us in this tribulation.

Chapter 29

One time, when we were seated at table with him and conversing, Augustine happened to say: 'Know that in this time of our misfortune I have asked God either to free this city which is surrounded by the enemy or, if something else appears better to Him, to make His servants strong in enduring His will, or at least to take them out of this world unto Himself.' When he had spoken these words for our instruction, together with him we then asked the same grace of the most high God for ourselves, for all our fellow bishops, and for those who were in the city. And, behold, in the third month of the siege Augustine succumbed to fever and was tormented with his last illness. Surely, the Lord did not deprive His servant of the fruit of his prayer, for what he asked for with tears and prayers he obtained in time both for himself and for the city. I also know that, when asked as a presbyter and bishop to pray for certain demoniacs, he begged God with tears and supplications, and the devils departed from the possessed. Likewise, when he was sick and confined to his bed, a certain man came with a sick relative and asked him to lay his hand upon him that he might be cured. Augustine replied that, if he had any such power, he certainly would have first applied it to himself. Thereupon, his visitor replied that he had had a vision and in his sleep had heard these words: 'Go to Bishop Augustine, what he may lay his hand upon him, and he will be healed.' When Augustine learned this, he did not delay doing it and immediately the Lord caused the sick man to depart from him healed.

Chapter 30

Now, I must by no means pass over in silence the fact that, when the afore-mentioned enemy was threatening us, Augustine was consulted in letters by the holy Honoratus, our fellow bishop of the church at Thiabe. His problem was whether or not bishops or clergy should withdraw from the churches at the approach of an enemy. In reply, Augustine indicated a greater source of fear at the hands of those who were the destroyers of Romania. This letter I have wished included in this text, because it is especially useful and even necessary for the life of God's priests and ministers.

'To our holy brother and fellow bishop, Honoratus, Augustine sends greetings in the Lord:

'I sent to your Grace a copy of the letter which I wrote to our brother and fellow bishop, Quodvultdeus, thinking that thus I would be relieved of the burden you imposed when you asked my advice upon a course of action amidst the dangers which have befallen our times. Although that letter was brief, I believe it omitted nothing which was necessary for me to say in reply and sufficient for the one who awaited it. I said, indeed, that those who wish and are able to move to places of safety should not be prevented, and that there should be no breaking of the ties of our ministry whereby Christ's love has bound us not to desert the churches which we ought to serve. Here, then, are the words, which I wrote in that letter: Since our ministry is so necessary for God's people, however few they may be, they should not remain without it. Thus we should pray to the Lord: "Be thou unto us a God, a protector, and a place of refuge."

'This advice, however, as you write, is not sufficient. You are worried that we are striving to act contrary to the Lord's precept and example when He tells us to flee from one city to another. We recall His words when He said: "And when they shall persecute you in this city, flee into another." Still, who would believe that the Lord wanted the flocks which He brought with His own blood to be abandoned by that necessary ministry without which they cannot live? Is this what He did when as a child He fled into Egypt, carried by His parents, not yet having established any churches which we might say were deserted by Him? When the Apostle Paul, to escape his enemy, was let down through the window in a basket and escaped his hands, did he deprive any church of his necessary ministry? Did not the other brethren who were living there supply what was needed? Indeed, it was in accordance with their wish that the Apostle acted, in order that he might be saved for the Church, since he alone was sought by the persecutor. Therefore, let Christ's servants, the ministers of His word and sacrament, do what He taught and permitted. Cetrainly, let them flee from one city to another, when one in particular is sought by the persecutors. Only, see to it that the Church is not abandoned by others who are not so persecuted, in order that they may give nourishment to their fellow servants, who they know could not otherwise live. However, when the danger is common to all—bishops, clergy, and laity—let not those who need others be abandoned by the ones they need. For this reason, either they should all move to places of safety, or those who must remain should not be abandoned by those who must supply their ecclesiastical needs. Let them live together or suffer together whatever the Father wishes them to endure.

'If it should happen that some suffer more, others less, or all equally, it is clear that they suffer for others who, although able to escape from such evils by flight, prefer to remain in order not to abandon the needs of others. This is the greatest proof of that charity which the Apostle John commends when he says: "As Christ laid down his life for us, so we ought to lay down our lives for the brethren." Both those who flee and those who cannot because bound by duties, if they are caught and made to suffer, clearly do so for themselves, and not for the brethren. On the other hand, those who suffer because of their unwillingness to abandon their brethren who needed them for their Christian welfare, without any doubt they lay down their lives for the brethren.

'Therefore, what we have heard a certain bishop say: "If the Lord has commanded us to flee in those persecutions where the fruit of martyrdom is possible, how much more should we flee useless sufferings when there is an invasion of hostile barbarians?"—this is really true and acceptable only for those not bound by ties of ecclesiastical duty. When, even though he could escape, a man does not flee from the attacks of the enemy, in order not to abandon the ministry of Christ (for without it men cannot live or become Christians), he finds a greater fruit of his charity than one who flees, not for his brethren's sake but his own, even if he is captured and suffers martyrdom for refusing to deny Christ.

'What, then, is it that you wrote in your former letter? You say, indeed: "If we must continue in our churches, I do not see what the advantage will be for ourselves or for the people, except that men will succumb before our very eyes, women will be dishonored, churches burned, we ourselves die of torture when something we do not possess is asked of us." Surely, God is able to hear the prayers of His family and to ward off disasters which they fear. However, because of something uncertain, there should not be a definite abandonment of duty, for, in that event, there is certain ruin for the people, not only in things pertaining to this life, but also in those of that other life which must be cared for

with incomparably greater attention and anxiety. Even if
our fear that something might happen in the places where
we are were certain, all the people on whose account we
should remain would have fled earlier and freed us from
the necessity of remaining. There is no one, indeed, who says
that ministers should remain when there no longer is anyone to whom they should minister. Thus, in truth, the holy
bishops fled from Spain when some of the people had already departed in flight, some were killed, others were scattered in captivity. Many more bishops stayed in the thick
of these dangers, because those on whose account they remained were there. Moreover, if some did desert their people,
this is exactly what we say should not happen. Such men,
indeed, were not influenced by divine authority, but were
either deceived by human error or constrained by fear.

'Why, then, do they think they should obey without dis-
crimination upon reading the command to flee from one
city to another, when they do not tremble at the thought of
the hireling who sees the wolf coming and flees because he
has no care for the sheep? Furthermore, why do they not
strive to understand those two true statements of the Lord
—the one where flight is either permitted or commanded,
and the other where it is blamed and censured—for thus
they would find them not contrary to each other, as in fact
they are not? How is this discovered, unles notice is made
of that which I discussed above, namely, that we, Christ's
ministers, should flee under the stress of persecution from
the places in which we are. This should happen, however,
only when there are no Christian people to whom to minister or when the necessary ministry can be performed by
others who have no reason for flight. So the Apostle fled,
as I mentioned above, let down in a basket, when he alone
was sought by the persecutor. Since the remaining ministers

were not under a similar strain, priests were not lacking
there nor the Church abandoned. The holy Athanasius,
Bishop of Alexandria, similarly fled when the Emperor Constantius gave orders to apprehend him in particular, while
the Catholic people who remained in Alexandria were by
no means deserted by the other ministers. However, when
the people remain and the ministers flee, taking away the
ministry, what else will this be but that damnable flight of
hirelings who have no care for the sheep? Indeed, the wolf
will come, not a man, but the Devil, who has frequently persuaded the faithful to become apostates when they were deprived of the daily ministry of the Lord's body. Therefore,
your weak brother for whom Christ died shall perish, not
through your knowledge, but your ignorance.

'As for those who are not deceived by error in this matter
but are overcome with fear, why do they not struggle
bravely against their terror, with God's compassion and help,
so that they may not experience evils incomparably more
burdensome and much more fearful? This happens when
love of God burns brightly and the pleasure of the world
does not exhale its fumes. Moreover, charity says: "Who
is weak, and I am not weak? Who is scandalized, and I am
not on fire?" Charity, however, is from God. Therefore,
let us pray that it may be given by Him who commands it.
For this reason, let us fear more lest Christ's sheep, who
will die some time by some kind of death, will be killed in
the heart by the sword of spiritual wickedness than bodily
by a sword of iron. Let us fear lest, when the inner sense
has been corrupted, purity of faith will die, rather than that
women will be violently dishonored in body. Chastity, indeed, is not spoiled by violence if it is preserved in the mind,
nor is it destroyed in the body when the will of the one who

suffers does not shamefully take pleasure in the flesh but without any real consent endures another's action. Let us fear lest living stones will be be destroyed when we desert them, rather than that the stones and wood of earthly buildings will be burned in our absence. Let us fear lest the members of Christ's body will be killed by a lack of spiritual nourishment rather than that the members of our body will be tortured when overcome by the enemy's attack. Not that these things are not to be avoided if possible; rather, they are to be endured if unavoidable without impiety—unless, perchance, someone asserts that he is not a wicked minister who withdraws his ministry which is necessary for devotion at the time when it is most essential.

'When these dangers have reached their height and there is no chance for flight, do we not consider how large a congregation, of both sexes and of every age, usually gathers in church? Some are eager for baptism, other for reconciliation, still others for acts of penance—all of them for the consolation, administration, and distribution of the sacraments. If, then, ministers are lacking, how much destruction comes upon those who depart from this world unregenerated or bound by sin? How great, moreover, is the grief of the faithful, their relatives, who will not have them with them in the rest of eternal life. Finally, how great is the groaning of all and how great the blasphemy of some because of the absence of ministers and their ministry? See what the fear of temporal evils effects and how great increase of eternal evils lies therein. If, however, ministers are present, there is help for all according to the measure of the strength which the Lord supplies. Some are baptized, others reconciled, none is deprived of the communion of the Lord's Body, all are consoled, edified, encouraged to ask God who is mighty to avert the evils which are feared. They are prepared, however, for either event, so that, if the chalice cannot pass from them, His will may be done who can wish no evil.

'You surely see now what you had said you did not see, namely, how much benefit Christians obtain if the presence of Christ's ministers is not wanting to them in the presence of evils. You also see the harm that is done by their absence, for they then seek their own, not the things which are of Jesus Christ, and they have not that charity of which we read: "It seeketh not her own"; nor do they imitate Him who said: "not seeking that which is profitable to myself, but to many, that they may be saved." He, too, would not have fled from the snares of that persecuting prince, if He had not wanted to save Himself for others who needed Him. Therefore, the Apostle says: "But I am straitened between two: having a desire to be disolved and to be with Christ, a thing by far the best; but to abide still in the flesh, is needful for you."

'At this point, someone may say that, when such dangers are threatening, God's ministers should flee in order to save themselves for the Church's benefit in more peaceful times. Some may do this, provided that others are not lacking to supply the Church's ministrations, which they deserve. Athanasius did this, as we mentioned above. Indeed, the Catholic faith, which his words and zeal defended against the Arian heretics, knew how necessary and beneficial to the Church it was that he remain in the flesh. However, when there is a common danger, there is a greater reason to fear that someone may be thought to do this, not from the desire to be of service, but from a fear of dying. If more harm results from the example of flight than good by the duty of living, on no condition should this be done. Finally, holy David, lest he be exposed to the dangers of battle, and perchance "the lamp of Israel be extinguished," withdrew from his persecutors. However, he did not act presumptuously; otherwise, he would have attracted imitators of his cowardice, who would have believed his action arose, not from thoughtfulness of the benefit to others, but from the confusion of his own fear.

'Another question arises, which we should not overlook. If, indeed, this usefulness is not to be disregarded, so that, when some disaster threatens, certain ministers should flee in order to be saved to care for those who will survive after the trouble, what should happen when all seem destined to perish unless some flee? What if the persecution is limited to this extent, that only the Church's ministers are pursued? What shall we say? Should the ministers abandon the Church in flight so it will not be left in a worse condition by them when they die? If, however, the laity are not sought after unto death, they can somehow hide their bishops and clergy, in accordance with God's help, in whose power all things are and who can, by His wonderful might, save even those who do not flee. Still, we are asking what we should do, that we may not be considered tempting God by expecting divine miracles in all circumstances. Certainly, when the danger is common to the laity as well as the clergy, the storm is not the same as the danger to merchants and sailors who are together on a ship. Far be it from us to value this ship of ours so lightly that the sailors, and especially the pilot, should abandon it in time of danger, even if they can escape by leaping into a small boat or even by swimming. In the case of those whom we think will perish because of our desertion, it is not their temporal death we fear, for that must come some time, but their eternal death. This can come if there is not watchfulness, and cannot come if there is. However, in the common danger of this life, why do we think that,

POSSIDIUS

wherever there is an attack by the enemy, all the clergy and not all the laity are going to die, so that those for whom the clergy are necessary will end this life together? Or why do we not expect that, as some of the laity will survive, so also shall some of the clergy, and these will be able to perform the necessary ministry?

'However, would that the discussion among God's ministers were over the question of who should remain and who should flee, lest the Church be abandoned by either the flight or the death of all! Such, indeed, will be the struggle among them when both are on fire with charity and both satisfy love. As far as I can see, if this discussion cannot be decided in any other way, those who should remain and those who are to flee must be chosen by lot. Indeed, those who say they should rather flee will either seem timid because unwilling to endure threatening danger or arrogant because deeming themselves more necessary to the Church so that they must be preserved. Furthermore, perhaps those who are better will choose to lay down their lives for their brethren, and thus those will be saved by flight whose lives are less useful because of less experience in counsel and government. Nevertheless, those who are wise and devout will oppose those whom they see ought to live and yet prefer to die rather than to flee. Thus, then, it is written: "The lot suppresseth contentions, and determineth even between the mighty." In difficulties of this sort, God is a better judge than men whether it is proper to call better men to the fruit of suffering and to spare the weak or to make the latter stronger in enduring misfortune and take them from this life since their lives cannot be as beneficial to the Church as that of the others. If there is a casting of lots, the procedure will be unusual, but, if so, who will dare to censure it? Only the ignorant or envious will fail to praise it in fitting words. If, however, this plan is unsatisfactory because there is no precedent available, let no one cause the Church's ministry, which is especially necessary and due in such great dangers, to cease. Let no one consider his own person in such a light that, even if he seems to excel in some grace, he proclaim himself more worthy of life and therefore of flight. Whoever thinks thus indeed pleases himself, but, if he says it, he displeases everyone.

'Surely, there are people who think that bishops and priests who do not flee, but remain in the midst of such dangers, deceive the people. The latter do not flee then, for they see their leaders remaining. However, it is easy to avoid this blame and reproach by addressing these people as follows: "Let not the fact that we are not fleeing from this place deceive you. We are staying here, not for our own sake but for yours, so that we may not fail to minister whatever we recognize as necessary for your salvation, which is in Christ. If, therefore, you wish to flee, you will release us from the bonds which hold us." This, I think, should be said whenever it seems truly advantageous to move to safer places. If at this statement all or some should say: "We are in His power whose wrath no one escapes no matter where he goes; moreover, His mercy can be found wherever one may be, even if he does not wish to go elsewhere, whether prevented by definite duties or unwilling to strive after uncertain places of refuge. Thus he will succeed, not in ending, but in exchanging, dangers"—undoubtedly they should not be abandoned by the Christian ministry. If, however, the people prefer to depart after hearing these words, the ministers who were remaining on their account need not say, for the people there no longer need their ministrations.

'Therefore, whoever flees when the Church's necessary ministry is not lacking because of his flight does what the Lord commanded or allowed. However, one who so flees that Christ's flock is deprived of the nourishment on which it lives, he is that hireling who see the wolf coming and flees because he has no care for the sheep.

'These facts, most beloved brother, I have considered and have written to you in truth and certain love, because you asked my advice. However, I have not commanded you, in case you find something better. Nevertheless, we can find nothing better to do in these dangers than offer prayers to the Lord, our God, that He may have pity on us. With His help, some prudent and holy men have merited to will and to accomplish this, namely, not to desert their churches and in the face of calumny not to depart in the least from the intention of their purpose.'

Chapter 31

Now, that holy man in the long life God gave him for the Church's welfare and happiness (indeed, he lived seventy-six years, almost forty of them as bishop or priest) used to say to us in intimate conversation that, even after receiving baptism, praiseworthy Christians and priests should not depart from the body wthout worthy and proper repentance. This he himself performed in the last illness which caused his death. He commanded the very brief penitential psalms of David to be written out, and during the days of his illness, as he lay in bed, he looked at the pages which were opposite him on the wall and read them with copious and continual weeping. Moreover, in order that no one might hinder his purpose, about ten days before he departed from the body he asked those of us who were present not to allow anyone to come to him except at the hours when the physician came to examine him or when nourishment was brought to him. His request was respected and fulfilled, and during all that time he had leisure for prayer. Up to his very last illness he preached the word of God in church incessantly, vigorously, and forcefully, with clear mind and sound judgment. With all the members of his body intact, his sight and hearing unimpaired, while we looked on and prayed at his bedside, 'he slept with his fathers,' as we read, 'wellnourished in a good old age.' After the Holy Sacrifice was offered, he was buried in our presence as we commended the repose of his body.

No will was made, because as a poor man he had nothing to leave. He always ordered the church's library, with all the books, to be carefully preserved for posterity. Whatever the church had by way of expenses or possessions he left in charge of his presbyter, who had the care of the church building. His relatives, whether in religion or not, he did not treat in the customary manner, both during his life and after his death. When he was still living, he gave them, if necessary, what he gave others, not that they might possess riches, but that they might not be in want, or at least less so. To the Church he left a very adequate number of clergy, as well as monasteries of men and women under their continent superiors, together with his library and books, including his own treatises and those of other holy men. Here, with God's help, his character and worth in the Church are discovered, and the faithful may find him still living. For this reason, a secular poet ordered a monument built for himself in a public place after his death, and composed this as the inscription, saying:

> 'O traveler, wouldst know that poets live again after death?

> What you now read, behold I speak! Your voice is
> but my breath.'

It surely is clear in his writings that this priest, so dear
and acceptable to God, lived uprightly and wisely in the
faith, hope, and charity of the Catholic Church, as far as
he could see with the light of truth. Those who read what
he has written on divine subjects derive profit therefrom;
however, I think that greater profit was derived by those who
were able to hear and see him speak when he was present in
church, especially those who knew his life among men. Not
only was he a scribe instructed in the kingdom of heaven,
bringing forth out of his treasure new things and old, and
one of those merchants who, when he had found a precious
pearl, sold what he had and bought it, but he is likewise
one of those concerning whom we read: 'So speak ye, and
so do.' Of these, the Saviour says: 'He that shall do and
shall teach men, he shall be called great in the kingdom of
heaven.'

Now, I earnestly beg your charity, who read these words.
You who bless the Lord, render thanks with me to almighty
God who has given me understanding as well as the will and
power to bring these facts to the knowledge of all, both now
and in the future. Moreover, I ask you to pray with me and
for me, that I may emulate and imitate in this world that
man, now dead, with whom, by God's grace, I lived intimately and pleasantly without any bitter disagreement for almost
forty years. Having done this, I will enjoy with him in the
world to come the promises of almighty God. Amen.

LIFE OF ST. ANTHONY
BY ST. ATHANASIUS

Translated by

SISTER MARY EMILY KEENAN, S.C.N.

Nazareth College

INTRODUCTION

THE EXTRAORDINARY importance of the *Life of Saint Anthony* can be attributed to a number of causes, but chief among them must be reckoned, first, the great holiness and unusual personality of the subject,[1] and, second, the unique authority and influence of the biographer, St. Athanasius,[2] and the veneration in which he was held.

It is only when the menace of the Arian heresy is grasped that the influence of St. Athanasius (296-373) can be understood. Arianism struck at the very heart of Christianity, the mystery of the Trinity, by asserting that Christ, the Son of God, the Second Person of the Trinity, was but a creature. If Arianism had not been crushed, Christianity, humanly speaking, would not have survived. In the mighty conflict that then raged, the Bishop of Alexandria was not only the indomitable leader in defending the divinity of Christ, but the personal inspiration of many of the other great thinkers

---

1 St. Anthony was born at Coma, which is today Queman-el-Arous. The abandoned fort in which he lived for twenty years was at Meimun. The mountain on which he finally made his home in 312 is in Qolzoûm, and bears his name today, Der Mar Antonios. Here, there still exists the ancient Coptic convent, Deir-el-'Arab. Cf. Leclercq, *DACL*, s.v. 'Monachisme.' Cardinal Newman beautifully portrays the character of St. Anthony in his *Historical Sketches,* 'Anthony in Conflict' and 'Antony in Calm.'
2 A very brief but succinct account of St. Athanasius is given in Campbell, *Greek Fathers* 47-53.

and writers, often more gifted than himself, who fought in the ranks of orthodoxy. This was Athanasius' greatest contribution to civilization.

All his writings clearly reflect the antithesis that exists between pagan and Christian thought, and this despite his Greek culture and distinctively Greek cast of mind. In this work, however, he gives in a simple, straightforward style the life of the man who was perhaps most typical of the reaction to pagan culture and ideals of that age.

The *Life* was written at the request of a group of 'foreign monks,' probably between 356 and 357, not long after the death of St. Anthony, while St. Athanasius himself was hidden in The Thebaid during the Arian persecution which was then raging.[3] Less than five years after its publication, Evagrius of Antioch translated it into Latin, and, in 384, as St. Augustine testifies, it had been read by officials of the imperial court at Trèves. There is also a very ancient Syriac version, as well as Armenian and Arabian translations.[4]

The number of ancient authors who testify to the authorship and date of the *Life* is impressive. Montfaucon has listed them in his *In Antonii vitam monitum,* which is reprinted in the Migne edition of his text of the *Life.* It was the Magdeburg Centuriators (1562) who made the first systematic attempt to discredit the *Life;* Weingarten's attack in 1877 was the last. His theory, fashionable for a time, was completely abandoned within a generation. Today, scholars are practically unanimous in their acceptance of the work

---

3 This is Leclercq's view; Cayré gives the year 360. A. Robertson, who wrote the notes for Ellershaw's translation, puts the date between 356 and 362. There variations depend on the interpretation of section 82 of the *Life.*
4 Cf. Leclercq, 'Monachisme.'

as a genuine historical record and as an authentic work of St. Athanasius.[5]

The *Life of Saint Anthony* is of major importance in the history of monasticism.[6] St. Anthony was not the first Christian hermit, it is true, nor was he a great organizer or legislator, but there can be no doubt that he was everywhere looked upon as the father of Christian monasticism. He is also regarded as the founder of the religious life, in the technical sense of the term, in all its various forms. The long ascetical sermon in the *Life* (section 16-34) can be considered the first monastic rule.

The mode of life prescribed by St. Anthony was really semi-eremetical in character, for the monks lived in separate huts or cells, and came together only occasionally for divine service or spiritual conferences. This form of monasticism became, under St. Anthony's direct influence, the norm in Northern Egypt from Lycopolis (Asyut) to the Mediterranean. It is represented in the Church today, at least in some measure, by the Carthusians in the West and by the semi-independent hermitages called Lauras in the East.

As the first biographical account of one who had achieved sanctity without martyrdom, the *Life of Saint Anthony* has been the pattern of countless 'Lives' of holy persons from the time of its publication to our own day.[7] Two of the earliest and most important works which stem from it are the *Lausiac*

---

5 The most satisfactory discussion of the historical and critical problems relating to the *Life of Saint Anthony* are to be found in Abbot Butler's *Lausiac History of Palladius,* I 197, 215-228; II 9-12.

6 There is a very extensive literature on this subject, but the two articles by Leclercq, 'Cenobitsme' and 'Monachisme,' in *DACL* are among the best treatments.

7 Such 'Lives' abounding in the miraculous were particularly numerous in the Middle Ages.

History of Palladius and St. Jerome's biographies of the
three solitaries, St. Paul, Malchus the Monk, and St. Hilarion.
It was, moreover, the inspiration of the vast iconography in
honor of St. Anthony,[8] and the theme of the 'temptation of
St. Anthony' has recurred frequently in literature and art.

The most famous instance of the influence of the *Life,*
however, is recorded in the *Confessions* of St. Augustine,
where the saint relates how Ponticianus, a fellow countryman
and an official at the imperial court, told of the extraordinary
effect a single reading of the life of Anthony had on two of
his comrades. They were so inflamed by it that they decided
to adopt such a life immediately, and, when the young women
to whom they were betrothed heard of their decision, they,
not to be outdone, determined to consecrate their virginity
to God.

More impressive still was the effect on St. Augustine himself, who, compelled, as it were, by Ponticianus' account, to
look squarely at himself, was so filled with horror and shame
at his own sordidness that, in order to escape it, he fled into
the garden where his moral conversion was finally accomplished.[9]

Because the struggles with the Devil and other extraordinary phenomena have such a large place in the *Life of St.
Anthony,* the modern reader not infrequently overlooks what
is actually the most important element in it, namely, the lesson of complete surrender to the call of Christ. Anthony
sought to live the perfect life of the Beatitudes as preached
by Christ, and the simple yet beautiful principles which he
shares with his brethren constitute a perfect pattern for true
Christian living in every age. The voice of Anthony, it has

8 Twelve reproductions are given in Maisie Ward, *St. Anthony of Egypt*
(London and New York 1950).
9 Cf. *Confessions* 8.6-8.

been well said, is not a voice calling us to the past, but to the supernatural.

Since there is no modern critical text of the *Vita sancti Antonii*, the text here used is that of Montfaucon, reproduced in Migne, *PG* 26.

SELECT BIBLIOGRAPHY

Text:

J. P. Migne, *Patrologia Graeca* 26 (Paris 1857) 835-976.

Translations:

H. Ellershaw, 'Life of Antony,' in *A Select Library of Nicene and Post-Nicene Fathers of the Christian Church*, Second Series, edited by H. Wace and P. Schaff, IV (New York 1907) 188-221.

J. B. McLaughlin, O.S.B., *St. Anthony the Hermit* (New York 1924).

Supplementary works:

E. C. Butler, *The Lausiac History of Palladius,* Vol. I, Prolegomena (Cambridge 1898); Vol. II, Text (Cambridge 1904).

J. M. Campbell, *The Greek Fathers* (New York 1929).

F. Cayré, *Manual of Patrology and History of Theology,* translated by H. Howitt, I (Paris 1936) 366-354.

H. Leclercq, 'Cenobitisme,' in F. Cabrol-H. Leclercq, *Dictionnaire d'archéologie chrétienne et de liturgie*, II. 2 (Paris 1910) 3074-3248. Cols. 3086-3088 are especially pertinent.

———, 'Monachisme,' *ibid*, XI. 2 (Paris 1934) 1802-1807.

J. H. Newman, *Historical Sketches* II (London and New York 1899) 94-126.

THE LIFE OF ST. ANTHONY

Preface

OU HAVE ENTERED into a noble contest with the monks of Egypt in undertaking to equal or surpass them in your training in the way of virtue, for now there are monasteries in your midst, and the name of monk is publicly esteemed. It is right, therefore, that everyone should praise your purpose; may God fulfill it in answer to your prayers.

You have asked me for an account of the blessed Anthony's way of life because you wish to learn how he began the practice of asceticism, what he was prior to it, how he died, and whether or not the things told of him are true, in order to train yourselves to zealous imitation of him. Most willingly have I accepted the task you imposed; indeed, merely to call Anthony to mind is of great profit to me, and I know that, when you have heard about him, you will not content yourselves with admiring the man, but you will also wish to imitate his way of life, for the life of Anthony is for monks an adequate guide in asceticism.

Do not hesitate to believe what you have heard from those who have brought you accounts of him; believe, rather, that they have told but little, for they certainly cannot have recounted all the details of his life. Even I—since you have urged me—notwithstanding all that I shall relate in my letter,

shall be writing but a few of the things I have remembered
about him. Therefore, do not cease questioning those who
sail from these shores, for it is probable that, when each one
has told what he knows, the account will not do Anthony
justice. For this reason, I had a mind, when I received your
letter, to send for some of the monks—especially those who
used to be with him most constantly—so that I might learn
further details and send you a more complete account. The
sailing season was closing, however, and the letter-carrier was
pressing me, so I have hastened to write for your reverent
consideration both what I myself know, for I saw him often,
and what I was able to learn from him, since I attended him
no little time, and served him personally.[1] In all the details
I have been concerned solely about the truth, so that no one
may be incredulous when he hears further details, nor, on the
other hand, think less of the man because he has heard so
little about him.

Chapter 1

Anthony was an Egyptian by birth. His parents were well
born and possessed considerable means, and since they were
Christians, he, too, was brought up a Christian. As a young
child, he was reared by his parents, knowing no one but them
and his home, and when he grew to boyhood and adolescence,
he refused to attend school because he wished to avoid the
companionship of other children. His whole desire was, as is
written of Jacob,[1] to dwell a plain man in his house.

---

1 Literally, 'poured water on his hands,' a Biblical expression which here
refers to the time that St. Athanasius spent as a disciple of St. Anthony,
whom he served as Eliseus served the Prophet Elias. Cf. 4 Kings 3.11.
According to R. Cellier, *Histoire génerale des auteurs sacres et ecclesi-
astiques* V (Paris 1735) 152, this was in 315.

---

1 Gen. 25.27.

He used to frequent the church with his parents and was very attentive as a child; as he grew older, he was respectful and obedient to his parents, and by paying close attention to passages read aloud, he carefully preserved for himself what was profitable in them. Although he had a moderately wealthy home, as a boy he did not trouble his parents for a variety of costly foods nor seek enjoyment in eating, but he was content solely with what he found and asked for nothing more.

Chapter 2

The death of his parents, when he was eighteen or twenty years old, left him with the responsibility of a very young sister, as well as of their home. Scarcely six months had passed since his parents' death, when, going to the church, as was his custom, he thoughtfully reflected as he walked along how the Apostles, leaving all things, followed the Saviour,[1] and how the faithful in the Acts of the Apostles, selling their possessions, brought the price of what they had sold and laid it at the Apostles' feet for distribution among the needy;[2] and he considered how great was the hope laid up for them in heaven. Pondering on these things, he entered the church.

It happened that the Gospel was then being read, and he heard the Lord saying to the rich man: 'If thou wilt be perfect, go, sell what thou hast, and give to the poor, and thou shalt have treasure in heaven; and come, follow me.'[3] As though God had inspired his thought of the saints and the passage had been read aloud on his account, Anthony left the church at once and gave to the villagers the property he had received from his parents—there were three hundred

1 Matt. 4.20.
2 Acts 4.35.
3 Matt. 19.21.

acres, fertile and very beautiful—so that he and his sister might not be in any way encumbered by it. He sold all their other worldly possessions and collected a large amount of money, which he gave to the poor, keeping a little for his sister's sake.

Chapter 3

On another occasion, as he was going into the church, he heard the Lord saying in the Gospel: 'Do not be anxious about tomorrow.'[1] He could remain no longer, but went out and gave even this to the needy. Later, entrusting his sister to virgins who were well known and faithful, he placed her in a convent[2] to be brought up, and then devoted himself to the practice of asceticism not far from his own house,[3] watching over himself strictly and patiently training himself. Monasteries were not yet as common in Egypt, and no monk knew the great desert, but anyone who wished to attend to his soul practiced the ascetical life alone, not far from his own village. Thus, there was in the neighboring village at the time an old man who had lived a solitary life from his youth. Upon seeing him, Anthony endeavored to equal him in virtue; so he, too, began to stay in the places near the village at first. If he heard of a zealous person anywhere else, he went forth from there like a wise bee and sought him out and did not return to his own place until he had seen him. After he had taken from him supplies, as it were, for traveling the road to virtue, he returned.

1 Matt. 6.34.
2 This is the earliest use of the word *parthenon* in the sense of 'convent' or 'nunnery.' Cf. E. C. Butler, 'Monasticism,' *Cambridge Medieval History* I (New York 1936) 521.
3 This practice had existed among Egyptian pagans and Egyptian Jews; Egyptian Christians continued it. Cf. *Lausiac Hisory* 1.229-230.

Here, then, he went through the first stages of the ascetical life, carefully weighing his resolution not to return to
his inheritance and not to recall his kindred, and directing
his whole desire and all his energies to strengthening his
spiritual practices. He labored with his hands, therefore, because he heard: 'If any man will not work, neither let him
eat,'[4] spending a part for bread and a part on the needy.
He prayed continually, because he had learned that one must
pray in secret without ceasing.[5] He paid such close attention
to what he heard read that nothing escaped him,[6] but he
remembered everything, his memory later serving him instead
of books.

Chapter 4

Training himself in these ways, Anthony was loved by
all. He was sincerely subject to the devout men whom he
visited and closely observed for himself the zeal and self-
denial which each had acquired: he noticed the courtesy of
one, the constancy of another in prayer; he observed one's
meekness, another's kindness; he attentively watched one as
he kept vigil and another in his love of study; he admired one
for his patience, another for his fasting and sleeping on the
ground; he watched closely the gentleness of one and the
forbearance of another; while in all he noted their devotion
to Christ and their love one for another. Having thus gathered
his fill, he returned to his own place of solitude, reflecting
thereafter on the special virtues of each one and striving
eagerly to exemplify all of them in himself. He was not
given to emulating persons his own age; yet he took care

4 2 Thess. 3.10.
5 Matt. 6.6; 1 Thess. 5.17.
6 Obviously, the Scriptures, which inspired and nourished his prayer.

that they should not surpass him in the higher things. He did this in such a way as to offend no one, but rather caused everyone to rejoice in him. All the villagers, therefore, and all lovers of the good who knew him, seeing what he was, called him dear to God. Some cherished him as a son; others, as a brother.

Chapter 5

The Devil, however, in his envy and hatred of the good, could not bear to see such steadfastness in a young person and attempted to use against him the methods in which he is skilled. He first tried to draw him away from the ascetical life by suggesting the memory of his property, anxiety about his sister, intimacy with his kindred, greed for money and for power, the manifold enjoyment of food, and the other pleasures of life, and finally the rigor of virtue and the great labor it entailed; he also hinted at the weakness of the body and the duration of time. In a word, he gathered up in his mind a great dust cloud of arguments, wishing to withdraw him from his upright purpose.

When, however, the Enemy saw that he was powerless against Anthony's resolution and that, instead, he was himself being defeated, by Anthony's firmness and overthrown by his great faith, and that he was not succeeding because of Anthony's continuous prayers, he then placed his confidence in the weapons 'in the navel of his belly,'[1] glorying in them—for they are his first snares against the young—and advanced against the youth. He troubled him by night and disquieted him so by day that even onlookers noticed the struggle that was taking place between the two. He suggested filthy thoughts; Anthony turned them away by his prayers.

1 Job 40.11.

He aroused carnal feelings, but Anthony, blushing in shame, fortified his body by faith, by prayers, and by fastings. The contemptible Enemy even dared to assume the appearance of a woman at night, imitating her every gesture solely to deceive Anthony; but he extinguished the burning oil of that illusion by meditating on Christ and reflecting on the nobility that is ours through Christ and on the spiritual nature of the soul.

Again, the Enemy suggested the softness of pleasure, but Anthony, in anger and grief, pondered on the threat of punishment by fire and the torment of the worm and, after weighing them against his temptations, came through them unharmed. All this but added to the confusion of the Enemy, for he who considered himself like to God was now mocked by a youth, and he who exulted over flesh and blood was routed by a man clad in flesh. For the Lord was assisting him, the Lord who took flesh for us and gave the body victory over the Devil, so that all who truly strive can say: 'Not I, but the grace of God with me.'[2]

Chapter 6

Finally, when the Serpent was unable to overthrow Anthony by such means and even saw himself driven out of his heart, he gnashed his teeth, as it is written;[1] and, as though driven to frenzy, he next came to Anthony as a black boy, his appearance matching his mind. He fawned upon Anthony, as it were; he no longer assailed him with thoughts, for, deceitful as he was, he had been cast out.

2 1 Cor. 15.10.

1 Ps. 111.10.

This time adopting a human voice, he said: 'I have deceived many, and I have overthrown many; yet now, when I attacked you and your works, as I have attacked others, I was powerless.'

Anthony then asked: 'Who are you who say such things to me? And at once he uttered a contemptible speech: 'I am a lover of fornication; I have undertaken to ensnare the young and entice them to it, and I am called the spirit of fornication. How many I have deceived who wished to be chaste! How many who practiced self-restraint have I by my seductions persuaded to change! I am he on whose account the prophet reproaches the fallen, saying: "You have been deceived by the spirit of fornication,"[2] for through me they were tripped up. I am he who often troubled you, but whom you as often overthrew.'

But Anthony thanked God and, taking courage against his adversary, said: 'You are, then, thoroughly despicable, for your mind is black and you are as weak as a child. Henceforth, I shall have no concern about you, for "the Lord is my helper and I will despise my enemies." '[3] At this the Evil One immediately fled, cringing at his words, fearing even to approach the man again.

Chapter 7

This was Anthony's first victory over the Devil, or rather this was the triumph, in Anthony, of the Saviour who 'has condemned sin in the flesh, in order that the requirements of the Law might be fulfilled in us, who walk not according

2 Osee 4.12.
3 Ps. 117.7.

to the flesh but according to the spirit.'[1] Anthony did not become negligent, however, nor did he act presumptuously, as if the Devil were under his power. Neither did the Enemy cease laying snares as though worsted, for again he went about like a lion,[2] seeking some occasion against him.

But Anthony, who had learned from the Scriptures[3] that the Enemy's wiles are numerous, persevered earnestly in his asceticism. He realized that, even if the Enemy had not been able to seduce his heart with bodily pleasures, he would undoubtedly try to ensnare him by other means, because the Devil is a lover of sin. More and more, then, he chastised his body and brought it into subjection,[4] lest, after triumphing in some matters, he should be dragged down in others. He therefore determined to accustom himself to a more rigorous way of life. People marveled at him, but he easily endured the hardship, for the eagerness of his spirit had become so a part of him that it was habitual; he would take even an insignificant occasion afforded by others to manifest great zeal in this matter. For he kept such long vigils that often he passed the whole night without sleep, and this not once, it was noted with wonder, but frequently. He used to eat once a day, after sunset; sometimes, however, after two days, and, frequently even after four. His food was bread and salt; his drink, water only. Of meat and wine there is no need even to speak, since nothing of this sort was found among the other holy men. A rush mat served him for sleep, but most of the time he lay on the bare ground. He refused to anoint himself with oil, saying that it was more becoming young men to show readiness in disciplining themselves and that they should not seek what would enervate the body, but

1 Rom. 8.3-4.
2 1 Peter 5.9.
3 Eph. 6.11.
4 1 Cor. 9.27.

rather accustom it to hardship, remembering the Apostle's words: 'When I am weak, then I am strong.'[5] The state of the soul, he said, is vigorous when the pleasures of the body are weakened.

He had come to this truly uncommon conclusion: he thought it proper to measure progress in virtue and retirement from the world for the sake of it not by time, but by earnestness of desire and stability of purpose. Accordingly, he himself took no account of the time which had passed, but day by day, as if beginning his ascetical life anew, he made greater efforts to advance, constantly repeating to himself St. Paul's saying: 'Forgetting what is behind, I strain forward to what is before.'[6] He also recalled the word of the Prophet Elias, who said: 'The Lord liveth before whose face I stand this day';[7] for he observed that in saying 'this day' the Prophet was not measuring the time which had passed, but daily, as though ever beginning, he endeavored to make himself such as one ought to be to appear before God—pure in heart and ready to submit to His will and to none other. And he used to say to himself that in the life of the great Elias the ascetic ought always to see his own, as in a mirror.

Chapter 8

Having strengthened himself in this manner, Anthony went out to the tombs that were at some distance from the village. Having requested an acquaintance to bring him bread at long intervals, he entered one of the tombs and, when the acquaintance had closed the door on him, he remained with-

---

5 2 Cor. 12.10.
6 Phil. 3.13.
7 3 Kings 18.15.

in alone. Now, the Enemy could not endure this. Fearing that in a short time Anthony would fill the desert with his asceticism, he came one night with a throng of demons and cut him so with lashes that he lay on the ground speechless[1] from the intense pain. Anthony declared that the pain was so severe that blows inflicted by men could not have caused him such agony.

By the providence of God, however, for the Lord is not unmindful of those who hope in Him, his acquaintance arrived the next day, bringing him the loaves. On opening the door, he saw Anthony lying on the ground apparently dead, so he picked him up and brought him to the village church, where he laid him on the ground. Many of his kinsmen and the villagers watched beside Anthony as if he were dead. About midnight, however, Anthony awakened, fully conscious, and, when he saw them all sleeping except his companion, he beckoned him to come to him and asked to be lifted again, without waking anyone, and carried back to the tombs.

Chapter 9

The man carried Anthony back, and, when the door was closed as before, he was again alone within. He could not stand up, because of the blows, but he prayed as he lay there and after his prayer called out: 'Here am I, Anthony; I am not going to flee from your blows, for, even if you inflict more on me, nothing shall separate me from the love of Christ.'[1] Then he sang: 'If camps shall stand against me,

---

1 It has been observed that the state which St. Athanasius here attributes to the activities of the Devil is very like a state of catalepsy. Cf. *DACL* XI 2.1803, s.v. 'Monachisme.'

---

1 Rom. 8.35.

my heart shall not fear.'[2] These were the ascetic's thought and words.

But the Enemy, a hater of the good, marveled that he had the courage to return after the blows, and, calling together his hounds, he passionately burst forth: 'You see that neither by the spirit of fornication nor by blows have we made this man cease, but that he even challenges us. Let us attack him in another way.' Evil schemes are easy for the Devil. During the night, therefore, the demons made such a din that the whole place seemed to be shaken to its foundations. They seemed to break the four walls of the room and to come in through them in the shape of beasts and reptiles; and suddenly the place was filled with the forms of lions, bears, leopards, bulls, serpents, asps, scorpions, and wolves, each of which was behaving in its natural manner. The lion kept roaring, ready to attack; the bull seemed to charge with its horns; though the serpent kept writhing, it never reached him; and the wolf kept checking itself as it rushed at him. The noises of all the apparitions together in the same place were terrible, and their outbursts of fury ferocious.

Anthony felt bodily pains even more severe, as they scourged and goaded him, yet he lay there unshaken, more vigilant in spirit than before. He groaned because of the pain of his body, but his mind was clear, and he said to them gaily: 'If you had any power, it would have been enough for one of you to come, but because the Lord has deprived you of your strength, you therefore try to frighten me by your numbers. That you take the shape of beasts is proof of your weakness.' And again he said, fearlessly: 'If you are strong enough, because you have received power against me, do not delay your attack, but, if you have no power, why do you needlessly trouble yourselves? For

2 Ps. 26.3.

faith in our Lord is a seal and a wall of safety for us.'
After numerous attempts, therefore, they gnashed their teeth
at him because they were mocking themselves and not him.

Chapter 10

Now, the Lord had thus far not been unmindful of
Anthony's conflict, but had been at hand to aid him. Looking up, Anthony saw the roof opening, as it were, and a ray
of light coming down toward him; suddenly, the demons
disappeared, and the pain of his body ceased at once; the
building was whole again. Realizing that help was at hand,
Anthony recovered his breath again, and, being relieved of
his pains, questioned the vision there before him: 'Where
were you? Why did you not appear at the beginning to end
my pains.' 'I was here, Anthony,' a voice answered, 'but
I waited to see your struggle. Because you have remained
firm and have not yielded, I will always be your helper, and
I will make your name known everywhere.'

Anthony arose and prayed, when he heard this, and was
so strengthened that he perceived that he had more strength
in his body than before. He was then about thirty-five years
old.

Chapter 11

On the following day, Anthony went forth with even
greater zeal for the service of God, and, upon meeting the
old man mentioned before, asked him to live with him in the
desert. The old man declined because of his age and because such a practice was not as yet customary, so Anthony
set off at once for the mountain by himself.

Again the Enemy saw his zeal and hoped to hinder him.

He threw in his path what seemed to be a large silver disc, but Anthony, recognizing the stratagem of the Evil One, stood and looked at the disc and then discomfited the Devil in it as he said: 'How did a disc get here in the desert? This is not a beaten pathway, and there is no trace of travelers here. It could not have fallen unnoticed, for it is very large. But, even if it had been lost, the loser would have found it had he turned back to look for it, because the place is a desert. This is a trick of the Devil. You shall not hinder my purpose by such means, Satan. Take this thing "with thee to perdition." '[1] And as Anthony said this, the disc vanished like smoke before the face of fire.

Chapter 12

Then, as he went on again, he saw in the road, not a deceptive image this time, but real gold scattered in the way. Whether the Enemy caused it, or whether some higher power was trying the athlete and showing the Devil that Anthony really cared nothing for money, he himself did not say, and we do not know. He did say that what appeared was gold. Anthony wondered at the quantity, but passed it by, stepping over it as if it were fire, without even turning back; he ran swiftly on so as to lose sight of the place and to forget its location.

Strengthened in his purpose more and more, he went steadily on to the mountain. On the other side of the river he discovered a fort which had been deserted for so long that it was full of reptiles; he crossed over and settled there. The reptiles immediately left the place, as if some one were pursuing them. He barricaded the entrance, after laying in

---

1 Acts 8.20.

bread for six months (the Thebans do this, and often it remains unspoiled for a whole year), and, since there was water within, he went down as into a shrine and remained there alone for one year. He neither went abroad himself nor saw any of those who came to him. Thus he devoted a long time to the practice of asceticism, receiving bread only twice a year from the room above.

Chapter 13

Those of his friends who came to him frequently spent the days and nights outside, since he did not allow them to enter. They used to hear what sounded like a turbulent crowd within, shouting and shrieking, as they screamed: 'Go away from our dwelling. What have you to do with the desert? You cannot hold out against our snares.'

At first, those outside thought that there were men who had entered by a ladder struggling with him, but, when they looked down through a hole and saw no one, they were alarmed and called to Anthony. He had disregarded the demons, but listened to the men and, coming to the door, advised them to go back home and not to be afraid, for the demons cause exhibitions of this kind against the timid. 'Make the sign of the Cross,' he said, 'and go away boldly, leaving these to make laughing stocks of themselves.' So they went away, fortified with the sign of the Cross, and he remained and was not harmed by them at all.

He did not become weary of the struggle, for the aid of a heavenly vision and the weakness of the Enemy brought him great relief from his labors and filled him with greater zeal. His friends used to come regularly, expecting to find him dead, but they would hear him singing: 'Let God arise, and let his enemies be scattered; and let them that hate him flee from before his face. As smoke vanisheth, so let them vanish away: as wax melteth before the fire, so let the wicked perish at the presence of God.'[1] And again: 'All nations compassed me about: and in the name of the Lord I have been revenged on them.'[2]

Chapter 14

Anthony spent nearly twenty years disciplining himself in this manner, neither going out, nor seldom being seen by anyone. As a result, many were eager to imitate his asceticism, and some of his acquaintances came and forcibly broke down the door and removed it. He came forth as from some shrine, like one who had been initiated in the sacred mysteries, and filled with the spirit of God. Then, for the first time, he was seen outside the fort by those who came to him. They were amazed to see that his body was unchanged, for it had not become heavy, as from lack of exercise, nor worn, from fasting and struggling with the evil spirits; he was just as they had known him before he had secluded himself.

The temper of his soul, too, was faultless, for it was neither straitened as if from grief, nor dissipated by pleasure, nor was it strained by laughter or melancholy. He was not disturbed when he saw the crowd, nor elated at being welcomed by such numbers; he was perfectly calm, as befits a man who is guided by reason and who has remained in his natural state.[1] Through him, the Lord healed many of those present

---

1 Ps. 67.2-3.
2 Ps. 117.10.

---

1 The state in which Adam and Eve were created, but which was damaged by the Fall.

who were suffering in body and freed others from evil spirits.

The Lord also gave Anthony grace in speech, so that he comforted many who were in sorrow and reconciled those who were at variance, urging all to prefer the love of Christ to anything in the world. And as he conversed with them, exhorting them to remember the good things to come and the love of God for us, who 'has not spared even his own Son but has delivered him for us all,'[2] he induced many to choose the solitary life. So from that time there have been monasteries[3] even in the mountains, and the desert was made a city by monks who had left their own city and enrolled themselves for citizenship in heaven.

Chapter 15

Once, when Anthony was obliged to cross the canal of the Arsenorites—the occasion was the visitation of the brethren —the canal was full of crocodiles. He simply prayed; then, he and all his companions entered it and passed through unharmed. Upon returning to his cell, he continued the same holy and strenuous labors. By frequent conferences he increased the zeal of those who had already become monks and stirred many others to a love of the ascetical life, and soon there were numerous cells because his speech drew men, and to all of them he acted as a father and a guide.

---

2 Rom, 8.32.
3 Literally, 'monasteries,' but in the original sense of solitary dwellings; probably huts, or cells, or grottoes. Cf. E. Fehrenbach, 'Cella,' *DACL* II. 2 2870.

Chapter 16

One day, when he went out because all the monks came to him and asked to hear a discourse, he spoke to them as follows in the Egyptian tongue: 'The Scriptures are sufficient for our instruction, yet it is good to encourage one another in the faith and to spur one another on by our words. Like children, then, you relate what you have learned to your father, and I, as your elder, will share with you my knowledge and experience. Let all make this resolution especially: not to give up once we have begun, not to become faint-hearted in our labors, and not to say. "We have spent a long time in the practice of asceticism." Rather, let us increase our zeal each day as if we were beginning anew, for, if measured by the ages to come, the whole of human life is very short, and all our time is as nothing compared with eternal life. In the world, everything is sold at its price, and measure is given for measure; the promise of eternal life, however, is bought for a trifle. For it is written, "The days of our years in them are threescore and ten years. But if in the strong they be fourscore years: and what is more of them is labour and sorrow."[1]

'If, then, we should spend eighty whole years, or even a hundred, in the practice of asceticism, we shall reign not merely for a hundred years, but forever. Our struggle is on earth, but it is not on earth that we shall receive our inheritance; our reward is promised in heaven. We put off a corruptible body and receive it back incorruptible.'

---

1 Ps. 89.10.

Chapter 17

'Therefore, children, let us not be faint-hearted nor think that we have labored a long time, nor that we are doing anything great, for "the sufferings of the present time are not worthy to be compared with the glory to come that will be revealed in us."[1] Let us not think, as we look at the world, that we have renounced something great, because the whole earth is very small when compared to the whole of heaven. Though we were lords of even the whole earth and gave it all up, it would be as nothing compared to the kingdom of heaven. It is as if a man should disregard one bronze coin in order to gain a hundred gold ones; so, a man who renounces the whole earth, though he be lord of it, gives up little and receives a hundredfold in return.

'And if the whole earth is not worth the kingdom of heaven, surely he who has left a few fields leaves nothing, as it were; even if he has given up a house or much gold, he ought not to boast nor grow weary. Moreover, we should consider that, if we do not relinquish these things for virtue's sake, we leave them behind later when we die and often, as Ecclesiastes reminds us,[2] to those to whom we do not wish to leave them. Why, then, do we not relinquish them for the sake of virtue, so that we may inherit a kingdom? Let none of us, therefore, give entrance to the desire for possessions, for what gain is it to acquire those things which we cannot take with us? Why not rather acquire those which we can take: prudence, justice, temperance, fortitude, understanding, charity, love of the poor, faith in Christ, gentleness, hospitality? If we obtain these, we shall find them there before us preparing a welcome for us in the land of the meek.'

---

1 Rom. 8.18.
2 Eccle. 2.18-19; 6.2.

Chapter 18

'With such thoughts, then, let a man persuade himself not to regard this matter lightly, especially if he considers that he is himself a servant of the Lord and owes service to his Master. Hence, as a servant would not dare to say: "I am not going to work today because I worked yesterday," and he would not refuse to do any work on the following days because he was counting the past, but would daily, as it is written in the Gospel,[1] show the same readiness to please his Master and avoid danger, so we, too, should persevere daily in the practical of asceticism, knowing that the Lord will not pardon us for the sake of the past if we are careless for a single day, but will be angry with us because of our negligence. Thus we have heard in Ezechiel.[2] Likewise, Judas, because of one night, lost all his previous labor.'[3]

Chapter 19

'Therefore, children, let us hold fast to the practice of asceticism and not grow careless. For, in this, we have the Lord working with us, as it is written: "To all that choose the good, the Lord works with them for good."[1] And in order to avoid negligence, it is well for us to reflect on the Apostle's saying, "I die daily";[2] for, if we also live as if dying daily, we shall not sin. That is to say, when we wake each day we should think that we shall not live until evening;

---

1 Luke 17.7.
2 Ezech. 3.20; 18.26.
3 John 6.71-72.

---

1 Rom. 8.28.
2 1 Cor. 15.31.

and again, when falling asleep, we should think that we shall not awaken; for our life is of its nature uncertain and is measured out to us daily by Providence. Living from day to day in such dispositions, we shall neither sin, nor desire anything inordinately, nor nurse angry feelings against anyone, nor lay up treasure on earth, but, as if daily expecting to die, we shall be poor and shall forgive everyone everything. We shall not take hold of the desire for women or for any other carnal pleasure, even to conquer it, but we shall turn from it as something we ignore,[3] ever striving and looking forward to the day of judgment. For, a greater fear and anxiety concerning the torment of hell always dispels the enticement of pleasure and rouses the languid soul.'

Chapter 20

'Now that we have begun and have entered on the way of perfection, let us press on the more so that we may reach the things that lie before.[1] Let no one turn back like Lot's wife, especially since the Lord has said: "No one, having put his hand to the plough and looking back, is fit for the kingdom of God."[2] To turn back is nothing other than to change one's purpose and to seek after worldly things again. Do not be fearful when you hear of perfection, nor be surprised at the word, for it is not far from us, nor does it exist outside of us; perfection is within our reach, and the practice of it is a very easy matter if only we will it. The Greeks go

---

3 That is, lust is to be avoided by flight from the occasions rather than by direct resistance, since direct resistance tends to make one dwell too much on the thing to be fought against. Cf. St. Thomas, IIa IIae, q.35,a.1 ad4um.

---

1 Phil. 3.13.
2 Luke 9.62.

abroad, even crossing the sea to become learned, but we have no need to go abroad for the sake of the kingdom of heaven, nor need we cross the sea for the sake of perfection; the Lord has already told us: "The kingdom of God is within you."[3]

'We need only to will perfection, since it is within our power and is developed by us, for, when the soul keeps the understanding in its natural state, perfection is confirmed. The soul is in its natural state when it remains as it was created, and its was created beautifully and exceedingly upright. For this reason, Josue, the son of Nave, commanded the people: "Incline your hearts to the Lord the God of Israel,"[4] and John: "Make straight his paths."[5] Rectitude of soul, then, consists in preserving the intellect in its natural state, as it was created. On the other hand, when the intellect turns aside and deviates from its natural state, the soul is said to be evil. Thus, the matter is not difficult; if we remain as we were made, we are in a state of virtue; but, if we think evil thoughts, we are accounted evil. If, then, perfection were a thing to be acquired from without, it would indeed be difficult; but, since it is within us, let us guard against evil thoughts and let us constantly keep our soul for the Lord, as a trust received from Him, so that He may recognize His work as being the same as when He made it.'

Chapter 21

'Let us strive not to be ruled by anger nor overpowered by concupiscence, for it is written that "the wrath of man does

3 Luke 17.21.
4 Jos. 24.23.
5 Matt. 3.3.

not work the justice of God,"[1] and "when passion has conceived, it brings forth sin; but when sin has matured, it begets death."[2] Living thus, let us watch constantly and, as it is written, keep our heart with all watchfulness,[3] for we have terrible and crafty enemies, the wicked demons, and we wrestle against them, as the Apostle said: "For our wrestling is not against flesh and blood, but against the Principalities and the Powers, against the world-rulers of this darkness, against spiritual forces of wickedness on high."[4]

'The number of evil spirits in the air around us is great, and they are not far from us. They differ greatly, and much could be said of their nature and of their distinctions, but such an account is for others greater than we are. At the present time, however, we need only to know their wiles against us.'

Chapter 22

'Therefore, we must first understand that the demons were not created demons, for God made nothing evil. They were created good, but, having fallen from heavenly wisdom, they have since then been continually flying about the earth. They deceived the Greeks by apparitions and, because they envy us who are Christians, they leave nothing unmoved in their desire to keep us from the way to heaven that we may not mount to the place from which they fell.

'A man has need of much prayer and self-discipline that he may receive from the Spirit the gift of discerning spirits and be able to know their characteristics—which of them are less evil, which more; what is the nature of the special pur-

1 James 1.20.
2 James 1.15.
3 Prov. 4.23.
4 Eph. 6.12.

suit of each of them, and how each of them is overcome and cast out. They have numerous changes of plots. The blessed Apostle and his followers knew this when they said: "We are not unaware of his devices,"[1] and we, from the temptations we have experienced from them, must, when oppressed by them, guide one another. Therefore, I, who have had some experience of them, speak to you as my children.'

Chapter 23

'If the evil spirits see each Christian, and especially each monk, laboring cheerfully and making progress, they first attack and tempt by putting snares in the way. Their snares are evil thoughts. We need not fear their suggestions, however, for by prayer and fasting and trust in the Lord they immediately fail.

'But, even when they have failed, they do not rest, but come back again, craftily and deceitfully. When they cannot deceive the heart openly with shameful pleasures, they attack again in another way and set themselves to cause great fear by devising empty images, changing their shapes, and taking the form of women, of wild beasts, of reptiles, of gigantic bodies, and of troops of soldiers. Even so, we need not fear their phantoms, for they are nothingness and quickly disappear, especially if one fortifies himself with faith and the sign of the Cross. Yet, they are bold and very shameless, for, even if they are overcome, they attack again in another way. They pretend to prophesy and foretell the future, and they appear as tall as the roof and of great width in order to seize stealthily by such phantoms those whom they were unable to ensnare by their arguments.

1 2 Cor. 2.11.

If here, also, they find the soul strengthened by faith and by the hope of its purpose, they then bring in their leaders.'

Chapter 24

Anthony said that they often appeared in that shape in which the Lord revealed the Devil to Job when he said: 'His eyes are as an image of the morning star. Out of his mouth go forth burning lamps, and watch-fires are shot forth; out of his nostrils goeth smoke of a furnace burning with a fire of coals. His breath is coals, and flame cometh forth out of his mouth.'[1]

'When the leader of the demons appears in this manner, the crafty one causes terror, as I said, by boasting, as the Lord convicted him of doing when He said to Job: "For he shall esteem iron as straw, and brass as rotten wood, and he thought the sea an unguent-box, and the infernal regions of the abyss as captive, and the abyss as a place for walking."[2] And by the Prophet: "The enemy said I will pursue and overtake."[3] And again, by another Prophet: "I shall seize the whole world in my hand as a nest, and as eggs that are left I shall take it up."[4] In a word, such are the things they try to boast and to proclaim so that they may deceive the devout.

'But, again, we, the faithful, must not fear his phantoms nor heed his words, for he lies and never speaks a word of truth. Although he talks and boasts of so many great things, he was drawn by the hook, like a dragon by the Saviour, and received the halter round his nostrils like a beast of

1 Job 41.9-12.
2 Job 41.18, 22-24 (Septuagint).
3 Exod. 15.9.
4 Isa. 10.14.

burden, and was bound like a runaway with a ring in his nostrils,[5] and his lips were pierced with an armlet. The Lord has caged him like a sparrow to be mocked by us;[6] he and his demons have been placed like scorpions and serpents to be trodden under foot by Christians.[7] A proof of this is that we are now living our kind of life in spite of him. Behold, he who threatened to dry up the sea and seize the world now cannot hinder our practice of asceticism, nor even prevent my speaking against him.

'Let us, then, not heed what he may say, for he lies, and let us not fear his empty visions, for they also are false. That which appears in them is not true light they are bringing, but the beginnings and the likeness of the fire prepared for them, and they will themselves burn in the flames by which they attempt to frighten men. They appear, of course, but they disappear again at once, hurting none of the faithful, but bearing with them the likeness of the fire that is destined to receive them. We should not, therefore, fear them on this account, for, by the grace of Christ, all their practices are to no purpose.'

Chapter 25

'But they are treacherous and ready to change and transform themselves into every shape. Often, without appearing, they even pretend to play the harp and to sing, and they recite passages from the Scriptures. Sometimes, when we are reading, they immediately repeat many times, like an echo, what we have read. When we are sleeping, they waken us to prayers, and this repeatedly, scarcely allowing us to sleep.

5 Job 40.19,24.
6 Job 40.24.
7 Luke 10.19.

At times, they even assume the appearance of monks, and they pretend to speak like pious men in order to deceive by this guise and then drag those whom they deceive wherever they will.

'We must not heed them, though they rouse us to prayer, though they counsel us to fast completely, though they pretend to accuse and reproach us for those things concerning which they were once in agreement with us. For they do this not for the sake of piety or of truth, but to lead the simple into despair, that they may say that asceticism is use- less, and to make men disgusted with the solitary life on the grounds that it is burdensome and very grievous, and to hinder those who live the life in spite of them.'

Chapter 26

'The Prophets sent by the Lord declared such as these wretched when he said: "Woe to him that giveth his neigh- bor a turbid drink to subvert him,"[1] for such devices and thoughts turn men away from the road which leads to virtue. The Lord Himself, even when the demons spoke the truth —for they spoke the truth when they said, "Thou are the Son of God"[2]—silenced them, nevertheless, and forbade them to speak, lest in the midst of the truth they oversow their own wickedness; He also wished to accustom us never to heed them even though they seem to speak the truth.

'It is unseemly that we who have the Holy Scriptures and the freedom of the Saviour should be taught by the Devil, who did not keep his own rank, but thinks now one thing, now another. Even when he quotes passages from the Scrip-

---

1 Hab. 2.15 (Septuagint).
2 Luke 4.41.

tures, the Saviour forbids him so speak in these words: "But thus to the sinner God hath said: Why dost thou declare my justices, and take my covenant in thy mouth?"[3] For the demons do everything—they talk, they make an uproar, they dissemble, they confuse—in order to deceive the simple. They make a din, laugh senselessly, and hiss, but, if no one heeds them, they afterwards weep and lament as though defeated.'

Chapter 27

'The Lord, then, being God, silenced the evil spirits, and it is fitting that we, learning from the saints, do as they did and imitate their courage. For, when they saw these things, they used to say: "When the sinner stood against me, I was dumb, and was humbled and kept silence from good things."[1] And again: "But I, as a deaf man, heard not, and as a dumb man not opening his mouth."[2]

'Let us, therefore, neither listen to them, since they are hostile to us, nor heed them, even if they rouse us to prayer or speak of fastings. Let us rather attend to our own purpose of self-discipline, and let us not be deceived by those who ever act deceitfully. We must not fear them even though they seem to attack us, even though they threaten death; they are powerless and can do nothing but threaten.'

3 Ps. 49.16.

1 Ps. 38.2.
2 Ps. 37.14.

Chapter 28

'I have already spoken of these things in passing but now we must not shrink from speaking about them at greater length. The warning will be a protection for you. Since the Lord dwelt among us, the Enemy has fallen, and his powers have been weakened. He does not submit quietly to his fall, however, in spite of his powerlessness, but keeps threatening like a tyrant, even if only with words. Let each of you consider the following, and he can despise the evil spirits.

'If they were confined to bodies such as ours, they could say: "When men hide themselves, we cannot find them, but if we do, we do them harm." If such were the case, we could escape them by hiding and by shutting the doors against them. But their nature is not like ours, and they can enter, even when the doors are shut, and take possession of all the air, they and their chief, the Devil. They are bent on evil and are ready to inflict injury, for, as the Saviour said, the Devil, the father of evil, is a murderer from the beginning.[1] Yet, we are still alive, spending our lives in defiance of them, so it is evident that they are powerless. This place is no hindrance to their plotting, nor do they regard us friends whom they should spare; neither are they lovers of goodness that they should amend. On the contrary, they are wicked and desire nothing so much as to injure those who love virtue and honor God. Since they have no power, they do nothing but threaten. If they had the power, they would not hesitate to use it, but would do the evil at once, since their purpose is toward this, and especially against us.

'Behold, we are now gathered together and are speaking against them, and they know that, as we advance, they grow

1 John 8.44.

weak. If, then, they had the power, they would not allow any of us Christians to live, for the service of God is an abomination to a sinner.[2] But, since they have no power, they only injure themselves, for they can do none of the things they threaten.

'Then, this also must be considered that we may not fear them: if they had any power, they would not come in a crowd, nor cause phantoms, nor use cunning devices by changing their appearances. It would be sufficient for only one to come and do whatever he could and wished to do, since anyone who has power does not destroy with phantoms nor frighten with tumults, but uses his power at once as he wills. But, since the evil spirits have no power, they play as upon a stage, changing their shapes and frightening children by the apparition of crowds and by their changed forms. On this account they are to be despised the more for their powerlessness.

'The true angel sent by the Lord against the Assyrians had no need of crowds nor apparitions from without, nor loud noises, nor clappings, but he used his power quietly and destroyed 185,000 at one time.[3] Powerless demons such as these, however, try to frighten, if only by empty phantoms.'

Chapter 29

'Should anyone ask, upon recalling the story of Job: "Why then did the devil go forth and do all these things against him: strip him of his possessions, destroy his children, and strike him with a grievous ulcer?" Let such a one know in reply that it was not the Devil who was powerful, but God

---

2 Eccli. 1.32.
3 4 Kings 19.35.

who delivered Job to him to be tried. He was unable to do anything, but asked, and received the power, and made use of it. For this reason, the Enemy is to be condemned the more, that, though he desired it, he had no power against one just man. If he had had the power, he would not have asked for it. And since he asked for it, not once, but a second time, it is evident that he is weak and powerless.

'But it is not to be wondered that he was powerless against Job, when he could not bring destruction on even his beasts, had God not permitted. He does not have power even against swine, for, as it is written in the Gospel: "They kept entreating him, saying, If thou cast us out, send us into the herd of swine."[1] If they have no power over swine, much less have they power over men made in the likeness of God.'

Chapter 30

'Therefore, we must fear God alone, and despise these evil spirits, having no fear of them at all. The more they do such things, the more we should intensify our ascetical exercises against them, for the great weapon against them is a virtuous life and confidence in God. They fear the fasting, the watching, the prayers, the meekness, and the silence of ascetics; their indifference to money and vainglory; their humility, love of the poor, their almsdeeds and their gentleness, but, above all, their devotion to Christ. The demons, therefore, do everything to prevent anyone tramping on them, for they know the grace the Saviour has given to the faithful against them when He said: "Behold I have given you power to tread upon serpents and scorpions, and over all the might of the enemy." '[1]

---

1 Matt. 8.31; Mark 5.12.

---

1 Luke 10.19.

Chapter 31

'Accordingly, if they pretend also to tell the future, pay no heed to them. Often, they tell us days beforehand that brothers are coming, and then brothers do come. It is not from concern for their hearers, however, that the demons do this, but in order to gain credence for themselves, and then, afterwards, when they have them in their power, to destroy them. Consequently, we must not heed them; we should refute them even as they speak, because we have no need of them. For, what wonder is it if, when they have seen the brothers starting on a journey, they outrun them and announce their coming, since their bodies are more subtle than men's? A man traveling by horse would also bring word beforehand, outstripping those who travel on foot. In this case, then, there is no need to wonder at them; they knew nothing beforehand which has not already taken place; God alone knows all things before they come to pass.[1]

'The demons, however, like thieves, run ahead and announce what is taking place. To how many are they now announcing our doings—that we are assembled and are speaking against them—before anyone of us goes forth to announce the news! A swift-footed boy could also do this, outstripping a slower person. What I mean is this. If someone starts to travel from the Thebiad or any other place, the demons do not know whether he will travel until he actually starts. But, when they have seen him setting out, they run ahead and announce it before he comes, and then after some days he arrives. Often, however, they prove false, because the travelers turn back.'

---

1 Dan. 13.42.

Chapter 32

'So, too, they sometimes idly talk about the rising waters of the river, for, having observed that there have been many heavy rains in the sections of Ethiopia, and knowing that the overflow of the river originates there, they run on ahead and tell it before the water comes into Egypt. Men could tell it, too, if they could run as swiftly as the demons do. And just as David's watchman, by going up to a high place, saw better who was coming than the one who stayed below, and, also, as he who ran ahead related before the others, not the things which had not yet occurred,[1] but those which were already in progress and taking place, so, too, the evil spirits choose to weary themselves in making these things known to others solely to deceive them.

'If Providence, however, should in the meantime decide otherwise concerning the waters or the travelers, for Providence can do this, the evil spirits have been deceived and those who heeded them have been tricked.'

Chapter 33

'It was in this way that the oracles of the Greeks originated and in times past they were deceived by the demons; but in this way, too, their deception was later brought to an end. For the Lord came and He has vanquished the evil spirits with that trickery of theirs. Of themselves they have no knowledge, but, like thieves, they pass on the things they see among others; they surmise rather than prophesy. If they sometimes chance to speak the truth, let no one wonder at

---

1 2 Kings 18.24.

them on this account. Physicians with experience of diseases
often foretell the symptoms when they observe the same diseases in others, for they judge from their experience. And
again, seamen and farmers, from this habit of observing the
condition of the atmosphere, predict stormy or calm weather.
No one could say on this account that they prophesy by divine
inspiration; they speak from experience and practice. If,
therefore, sometimes the evil spirits also say these things by
conjecture, do not marvel at them because of it, nor heed
them. What advantage is it to the hearers to learn from them
days beforehand what is to happen? What sort of anxiety
is this—to know such things, even if one could truly know
them? It is not conducive to virtue, nor is it in any way a
mark of a good character. None of us is judged by what he
does not know, and no one is accounted blessed because of
his learning and knowledge; but for these things each one
will be judged: if he has kept the faith and truly observed
the Commandments.'

Chapter 34

'We must not, then, attach great importance to these
matters, nor live a life of self-denial and toil in order to
know the future, but in order to please God by living uprightly. Neither ought we to pray to know the future nor
ask it as a reward of our austere life, but we ought to pray
that the Lord may be our fellow worker in gaining victory
over the Devil. If we care to know the future, even once,
let us be pure in mind, for I believe that, when a soul is
perfectly pure and has persevered in its natural state, it
becomes clear sighted and is able to see more and further
than the evil spirits, since it has the Lord to reveal things
to it. The soul of Eliseus was such as this when he watched

what was done by Giezi, and saw the armies standing at his side.'[1]

Chapter 35

'Therefore, whenever demons come to you by night and wish to tell the future, or say: "We are angels," pay no attention to them, for they lie. And even if they praise your practice of asceticism and call you blessed, do not hearken or act as if they were there at all; instead, bless yourselves and the house, and pray, and you will see them vanish. For they are cowards, and they greatly fear the sign of the Lord's Cross, since it was on the Cross that the Saviour robbed them of their prey and put them to open shame. If, however, they shamelessly persist, dancing and subtly transforming themselves with their apparitions, do not shrink from them in fear nor heed them as if they were good spirits.

'It is possible, with the help of God, easily to distinguish the presence of the good and the bad; a vision of the holy ones is not agitated. "He shall not protest and cry out; none will hear his voice." It occurs so quietly and gently that joy and gladness and confidence are at once born in the soul, for the Lord who is our joy, and the power of God the Father, is with the holy ones. The soul's thoughts remain untroubled and calm, so that, enlightened of itself, it contemplates those who appear. A longing for the heavenly things to come takes possession of it, and it would wish to be wholly united to them if it could depart with them. If, however, some people, being human, are struck with fear at the vision of good angels, the visitants at once dispel this fear by their charity, as Gabriel did for Zachary,[2] and the angel who appeared

---

1 4 Kings 5.26; 6.17.

---

1 Isa. 42.2; Matt. 12.19.
2 Luke 1.13.

to the women at the holy sepulchre,[3] and the angel that said to the shepherds in the Gospel: "Fear not."[4] Their fear is not from timidity of soul, but from the full knowledge of the presence of higher beings. Such, therefore, is the vision of holy ones.'

Chapter 36

'The assault and appearance of the evil ones is troubled with clamor, din, and shouting, such as the disturbance of rough youths and robbers might be. From this there follows immediately apprehension of soul, confusion and disorder of thought, dejection, hatred toward ascetics, spiritual sloth, affliction, the memory of one's family, and fear of death; presently, there is craving for evil, a contempt for virtue, and instability of character.

'Whenever, then, you are fearful upon seeing someone, if the fear is immediately taken from you, and in its place there comes joy inexpressible, cheerfulness, confidence, renewed strength, calmness of thought, and the other signs I have named before—courage and love of God—be of good heart and pray; the joy and the settled state of the soul prove the sanctity of the one who is present. Thus Abraham rejoiced when he saw the Lord,[1] and John leaped for joy at the voice of Mary the Mother of God.[2] But if during an apparition there is confusion and noise from without, and earthly display, and threatening of death, and such things as I have mentioned before, know that it is the visitation of the evil ones.'

---

3 Matt. 28.5.
4 Luke 2.10.

---

1 John 8.56.
2 Luke 1.41.

Chapter 37

'Let this likewise be a sign to you: whenever the soul continues to be fearful, it is the Enemy who is present, for the
evil spirits do not dispel the fear of their presence as the
great Archangel Gabriel did for Mary and Zachary,[1] and
as the angel who appeared to the women at the tomb.[2]
On the contrary, whenever they see men afraid, they re-
double their phantoms so as to terrify them the more, that
then they may come upon them and mock them, saying:
"Fall down and worship us."[3]

'In this manner they deceived the Greeks, for among them
they were erroneously taken for gods. But the Lord has not
permitted us to be deceived by the Devil, because, when he
appeared to Him, He rebuked him and said: "Begone, Satan!
for it is written: 'The Lord thy God shalt thou worship and
him only shalt thou serve.' "[4] Accordingly, let us despise the
Crafty One more and more, for, what the Lord said He
said for our sake, that when the devils hear the same words
from us they may be put to flight through the Lord, who rebuked them in those words.'

Chapter 38

'We must not boast of casting out devils, nor be elated at
the healing of diseases, nor should we admire only the man
who casts out devils, and account that one useless who does
not. A man should observe carefully the discipline of each
monk, and either imitate it, strive to excel it, or correct it.

1 Luke 1.13,30.
2 Mark 16.6.
3 Matt. 4.9.
4 Matt. 4.10.

To work miracles is not ours; that is the Saviour's work. At any rate, He said to His disciples: "But do not rejoice in this, that the spirits are subject to you; rejoice rather in this, that your names are written in heaven."[1]

'The fact that our names are written in heaven is evidence of our virtuous life, but to cast out devils is but the charismatic gift of the Saviour who bestowed it. To those who boasted of their miracles and not of their virtues, saying: "Lord, did we not cast out devils, in thy name, and work many miracles in thy name?"[2] He answered: "Amen, I say to you I know you not." For the Lord knows not the ways of the unholy.[3]

'As I have said before, we ought always to pray to receive the grace of discerning spirits in order that, as it is written, we may not trust every spirit.'[4]

Chapter 39

'I would not wish to cease speaking and to say nothing about myself, content with what I have just told you. But that you may not think that I am merely talking, and may believe that I am speaking from experience and speaking the truth, I am repeating, not for myself but for love of you and for your encouragement, what I have observed of the practices of the evil spirits, even if by doing so I make myself a fool. The Lord who hears knows this and knows the purity of my conscience.

'How often have the evil spirits called me blessed, and I have cursed them in the name of the Lord! Often, they

---

1 Luke 10.20.
2 Matt. 7.22-23.
3 Ps. 1.6.
4 1 John 4.1.

have foretold the rising of the river, and I said to them: "And why are you concerned about this?" Once they came threatening, and surrounded me like soldiers in full armor. Sometimes, they filled the house with horses and wild animals and serpents, but I sang the psalm, "Some trust in chariots, and some in horses: but we will call upon the name of the Lord our God,"[1] and at these prayers they were turned back by the Lord.

'Once, they came in the dark, assuming the appearance of light, and said: "We have come to light you, Anthony." But I closed my eyes and prayed and the light of the unholy ones was put out at once. A few months later, they came as if singing psalms and babbling from the Scriptures. "But I, as a deaf man, heard not."[2] Once, they shook the cell, but I prayed and remained unshaken in mind. Afterwards, they came again, pounding, hissing, leaping, but as I prayed and lay singing the psalms to myself, they immediately began to wail and lament as if exhausted, and I glorified the Lord who had humbled them and made an example of their blindness and fury.'

Chapter 40

'Once, a very tall demon appeared with a procession of evil spirits and said boldly: "I am the power of God, I am His providence. What do you wish that I grant you?" I then blew my breath at him, calling on the name of Christ, and I tried to strike him. I seemed to have succeeded, for, immediately, vast as he was, he and all his demons disappeared at the name of Christ.

1 Ps. 19.8-9.
2 Ps. 37.14.

'Once when I was fasting, the Deceiver came to me as a monk with a vision of loaves, and counseled me, saying: "Eat and cease from your many hardships; even you are a man and will become weak." But I perceived his artifice and rose to pray. He could not endure this, for he departed, appearing as smoke as he went out through the door. How often in the desert he showed me a vision of gold, merely to have me touch it and look at it. But I sang a psalm against him, and the illusion vanished.

'Frequently, the demons struck me blows, but I kept saying: "Nothing will separate me from the love of Christ,"[1] and at this they struck one another instead. It was not I, however, who stopped them and brought them to nought, but it was the Lord, who says: "I was watching Satan fall as lightning from heaven."[2] Mindful of the Apostle's saying,[3] children, I have applied the Lord's words to myself so that you may learn not to be faint-hearted in the ascetical life and not to fear the delusions of the Devil and his demons.'

Chapter 41

'Since I have become a fool in discussing these things with you, take this also for your safety and assurance, and believe me, for I do not lie.

'Once, some one knocked at the door of my cell, and, going out, I saw a great, towering figure. When I asked: "Who are you? he said: "I am Satan." Then when I asked: "Why are you here?" he said: "Why do the monks and all other Christians blame me without cause? Why do they curse

1 Rom. 8.35.
2 Luke 10.18.
3 1 Cor. 4.6.

me hourly?" To my question, "Why do you molest them?"
he answered: "It is not I who molest them, but they disquiet
themselves, for I am powerless. Have they not read that 'The
swords of the enemy have lost their edge forever; thou hast
rooted up their cities.'[1] I no longer have a place, a weapon, a
city. There are Christians everywhere, and, now, even the
desert has been filled with monks. Let them watch over themselves and not curse me without cause." Then, marveling
at the grace of the Lord, I answered: "You always lie and
never speak the truth, but this time, however, you have spoken
truly even though against your will, for Christ has come and
made you powerless. He has cast you down and stripped
you." When he heard the Saviour's name, he vanished, for
he could not endure its burning heat.'

Chapter 42

'If, then, even the Devil himself admits that he is powerless, we ought utterly to despise both him and his demons.
The Enemy with his hounds has but so many stratagems, and
we who have learned his weakness can look upon them with
contempt. Let us, therefore, not be disheartened in this matter, nor succumb to cowardice of soul, nor invent terrors
for ourselves, saying: "But if a demon should come and
overthrow me, or lift me up and hurl me down, or come
suddenly upon me and molest me?" We should not even
think of such things, nor should we be sad as if we were
lost. We should take courage, rather, and be always joyful
as men who have been saved.

'Let us bear in mind that the Lord who defeated and
vanquished them is with us. And let us always carefully con-

---

1 Ps. 9.7.

sider this fact, that, while the Lord is with us, our enemies will do nothing to us; they will conform themselves to the attitudes they find in us when they come, and thus they will adapt their phantoms to our dispositions. If they find us fearful and disquieted, they attack at once, like thieves when they find the place unguarded; and whatever we ourselves are thinking, this they carry out and more. If they see us anxious and afraid, they increase our fear the more by apparitions and threats, and our poor soul is tormented accordingly in these ways.

'If, however, they find us rejoicing in the Lord, and meditating on the good things to come, thinking on these things of the Lord, and reflecting that all things are in His hands, and that no evil spirit has any strength against a Christian, nor any power at all over any one—seeing the soul safeguarded by such thoughts, they turn away in confusion. Thus, when the Enemy saw Job fenced about with these thoughts, he withdrew from him, but, finding Judas undefended, he captured him. If, then, we would despise the Enemy, we must keep our thoughts always on the things of the Lord, and let our soul ever rejoice in hope. We shall see that the artifices of the demons are as smoke, and that, instead of pursuing, they themselves are put to flight, for they are, as I have said before, very cowardly, and are always expecting the fire which is prepared for them.'

Chapter 43

'Keep this, also, as a sign for your protection against them. Whenever an apparition occurs, do not be overcome with fear at the outset, but, whatever it be, first boldly ask: "Who are you and why are you here?" If it is a vision of angels or of saints, they will reassure you and turn your fear into joy. But, if it is anything diabolical, it immediately loses all strength on seeing your resolute spirit, for, simply to ask: "Who are you and why are you here?" is proof of calmness. Thus, when the son of Nave inquired,[1] he received an answer, and the Enemy did not escape when Daniel questioned him.'[2]

Chapter 44

While Anthony spoke of these things, all were filled with joy. In some, the love of virtue increased; in others, carelessness was overcome; and in others, self-conceit was curbed. All were persuaded to despise the snares of the Devil, and everyone marveled at the grace which the Lord had given to Anthony for the discerning of spirits. So the cells in the hills were like tabernacles filled with heavenly choirs singing psalms, studying, fasting, praying, rejoicing in the hope of things to come, laboring in order to give alms with love and harmony one toward another.

And truly, one could see a land set apart, as it were—a land of piety and justice. For neither wrong-doer nor wronged was there, nor complaint of the tax-collector, but a great number of ascetics, all of one mind toward virtue. As one looked again on the cells and on the regularity of the monks, one cried aloud, saying: 'How beautiful are thy tabernacles, O Jacob, thy tents, O Israel! As woody valleys: as watered gardens near the rivers: as tabernacles which the Lord hath pitched: as cedars by the waterside.'[1]

---

1 Jos. 5.13.
2 Dan. 13.51-59.

---

1 Num. 24.5-6.

Chapter 45

Anthony returned alone to his own cell as usual and intensified his spiritual life. Often each day he sighed at the thought of the mansions of heaven, as he longed for them and reflected on the shortness of man's life. He was filled with shame when going to eat and sleep and when caring for the other needs of the body, as he thought of the spirituality of the soul. Frequently, when he was to eat with many other monks, when he recalled the food of the spirit, he excused himself, and went at a distance from them, thinking it cause for shame that he should be seen eating by others. He used to eat when alone, however, because of bodily necessity and often, too, with the brethren, and, though ashamed on their account, he spoke freely, because of the words of help he gave them.

He used to say that we should give all our time to the soul rather than to the body, but that we ought to allow a little time to the body. In general, however, we should rather devote our time to the soul and seek its profit so that it may not be dragged down by the pleasures of the body, but that the body may be made subject to the soul, instead, for this is what the Saviour said: 'Do not fret over your life, how to support it with food, over your body, how to keep it clothed. Do not seek what you shall eat or what you shall drink; and do not exalt yourselves! (for after all these things the nations of the world seek); but your Father knows that you need these things. Seek first the kingdom of God, and all these things shall be given you besides.'[1]

---

1 Luke 12.22; 29-31.

Chapter 46

After this, the persecution which then occurred under Maximinus laid hold upon the Church. When the holy martyrs were led to Alexandria, Anthony quit his cell and followed them, saying: 'Let us also go that we may enter into the contest if we are called, or else that we may look on those who are contending.' He longed for martyrdom, but, as he did not wish to give himself up, he ministered to the confessors in the mines and in the prisons. In the court of justice he was very zealous in stirring to generosity in their struggles those who were summoned, and in receiving those who were to undergo martyrdom and accompanying them to the end.

The judge, seeing the fearlessness of Anthony and his companions, and their zeal in this work, gave orders that no monk should appear in the court nor even remain in the city. All the others thought it well to hide themselves that day, but Anthony heeded the command to this extent that he washed his tunic the more, and on the following day stood on a high place out in front, where he was in plain view of the prefect. Then, while all wondered at this, and the prefect saw him, as he went through with his escort, Anthony stood there calmly, showing the eagerness that we Christians have. He was praying that he, too, might be martyred, as I have said before, and he grieved because he had not yet been called to be a martyr, but the Lord was keeping him to help us and others, that he might teach many the practice of asceticism that he had himself learned from the Scriptures. Many, on merely seeing his manner of acting, were eager to imitate his mode of life. He again ministered to the confessors as before, wearying himself in serving them as if he were a prisoner with them.

Chapter 47

When, at length, the persecution had ceased and the blessed Bishop Peter had died a martyr, Anthony departed and again retired to he cell. There, he was daily a martyr to conscience in the sufferings he endured for the faith. He practicsed a much more intense asceticism, for he fasted constantly and wore a garment made of skin, the inner lining of which was of hair. He kept this even until his death. He never bathed his body with water to cleanse it. nor did he even wash his feet; he would not allow them to put in water at all without necessity. No one ever saw him unclothed, nor did anyone, except when he died and was buried, see Anthony's body uncovered.

Chapter 48

After he had withdrawn and had resolved to spend a fixed time during which he himself would neither go outside nor receive anyone, Martinianus, a captain of the soldiers, came and disturbed him, for he had a daughter troubled by an evil spirit. The captain stayed a long time, knocking at the door asking him to come and pray to God for the child, but Anthony did not allow the door to be opened. Leaning out from above, he said, 'Man, why do you keep crying out to me? I am only a man like yourself. If you believe in Christ, whom I serve, go, and, according as you believe, pray to God and it will be done.' Immediately, therefore, believing and calling upon Christ, Martinianus went away with his daughter made clean from the evil spirit. The Lord effected many other things also through Anthony, for He said: 'Ask and it shall be given to you.'[1]

---

1 Luke 11.9.

Many of the sufferers simply slept outside his cell, since he did not open the door, and they were cleansed because they believed and prayed sincerely.

Chapter 49

As he saw that many crowded to him, and that he was not permitted to withdraw according to his resolution, as he wished, fearing that either he would become proud because of the things the Lord was accomplishing through him,[1] or that someone would think more highly of him than the truth warranted, after considering the matter, he set out for the upper Thebiad among those who did not know him. He had even gotten the loaves from the brethren, and was sitting on the bank of the river watching for a boat to pass, so that he might board it and go with them.

While he was thinking of this, a voice came to him from above: 'Anthony, where are you going, and why?' He was not frightened, for he was accustomed to be called in this way frequently, so he listened and answered: 'The crowds do not allow me to be alone. I therefore wish to go into the upper Thebiad because there are many annoyances for me here, but chiefly because people ask me things beyond my power.' And the voice said to him: 'Even though you go up into the Thebiad, or down into the pasture lands, as you are planning, you will have to endure a doubly great burden. If, however, you wish to be really alone, go up now into the inner desert.'

'And who will show me the way, Anthony asked, 'for I do not know it?' Immediately, he was shown some Saracens starting out in that direction. He went forward to meet them,

---

1 2 Cor. 12.6.

and, when he asked to go with them into the desert, they
welcomed him gladly, as if by the command of Providence.
He traveled with them three days and three nights, until he
came to a very high hill, at the foot of which there was
water, very clear, and sweet, and very cold. Beyond, there
was level ground and a few wild date palms.

oasis

Chapter 50

Anthony, moved by God, as it were, was delighted with
the place, for it was this spot which the voice had spoken
of when he was on the river bank.

After he had received bread from his fellow travelers to
start with, he remained alone on the hill, with no one else
with him, for from then on he kept that place as one who
had discovered his own home. The Saracens, having seen
Anthony's earnestness, used to travel that way purposely and
were glad to bring him bread, and sometimes he had also
a little frugal refreshment from the date palms. Later, when
the brethren learned the place, like children mindful of their
father, they were careful to send him bread. But, when Anthony saw that because of the bread some were being put to
trouble and hardship, he decided to ask some of those who
came to him to bring him a two-pronged hoe, an axe, and
a little grain. When they brought these things, he went over
the ground around the hill, and found a small plot that was
suitable, which he tilled and sowed, for he had water in
abundance from the spring. He did this every year, and had
bread as a result, rejoicing that he would trouble no one on
this account, and that he was keeping himself from being a
burden in any way.

Later, when he saw that people were coming to him again, he raised a few vegetables also, that the visitors might have some little refreshment after the weariness of that hard journey. At first, however, the beasts in the desert often used to damage his crop and his garden when they came for water, but, having caught one of them, he said graciously to all: 'Why do you harm me when I do you no harm? Go away, and, in the name of the Lord, do not come near these things any more.' Afer that, as if fearing his command, they no longer came near the place.

Chapter 51

He was then alone on the inner mountain, devoting himself to his prayers and spiritual exercises. The brethren who served him, however, asked that they might come each month to bring him olives, pulse, and oil, for he was now an old man.

The many wrestlings he endured while he dwelt there we have learned from those who visited him; wrestlings, not against flesh and blood, as it is written,[1] but against opposing demons, for there also the brethren heard the tumults, and the sound of many voices, and the clash of weapons, as it were; and at night they saw that hill filled with wild beasts, and they saw him fighting as with invisible foes, and praying against them. He comforted his visitors, but he himself fought as he knelt and prayed to the Lord. It was indeed remarkable that, though alone in such a wilderness, he was not frightened away by the demons who attacked him, nor alarmed at the wildness of the four-footed beasts and creeping things, although they were numerous, but he truly trusted

---

1 Eph. 6.12.

the Lord like Mount Sion, as the Scripture says,[2] with a serene and tranquil mind, so that the demons fled instead, and the wild beasts kept peace with him, as it is written.[3]

Chapter 52

The Devil, therefore, watched Anthony and gnashed his teeth against him, as David sings in the psalm,[1] but Anthony was consoled by the Saviour and remained unharmed by the Devil's wickednes and his many arts.

The Devil set wild beasts on him as he watched at night, and nearly all the hyenas in that desert came out from their dens and surrounded him. He was in their midst, and each with open mouth threatening to bite him, but he was aware of the enemy's craft, and said to all of them: 'If you have received power over me, I am ready to be devoured by you, but, if you are sent by evil spirits, go without delay, for I am a servant of Christ.'

They fled when Anthony said this, as if driven by the whip of his words.

Chapter 53

A few days later, as he was busy at his work—for he was careful to work hard—someone stood at the door and pulled the plait he was making, for he was weaving baskets, which he gave to visitors in exchange for what they brought. He rose and saw a beast resembling a man as far as the thighs, but with legs and feet like an ass. Anthony simply blessed

2 Ps. 124.1.
3 Job 5.23.

1 Ps. 34.16.

himself and said: 'I am a servant of Christ; if you have been sent against me, here I am.' The beast with its evil spirits fled so fast that in its speed it fell and died. The death of the beast marked the defeat of the demons, for they were doing everything in their power to drive him from the desert, but they could not.

Chapter 54

Once, because he had been asked by the monks to return after a time and visit them in their places, he set out with the monks who had come to meet him. A camel carried the loaves and the water for them, since the entire desert is without water; there is none at all to drink, except on that one mountain where Anthony had his cell, and it was from here they had drawn the water. When, therefore, the water failed on the way, and the heat was intense, they were all in danger. After searching around and finding no water, they were no longer able to walk, so they lay down on the ground; they let the camel go, for they despaired of themselves.

The old man, seeing all in danger, was much grieved; with a groan he went a little distance from them, and knelt and prayed with extended arms. At once, the Lord caused a spring to come forth where he had stopped to pray, and all drank and were refreshed. After filling their water-skins, they searched for the camel and found it; the rope had chanced to encircle as stone and in this way was held fast. When they had brought the animal back and watered it, they placed the skins on it and went on their way unharmed.

When Anthony came to the outer monasteries, all the monks embraced him, for they looked on him as a father. And he, as though bringing supplies from his hill, refreshed and aided them with his words. There then was joy in the hills again, and eagerness to advance, and encouragement because of their mutual faith. He, too, rejoiced when he saw the zeal of the monks, and learned that his sister had grown old in her virginity and was guiding other virgins.

Chapter 55

After some days, Anthony went back to the mountain. From that time on, many people came to him, and even some who were sufferers ventured to come. For all the monks who came to him he always had this advice: to trust in the Lord and to love Him, to guard themselves from impure thoughts and the pleasures of the flesh, and, as is written in Proverbs,[1] not to be led astray by feasting of the stomach; to flee vainglory, to pray always, to sing psalms before sleep, and, on awakening, to repeat by heart the Commandments in the Scriptures, and to remember the deeds of the saints so that the soul, conforming itself to their precepts, might train itself to imitate their zeal.

He counseled them especially to heed constantly the Apostle's word: 'Do not let the sun go down upon your anger,'[2] and to consider that this was spoken about all the Commandments alike; the sun should not go down, not simply on our anger, but on any other of our sins, for it is right and necessary that the sun should not condemn us for any evil by day, nor the moon for any sin, not even an evil thought, by night. 'To preserve this disposition,' he said, 'it is well to hear and heed the Apostle, for he says, "Put your

---

1 Prov. 24.15 (Septuagint).
2 Eph. 4.26.

own selves to test and prove yourselves."[3] Daily, therefore, let each one take account with himself of the actions of the day and the night. If he has sinned, let him cease; and if he has not, let him not boast, but persevere in good, without growing negligent, nor condemning his neighbor, nor justifying himself till the Lord come who searches hidden things, as the blessed Apostle Paul said. Often, we are unaware of what we do, and we do not know, but the Lord sees everything. Entrusting judgment to Him, then, let us sympathize with one another, bearing one another's burdens; but let us judge ourselves and be earnest in filling up the things in which we are lacking.

'As a safeguard against sin, let the following be observed: Let us note and write down our deeds and the movements of our soul as if we were to tell them to each other. If we are utterly ashamed to have them known, be assured that we shall cease sinning and even cease thinking anything evil. For, who wishes to be seen sinning, or, when he has sinned, does not pretend otherwise because he wishes to escape notice? Therefore, just as we would not commit fornication in the sight of each other, so if we write our thoughts as if to tell them to one another, we shall guard ourselves the better from foul thoughts through shame of having them known. Let the written account serve us instead of the eyes of our fellow monks, so that, blushing at the writing as at being seen, we may not even think an evil thought, and, moulding ourselves in this way, we shall be able to bring the body into subjection, to please God, and to trample on the snares of the enemy.'

---

3 2 Cor. 13.5.

Chapter 56

Such were the counsels Anthony gave to those who came to him. He sympathized and prayed with those who were suffering, and the Lord often heard him, as he showed in many ways. When he was heard, he did not boast, nor did he murmur when not heard, but he always gave thanks to the Lord and encouraged the sufferers to be patient and to know that healing belonged neither to him nor to any man, but to God alone, who works when He wills and toward whom He wills. The sufferers, therefore, received even the words of the old man as healing, having learned not to be downcast, but rather to suffer in patience; and those who were cured learned not to thank Anthony, but God alone.

Chapter 57

A man named Fronto from the court had a terrible disease, for he kept biting his tongue and was in danger of injuring his eyes. He came to the mountain and asked Anthony to pray for him. After he had prayed, Anthony said to Fronto: 'Go, now, and you shall be healed.' Fronto objected and remained in the house for days, but Anthony kept saying: 'You cannot be healed while you remain here. Go away and, when you reach Egypt, you will see the sign which is being done in you.' The man believed and went away, and, when he had only come within sight of Egypt, he was cured of his disease and made well, according to the work of Anthony which he had learned from the Saviour in prayer.

Chapter 58

A young girl from Busiris in Tripoli had a dreadfully offensive disease. The discharge from her eyes, nose, and ears
fell to the ground and immediately turned to worms, and
her body was paralyzed and her eyes were crossed. Her
parents, hearing of the monks who were going to Anthony,
asked to journey with them with their daughter, for they
had faith in the Lord who had healed the woman troubled
with an issue of blood.[1] And when the monks consented,
the parents and the child remained beyond the mountain with
Paphnutius, the confessor and monk, while the others went
in.

When they wanted merely to tell about the girl, Anthony
interrupted them and described the child's disease and how
she had traveled with them. When they asked that she and
her parents also be admitted to come to him, he would not
allow it, but said: 'Go, and if she is not dead, you will find
her cured. For this is not my doing that she should come to
me, a wretched man; healing is from the Saviour who shows
His mercy in every place to those who call upon Him. To
her prayers, therefore, the Lord has been gracious, and His
love has revealed to me that He will heal the child's sickness
while she is there.' The miracle then took place, for they
went out and found the parents rejoicing and the girl now
in sound health.

Chapter 59

Two of the brethren were coming to him when, on the
way, the water failed. One died, and the other was on the
point of dying; he no longer had strength to go on, and lay

1 Matt. 9.20.

on the ground awaiting death. But Anthony, sitting on the mountain called two monks who happened to be there and said urgently to them: 'Take a jar of water and run down the road toward Egypt. Two monks were on their way, but one has just died; the other also will die if you do not hasten. This has just been shown to me as I prayed.'

The monks went, therefore, and found one monk lying dead, and they buried him; they revived the other with water and brought him to the old man, for the distance was a day's journey. If anyone asks why Anthony did not speak before the other died, such a question is amiss, for the sentence of death was not from Anthony, but from God, who decreed death for the one and revealed the dangerous state of the other. In Anthony this only is wonderful, that, while sitting on the mountain, he kept his heart recollected, and the Lord revealed to him things taking place at a distance.

Chapter 60

On another occasion, also, as he was sitting on the mountain, he looked up and saw one being borne along in the air, and there was great rejoicing among all who met him. Wondering then, and thinking such a company blessed, he prayed to learn what is might be. Immediately, a voice came to him that this was the soul of the monk Amun in Nitria, who had persevered as an ascetic until old age. Now, the distance from Nitria to the mountain where Anthony was is thirteen days' journey. Those who were with Anthony, therefore, seeing the old man in wonder, asked to know why, and heard that Amun had just died. He was well known, because he often came there, and also because many miracles had been worked through him.

Once, when Amun had to cross the river called Lycus, when the waters were at flood tide, he asked his companion Theodore to keep at a distance from his so that they might not see each other naked as they swam across the river. Theodore then went away, but Amun was again ashamed even to see himself unclothed. While he was pondering, therefore, filled with shame, he was suddenly carried over to the other side. Theodore, himself a devout man, came near, and seeing that Amun, who had gotten the start of him, was not even wet from the water, asked to know how he had crossed. When he saw that Amun was reluctant to say, he seized his feet and declared that he would not let go of them until he had learned this from him. Amun, seeing Theodore's determination, especially from his speech, asked him in turn not to tell anyone until his death, and then told him that he had been carried across and set down on the other side; that he had not walked on the water, for this was altogether impossible to men, and possible only to the Lord and to those to whom He granted it, as He did to the great Apostle Peter.[1] Theodore told this incident after Amun's death.

The monks to whom Anthony spoke of Amun's death noted the day, and when, thirty days later, the brethren came from Nitria, they inquired and learned from them that Amun had fallen asleep on the day and hour when the old man had seen his soul carried upward. Both they themselves and the others wondered at the purity of Anthony's soul, that he should learn at once what had happened at a distance of thirteen days' journey, and should see the soul being led heavenward.

1 Matt. 14.29.

Chapter 61

Count Archelaus once met Anthony on the outer mountain, asked him merely to pray for Polycratis, an admirable and Christ-like virgin of Laodicea. She was suffering terribly in the stomach and side from her excessive penances, and her whole body was weak. Anthony prayed, therefore, and the count noted the day the prayer was made. When he returned to Laodicea, he found the virgin well, so he asked when and on what day she was relieved of her sickness, and brought out the paper on which he had noted the time of the prayer. Upon learning the time, he at once showed the writing on the paper, and all wondered, for they recognized that the Lord had freed her from her pains while Anthony was praying for her and invoking the goodness of the Saviour in her behalf.

Chapter 62

Anthony often told days beforehand—sometimes even a month—those who were coming to him and the reason for their coming. Some came simply to see him, some because of sickness, and others because they were suffering from devils. No one thought the weariness of the journey either a trouble or a loss. for each one returned conscious that he had been helped. Although Anthony foretold such things and foresaw them happening, he used to ask that no one should admire him on this account, but rather marvel at the Lord, who has granted us the grace to know Him according to our capacity.

Chapter 63

On another occasion, he again went down to the outer
monasteries, where he was asked to enter a boat and pray
with the monks. He alone perceived a foul and terribly
acrid odor. The men on the boat said that the fish and pickled
meat in the vessel were causing the odor, but Anthony said
that the foul odor was due to something else. Even as he was
speaking, a young man with an evil spirit suddenly cried
out; he had come on earlier and was hiding in the boat.
When rebuked in the name of our Lord Jesus Christ, the evil
spirit went out of the man and he was made whole, and everyone knew that the evil spirit had caused the foul odor.

Chapter 64

Another man, one of the nobles who had a devil, came
to him. This devil was so terrible that the possessed man did
not know that he was coming to Anthony; he even used to
eat the excrement from his own body. Those who brought
him begged Anthony to pray for him, and Anthony, in pity,
prayed and watched with the young man during the whole
night.

Toward dawn, the youth came and suddenly attacked
Anthony, and gave him a push. His companions were indignant, but Anthony said: 'Do not be angry with him, for
it is not he, but the devil, who is in him; the devil has done
this in his fury at being rebuked and commanded to go into
waterless places. Give glory to God, therefore; his attacking me
in this way is a sign to you that the devil has departed.' At
Anthony's words, the young man was immediately made

whole, and then, having recovered his right mind, he realized where he was, and embraced the old man, as he gave thanks to God.

Chapter 65

A number of the monks have related, and their stories agree, many other things similar to this that Anthony did. Yet these are not so marvelous as other even greater wonders seem to be.

Once, about the ninth hour, when he had stood up to pray before eating, he felt himself carried away in spirit, and, incredible as it may seem, as he stood he saw himself from outside himself, as it were, being guided through the air by certain beings; then he saw malign and terrifying beings stationed in the air who were endeavoring to hinder his passage. When his guides resisted them, they demanded an accounting to determine whether or not he was answerable to them. When, however, they wished to take an account from his birth, Anthony's guides prevented them, saying: 'The Lord has wiped out his faults from the time of his birth, but you may take an account from the time he became a monk and promised himself to God.' Then, after they accused him but proved nothing, his way became free and unhindered, and immediately he saw himself coming, as it were, and re-entering himself, and again he was Anthony as before.

He forgot to eat, and remained the rest of the day and all of the night groaning and praying, for he was astonished to see against how many enemies we wrestle, and with what great difficulties we have to pass through the air. He remembered that the Apostle had meant this when he said:

'according to the prince of the power of the air about us.'[1]
For, here, the enemy has power to fight and to try to hinder
those who pass through. For this reason, Anthony exhorted
particularly: 'Take up the armor of God, that you may be
able to resist in the evil day';[2] 'so that anyone opposing may
be put to shame, having nothing bad to say of us.'[3]

Having learned this, let us remember the Apostle's word:
'Whether in the body, I do not know, or out of the body, I
do not know, God knows.'[4] But Paul was caught up into the
third heaven, and heard inexpressible words, and returned,
whereas Anthony saw himself entering the air and struggling
until he was proved free.

Chapter 66

He had this grace, also, from God. If ever he was per-
plexed about anything, when he searched within himself as
he sat alone on the mountain, the solution was revealed to
him by Providence in prayer. He was one of the blessed
who are taught of God, as it is written.[1] Afterwards, he discussed with some of those who came to him the life of the
soul and the nature of the place it will have hereafter, and
on the following night someone from above called him,
saying: 'Anthony, arise, go out and look.' He went out, therefore, for he knew which voice to obey, and, looking up, he
saw a towering figure standing formless and terrifying, reaching to the clouds, and he saw people going upward, as if

1 Eph. 2.2.
2 Eph. 6.13.
3 Titus 2.8.
4 2 Cor. 12.2.

1 John 6.45.

on wings. The figure was stretching out its hands, and it stopped some, but others, by flying above it, passed over it and rose without further trouble. The towering figure then gnashed its teeth at these, but exulted over those who fell.

Then a voice came to Anthony: 'Understand the vision,' and his mind was opened and he understood that it was the passing souls, and that the towering figure was the power and prevents them from passing, but he is unable to seize those who have not yet yielded to him, as they pass above him.

After this vision, which he took as another reminder, as it were, Anthony strove the more to advance day by day. He was reluctant to relate these things to others, and continued long in prayer, wondering at them within himself. When his companions pressed him with their questions, however, he was compelled to speak, as a father who cannot withhold things from his children. He thought that, since his own conscience was blameless, the telling would help them, for they would learn that the ascetical life bears good fruit, and that visions frequently are a solace for its hardships.

Chapter 67

Anthony was of a patient disposition and humble of heart. Great as he was, he reverenced the law of the Church to an extraordinary degree, and wished every cleric to be shown more honor than himself. He was not ashamed to bow his head to bishops and priests, and, whenever a deacon came to him for help, he discussed what was necessary to help him, but gave place to him in the matter of prayer, for he himself was not ashamed to learn. Often, he would ask questions and beg to hear from his companions, and, if someone said anything useful, he acknowledged that he was helped by it. His countenance was extraordinarily beautiful. This was likewise a gift from the Saviour, for, even if he was with the company of monks and someone who had not known him before wished to see him, immediately upon coming up to them he would pass the others by and run straight to Anthony, as if drawn by his eyes.

Not that he was taller or of larger build than the others; it was the serenity of his disposition and the purity of his soul that were extraordinary. His soul was tranquil; hence, his exterior senses were untroubled and his face radiated the inner joy of his soul. One realized the state of his soul from the movements of his body, according to the Scripture: 'A glad heart maketh a cheerful countenance; but by grief of mind the spirit is cast down.'[1] Thus Jacob knew that Laban was devising a plot, and said to his wives: 'Your father's countenance is not as yesterday and the day before.'[2] Thus, also, Samuel recognized David, for he had joyous eyes and teeth as white as milk.[3] Thus, also, was Anthony recognized, for he was never troubled because his soul was calm and never gloomy, because he had a joyful heart.

Chapter 68

Anthony's devotion to the faith was most extraordinary. He never held communion with the Meletian schismatics, because he knew their wicked apostasy from the beginning; nor did he have friendly dealings with the Manichaeans or

---

1 Prov. 15.13.
2 Gen. 31.5.
3 1 Kings 16.12.

any other heretics, except in so far as to admonish them to be
converted to piety, for he believed and maintained that friendship and association with them was harmful and destructive
to the soul. He likewise detested the heresy of the Arians, and
charged everyone not to go near them and not to hold their
false belief. On one occasion, when some of the Ariomanites[1]
came to him, after he questioned them and learned that they
were wanting in piety, he drove them from the mountain,
for he said that their words were worse than the poison of
serpents.

Chapter 69

Once, also, he was filled with indignation and wrath against
the Arians, when they falsely asserted that he was of the
same mind as they. Then, at the request of the bishops and
all the brethren, he came down from the mountain and
went into Alexandria, where he publicly denounced the
Arians, declaring that this was the last heresy, the forerun-
ner of Antichrist. And he taught the people that the Son
of God is not a creature and that He is not begotten from
nothingness, but that He is the eternal Word and Wisdom
of the substance of the Father. It is impious, therefore, to
say that there was a time when He was not, for the Word
was always co-existing with the Father.

'Have no fellowship, then, with these impious Arians,'
he said, 'for there is no fellowship between light and darkness.[1] You are devout Christians, but they, when they say
that the Son and Word of God the Father is a creature,[2]

---

1 A title originally enjoined by Constantine because of the fanatical
   character of the Arians. Cf. J. H. Newman, *St. Athanasius* (London
   and New York 1900) 377-379.

---

1 2 Cor. 6.14.
2 Cf. Newman, *op. cit.* 34-36, for a summary of the Arian tenets.

differ in no way from the pagans who worship the creature instead of God the Creator. You may be sure that the whole of creation is angry with them, because they count among creatures the Creator and Lord of all, by whom all things were made.'

Chapter 70

The people all rejoiced when they heard so great a man anathematize the heresy which was making war against Christ, and all the townspeople hurried out to see Anthony. The Greeks and their so-called priests also came into the church, saying: 'We beg to see the man of God,' for everyone called him this.

Here, too, the Lord cleansed many from devils through him and healed those whose minds were affected. Many of the Greeks asked only to touch the old man, believing they would be helped. In those few days, doubtless, as many became Christians as one would otherwise have seen converted in a year. Some thought that he was annoyed by the crowds, and they were keeping the people away from him, but he was not at all disturbed and said: 'These people are no more numerous than the evil spirits with whom we wrestle on the mountain.'

Chapter 71

When he was leaving and we were seeing him on his way, a woman behind us cried out, as we came to the gate: 'Wait, man of God, my daughter is grievously troubled by a devil; wait, I beseech you, lest I injure myself by running.' The old man heard and, at our request, waited willingly.

When the woman drew near, the child was hurled to the

ground, but, after Anthony prayed and spoke the name of Christ, the child rose up healed, for the unclean spirit had gone out of her. The mother blessed God, and everyone gave thanks, and Anthony, too, rejoiced as he set out for the mountain as for his own home.

Chapter 72

Anthony was unusually prudent. The extraordinary thing was that, although he had no education, he was a discerning and intelligent man. At any rate, two Greek philosophers once came to him, thinking they would try their skill on him. He was on the outer mountain, and, having recognized the men from their appearance, he went out to them and, by means of an interpreter, asked: 'Why have you philosophers put yourselves to so much trouble to come to a foolish man?' And when they answered that he was not a foolish man, but a very wise one, he replied: 'If you have come to a fool, your labor is useless, but, if you think me wise, become what I am, for we ought to imitate the good. Had I gone to you, I should have imitated you, but, since you have come to me, become what I am, for I am a Christian.' They went away, wondering, for they saw that even the devils feared Anthony.

Chapter 73

Certain others, and they, too, were philosophers, met him on the outer mountain, intending to mock him because he had had no schooling. Anthony said to them: 'What do you say? Which is first: the mind or letters? And which is the cause of which: the mind of letters, or letters of the mind?'

And when they answered that the mind is first and that it is the inventor of letters, Anthony said: 'Then one who has a sound mind has no need of letters.'

This astounded both the philosophers and the bystanders, and they went away marveling that they had seen such intelligence in an unlettered man.[1] For he did not have the rough manners of one who had been reared on the mountain and who had grown old there, but he was both gracious and courteous. His speech was seasoned with the divine salt; hence, no one bore him any ill will; on the contrary, all who went to see him were delighted with him.

Chapter 74

Afterwards, of course, some others came, and they were of those who were considered learned by the Greeks. They asked him for an explanation of our belief in Christ, and attempted to argue about the preaching of the holy Cross, with the intention of scoffing at it. Anthony waited a little, and, having first deplored their ignorance, said to them through an interpreter: 'Which is nobler, to confess the Cross, or to attribute adultery and paederasty to those whom you call gods? Our choice is proof of manliness, a token of our contempt of death, but yours is the passion of lust. Then, is it better to say that the Word of God was not changed, but, remaining the same, took a human body to save and help men, so that, having shared our human birth, He might make men partakers of the divine and spiritual nature;[1] or to liken the divine to senseless things, and then to

1 'Unlettered,' in the sense that he did not know Greek.

1 Cf. St. Athanasius, *De incarnatione verbi* 54.3 (*PG* 25.198).

worship four-footed creatures, serpents, and the images of
men? For, these are the things you wise men worship. How
do you dare scoff at us for saying that Christ has appeared
as man, when you, drawing the soul down from heaven,
maintain that it has strayed and fallen from heaven's vault
into the body? And would that it were only into a human
body, and that it did not pass on and change into four-footed
creatures and serpents.

'Our faith teaches that Christ came for the salvation of
men, but you err because you declare that the soul is ingenerate.[2] We believe in the power of Providence and His
love for men, and we hold that Christ's coming in the flesh
is not impossible with God. But you, maintaining that the
soul is an image of the Mind, ascribe falls to it and in your
myths represent it as changeable. And now you are asserting
that the mind itself is changeable by reason of the soul, for,
whatever the nature of the image, such must be the nature
of that of which it is the image. When you hold such views
about the mind, consider well that you are blaspheming also
the Father of the Mind.'[3]

Chapter 75

'As for the Cross, which would you say is better: to submit
to the Cross without shrinking from any kind of death what-

---

2 Newman, *op cit.* 374f., translates 'ingenerate.' Under this term were
  included, according to the particular philosophy or heresy in question,
  'the universe, matter, the soul of man, as well as the Supreme Being,
  and the Platonic *ideas*.'
3 St. Anthony is here refuting the teaching of the Neo-Platonists. Ploti-
  nus held that the Mind, or *Nous,* was the first emanation from the
  One, and that it was in the *Nous* that multiplicity first appeared. For
  pertinent citations, cf. F. Copleston, *A History of Philosophy* I (West-
  minister, Md. 1946) 464.

soever when wicked men are plotting against you, or to relate mythical tales of the wanderings of Osiris and Isis, and the plots of Typhon, and the flight of Chronos, and the devouring of his children, and the slaying of fathers? For, this is what your wisdom consists of. If you mock the Cross, why do you not marvel at the Resurrection? Those who tell of the one wrote of the other, also. Or why, when you mention the Cross, are you silent concerning the dead who were raised to life, the blind who regained their sight, the paralytics who were cured, the lepers who were cleansed, the walking on the sea, and the other signs and wonders which prove Christ is not merely man, but God? You seem to me to be doing yourselves a grave injustice, and you seem not to have really read our Scriptures. Read them and see that the things Christ did prove Him to be God who dwells among us for the salvation of mankind.'

Chapter 76

'But tell us of your own teachings. Yet, what more could you say about senseless creatures than that they are senseless and gross? But if, as I hear, you wish to say that these things are told among you as myths, that you make the rape of Persephone an allegory of the earth, and Hephaestus' lameness an allegory of fire, and Hera of the air, Apollo of the sun, Artemis of the moon, and Poseidon of the sea, you are, nevertheless, not worshiping God; you are serving the creature instead of the God who created all things.

'If you have devised such tales because of the beauty of creation, it was fitting that you stop short at admiration, and not make gods of creatures by offering them the honor due their Creator. If such be the case, it is time that you pay the honor due the architect to the house he has built, or that due the general to the soldier. What, then, do you say to these things, that we may determine whether there is anything about the Cross that deserves mockery?'

Chapter 77

The learned ones were at a loss, and kept turning this way and that, so Anthony smiled and again spoke through an interpreter.

'A mere glance proves that these things are false, but, since you rely on logical reasoning, for this is your special art, and since you wish that we should not even worship God without convincing arguments, tell me first how things, but especially the knowledge of God, are accurately known: through logical demonstrations, or through the operation of faith? And which is higher: an active faith or a logical demonstration?'

When they answered than an active faith is higher and is accurate knowledge, Anthony said: 'You are correct, for faith comes from the disposition of the soul, but dialectic is from the skill of those who devised it. Therefore, to those who have an active faith, proof by reasoning is unnecessary and probably useless. For you are trying to establish by arguments what we know by faith, and often you cannot even express what we know. The operation of faith is, then, better and surer than your sophistical deductions.'

Chapter 78

'Furthermore, we Christians do not hold the Mystery[1] in the wisdom of Greek reasonings, but in the power of faith abundantly given to us by God through Jesus Christ. In proof of this claim, see that we, without having learned letters, believe in God, knowing from His works His providence over all things.

'To show that our faith is an active faith, see, now, that we rely on our faith in Christ, whereas you rely on sophistical disputations. Yet, the portents of the idols are disappearing among you, whereas among us the faith is spreading everywhere. And you with your syllogisms and sophistries make no converts from Christianity to Hellenism, but we, teaching faith in Christ, expose your superstitions, for all are recognizing that Christ is God and the Son of God. With all your eloquence of language, you do not hinder the teaching of Christ, while we, by invoking Christ crucified, drive away all the demons whom you fear as gods. Where the sign of the Cross is made, magic loses its power and sorcery fails.'

Chapter 79

'Tell me, therefore, where now are your oracles? Where are the incantations of the Egyptians? Where are the delusions of the magicians? When did all these lose their power and cease but at the coming of the Cross of Christ? Is it the

1 The word *musterion* here seems to be synonymous with the Christian religion. For the various meanings in the Christian sense, cf. F. Prat, *The Theology of Saint Paul*, translated from the tenth French edition by J. L. Stoddard, II (Westminster, Md. 1927) 383-385.

Cross, then, that is deserving of scorn, and not rather the things which it has made void and proved worthless?

'This, also, is cause for wonder, that your teaching was never persecuted, but was even honored by men throughout the country, while the followers of Christ are persecuted; yet it is our teaching, not yours, that is flourishing, and spreading. Your teachings perish in spite of praise and honor; faith in the teaching of Christ, however, has filled the world, notwithstanding your mockery or the frequent persecution of rulers. For, when did the knowledge of God so shine forth? When did chastity and the virtue of virginity so manifest itself, or when was death so despised, as since the Cross of Christ appeared? No one doubts this who sees the martyrs scorning death for the sake of Christ, or beholds the virgins of the Church who keep their bodies pure and undefiled for His sake.'

Chapter 80

'These proofs are sufficient to show that faith in Christ is the only true worship. Even now, you who seek conclusions based on arguments are without faith. But, "not in the persuasive words of Greek wisdom," as our teacher said,[1] do we set forth arguments; we win men by faith which plainly anticipates the process of arguments.

'See, there are here present some who are suffering from evil spirits.' They were persons who had come to him because they were troubled by demons; he brought them into the midst and said: 'Either cleanse them by syllogisms and by any art or magic you wish, while you call upon your idols, or, if you cannot, cease your contention with us, and you shall see the power of the Cross of Christ,' At these words, he

---

1 1 Cor. 2.4.

invoked Christ and made the sign of the Cross over the sufferers two or three times. Immediately, the men stood up, now
perfectly sound in mind, blessing the Lord.

The so-called philosophers were astonished and genuinely
amazed at the wisdom of the man and at the miracle which
had been worked. Anthony said: 'Why do you wonder at
this? It is not we who do it, but Christ who works these
things through those who believe in Him. Do you, also, believe, therefore, and you shall see that what we have is not
a trick of words, but faith which works through love for
Christ. If you obtain it, you will no longer seek proofs by
arguments; you will account faith in Christ sufficient.'

These were Anthony's words, and they marveled at them,
and, after embracing him and acknowledging the help they
had received from him, they went away.

Chapter 81

Anthony's fame reached even the emperors, for, when Constantine Augustus and his sons Constantius and Constans,
the Augusti, learned these things, they wrote to him as to a
father and begged an answer from him. He, however, considered the documents of no great importance and was not
elated over the letters; he remained just as he had been before the emperors wrote to him. When the letters were brought
to him, he summoned the monks and said: 'Do not be astonished if an emperor writes to us, for he is a man; wonder,
rather, that God has written the law for men and has spoken
to us through His own Son.'

He did not wish to accept the letters, pleading that he
did not know how to answer them. But, when the monks
urged that the emperors were Christians, he permitted the

letters to be read, lest they should take offense on the ground that he had wilfully disregarded them. He wrote an answer expressing approval of the emperors because they worshiped Christ, and advising them in the interests of their salvation not to think much of things present, but to remember the judgment to come, and to know that Christ alone is the true and everlasting King. He begged them to be lovers of their fellow men, to show concern for justice, and to care for the poor. They were glad to receive his letter. Thus, everyone loved him and all sought to have him as a father.

Chapter 82

Although he was recognized as such a great man, and gave such wise answers to those who came to him, he returned once more to the inner mountain and went on with his customary exercises. Frequently, when sitting or walking with those who come to him, he held his peace, as it is written in Daniel,[1] and after a time he would resume his conversation with the brethren. His companions realized that he was seeing some vision. For, often, on the mountain he saw what was happening in Egypt and described it to Serapion the bishop,[2] who was within and saw Anthony held by the vision. Once, as he sat working, he fell into an ecstasy, as it were, during which he kept sighing deeply. After a while, he turned to his companions with a deep groan and, trembling, fell on his knees to pray, where he remained a long time.

When the old man arose, he was weeping. His companions,

---

1 Dan. 10.15.
2 Bishop of Thumis and a correspondent of St. Athanasius. Cf. *PG* 26.530.

trembling and fearful, then asked to be told what he had seen, and gave him no peace until they compelled him to speak. Then with a loud groan he said: 'My children, it is better to die before what I have seen in this vision takes place.' And when they questioned him further, he said as he wept: 'Wrath is to fall upon the Church, and she will be delivered up to men who are like senseless beasts. I saw the table of the Lord, and mules standing around it on all sides in a circle and kicking what was within, as beasts kick when they leap in wild confusion. Surely, you heard how I kept sighing, for I heard a voice saying "My altar shall be made an abomination." '

This was what the old man saw, and two years later the present onset of the Arians occurred. They plundered churches, and, after seizing the vessels, not only had the pagans carry them away, but even forced pagans from the workshops to attend their meetings, and in their meetings, and in their presence did what they wished upon the sacred table. Then we all understood that the kicking of the mules had signified to Anthony beforehand what the Arians, like brute beasts, are now doing.

After this vision he comforted his companions, saying: 'Do not lose heart, children, for, as the Lord has been angry, so will He heal again and the Church shall quickly recover her own good order and shall shine as she has shone. You will see the persecuted restored and impiety retreating into its own hiding places, and the true faith everywhere speaking openly with all freedom. Only, do not defile yourselves with the Arians, for their teaching is not of the Apostles, but of the demons and their father, the Devil; indeed, it is the barren and senseless product of a distorted mind, resembling the senselessness of the mules.'

Chapter 83

Such were the powers of Anthony. We must not doubt that these many wonders were performed by a man, for it is the promise of the Saviour, who said: 'If you have faith, like a mustard seed, you will say to this mountain, "Remove from here"; and it will remove. And nothing will be impossible to you.'[1] And again: 'Amen, Amen, I say to you, if you ask the Father anything in my name, he will give it to you. Hitherto·you have not asked anything in my name. Ask, and you shall receive.'[2] And it is He who said to His disciples and to all who believe in Him: 'Cure the sick, cast out devils, freely you have received, freely give.'[3]

Chapter 84

Accordingly, Anthony healed, not as one commanding, but by praying and by calling on the name of Christ, so that is was evident to all that he was not the doer, but the Lord, who, through Anthony, showed His love for mankind and healed the suffering. Only the prayer was Anthony's, and the self-denial for the sake of which he had settled on the mountain, where he rejoiced in the contemplation of divine things. It distressed him, however, that he was troubled by so many people and dragged to the outer mountain, for even all the judges used to ask him to come down from the mountain, because it was impossible for them to go in there on account of the litigants who were following them. They asked him to come that they might only see him, and when, therefore, he avoided and refused to go to them, they stayed on and sent

1 Matt. 17.19.
2 John 16.23.
3 Matt. 10.8.

the prisoners, escorted by soldiers, up to him instead, so that he might come down on their account. At their urging, therefore, and at sight of the culprits lamenting, he used to go to the outer mountain. Again his trouble was not wasted, for he was a help to many and benefited them by his coming. He helped the judges, counseling them to prefer justice to all else, and to fear God, and to know that with what judgment they judged they would be judged. Nevertheless, he loved more than all else his dwelling on the mountain.

Chapter 85

Once, when he was thus importuned by some who were in distress and the commander had begged him through many messengers to come down, he went down and spoke briefly on the things relating to salvation and on their own needs. He was hastening back, when the duke, as he is called, asked him to stay. Anthony said that he could not remain with them longer, and he convinced him by an apt comparison. 'As fish, if they remain long on dry land, die,' he said, 'so monks who linger among you and spend time with you grow lax. We must therefore hasten to the mountain as the fish to the sea, lest while we linger we forget the inner life.' The officer, after hearing this and many other things from him, was amazed and said that truly this was a servant of God, for how could an unlettered person have such great understanding, if he were not beloved of God.

Chapter 86

There was one officer named Balakios, who bitterly persecuted us Christians because of his zeal in behalf of the detestable Arians. Since, in his cruelty, he was beating virgins and stripping and flogging monks, Anthony sent him a letter containing the following message: 'I see wrath coming upon you. Cease, therefore, persecuting Christians, lest the wrath, at length overtake you, for it is even now imminent.' But Balakios laughed and, throwing the letter on the ground, spat upon it. He also insulted the bearers and ordered them to take this message back to Anthony: 'Since you are concerned about the monks, I shall presently come in to you, also.' Five days had not passed when the wrath overtook him. Balakios and Nestorius, the prefect of Egypt, were going out on horse to the first stopping place from Alexandria, called Chaireos. The horses belonged to Balakios and were the quietest of all that he raised. They had not yet reached their destination when the horses began to play with each other, as horses do. Suddenly, the quieter horse, on which Nestorius was riding, threw Balakios and bit him, tearing his thigh so badly with its teeth that he was immediately taken back into the city, where he died within three days. And everyone marveled because Anthony's prediction had been quickly fulfilled.

Chapter 87

Such was the warning he gave to the cruel. He so instructed others who came to him that they at once forgot their lawsuits and called those blessed who had withdrawn from the world. He so championed those who were wronged that one would think that he himself, not others, was the injured one. He proved such a source of benefit to all that many soldiers and many of the wealthy laid aside the burdens of their life and became monks thereafter. In short, he was a physician, as it were, given to Egypt by God. For, who came in

sorrow who did not return rejoicing? Who came mourning
for his dead and did not quickly put aside his grief? Who
came in anger and was not converted to kindliness? Who
came weary in his poverty and, upon hearing and seeing
Anthony, did not despise wealth and find consolation in his
poverty? What monk grown careless came to him but did
not become stronger? What youth came to the mountain and
having seen Anthony did not straightway renounce pleasure
and love self-restraint? Who came to him tempted by the
Devil and was not relieved? Who came troubled in thought
and did not gain peace of mind?

Chapter 88

For this was another remarkable feature of Anthony's asceticism, that, having the gift of discerning spirits, as I have
said before, he knew their movements and was aware of the
object toward which each directed its attention and attack.
Not only was he himself not trifled with by them, but, by
encouraging those monks who were troubled in their thoughts,
he taught them how they could defeat the tempters' plots,
by explaining their weakness and wickedness. Thus, each
one, as though anointed by him for the conflict, went down
emboldened against the designs of the Devil and his demons.

And how many young women who, though they had
suitors, seeing Anthony only from a distance, remained virgins for Christ! People came to him from foreign lands,
also, and, having received help with all the others, returned
as if sent forth by a father. Since his death, all are like fatherless orphans, comforting each other with only his memory
and holding fast to his admonitions and counsels.

Chapter 89

It is fitting, too, that I tell how he died and that you listen, since you are eager to hear, for in this also he is worthy of imitation. He was visiting the monks on the outer mountain, as was his custom, and, having learned from Providence that his end was near, said to the brethren: 'This is the last visit I shall make to you; I wonder if we shall see each other again in this life. It is time for me to be set free, for I am near a hundred and five years.' They wept when they heard this and embraced the old man and kissed him. But he spoke joyously, as if departing from a foreign city to set out for his own. He exhorted them not to be negligent in their labors nor to lose heart in their practice of asceticism, but to live as if they were to die daily. They were to be zealous in guarding their souls from foul thoughts, as he had said before, to emulate the saints, and not to go near the Meletian schismatics, 'for you know their wickedness and profane purpose,' he said. 'And have nothing to do with the Arians, for their impiety is evident to all. Do not be troubled if you see judges protecting them, for it will cease; their show of power is both mortal and short-lived. Therefore, keep yourselves all the more uncontaminated by them, and preserve the tradition of the Fathers and, above all, the holy faith in our Lord Jesus Christ, which you have learned from the Scripture and of which I have often reminded you.'

Chapter 90

When the brethren urged him to remain with them and die there, he refused for many reasons, as he implied by his silence, but for this one in particular. The Egyptians like to performe the funeral rites for the bodies of devout men when they die, especially the holy martyrs, and to wrap them in fine linen. They do not bury them in the earth, but place them on couches and keep them at home with them, thinking in this way to honor the departed.

Anthony had often asked the bishops to give orders to the people about this matter and had likewise shamed laymen and rebuked women, saying that this was not lawful nor at all reverent. The bodies of both the Patriarchs and Prophets are preserved in tombs even until now, and the very body of the Lord was placed in a tomb and a stone was placed against and concealed it until He rose on the third day. In saying this, he showed that a man violates the law in not burying the bodies of the dead, even though they be holy. For, what is greater or holier than the Lord's body? Many, therefore, after they heard him, thereafter buried their dead in the ground, and thanked the Lord for having been taught rightly.

Chapter 91

Knowing this custom and fearing that they might treat his body in this manner also, Anthony hastened on, after taking leave of the monks on the outer mountain, and returned to the inner mountain where he usually stayed. He became ill after a few months. Having called those who were with him —there were two who stayed in the house, who had been living the ascetical life for fifteen years and who attended him because of his great age—he said to them: 'I am going the way of my father, as it is written,[1] for I see that I am called by the Lord. Be watchful and do not undo your long practice of asceticism, but be zealous in keeping your resolution as if

1 Jos. 23.14.

you were but beginning now. You know how the demons
plot against you, you know how fierce they are, yet how
feeble in strength. Do not fear them, therefore, but always
breathe Christ, and trust in Him. Live as though dying
daily, giving heed to yourself and remember the counsels
you have heard from me. Have no fellowship with the
schismatics nor with the heretical Arians. You know how
I also avoided them in view of their false, anti-Christian
heresy. Be ever more earnest in striving to be united first
with the Lord, then with the saints, that after death they
also may receive you as familiar friends into everlasting
dwellings. Ponder these things and heed them, and, if you
have any care for me, remember me as a father. Do not
permit anyone to take my body to Egypt, lest they should
place it in their houses; that is the reason I entered the
mountain and came here. You also know how I always reproved those who do this and bade them cease the practice.
Therefore, perform the last rites for my body yourselves and
bury it in the earth, and observe my request so that no one
but you alone may know the place. For, at the resurrection
of the dead, I shall receive it back incorruptible from the
Saviour. Divide my garments: give one sheepskin to Athanasius the bishop, together with the cloak which I used to lie
on, which he gave me new, but it has worn out with me.
Give the other sheepskin to Serapion the bishop, and you
keep the hair-cloth garment. For the rest, God be with you,
children, for Anthony is departing and is with you no more.'

Chapter 92

When he finished speaking and they had embraced him,
he raised his feet from the ground, and as if he were looking
and cease but at the coming of the Cros of Christ? Is it the

upon friends coming toward him on whose account he was very glad, for his countenance was joyful as he lay there, he then died and was taken to his fathers. And now, as he had commanded them, they prepared his body and wrapped it up and buried it in the earth; and no one to this day knows where it is buried but these two alone. And each of us who received a sheepskin from blessed Anthony and the cloak that he wore out guards it as a great treasure; even to look at it is like seeing Anthony, as it were, and to wear it is to take up his counsels with great joy.

Chapter 93

This is the end of Anthony's life in the body, as the preceding was the beginning of his life of asceticism. And if these are but insignificant things compared with his virtue, yet judge from them what kind of man Anthony, the man of God, was, who from youth to such great age kept his eagerness for the ascetical life and never yielded to the desire of costly food because of his old age nor changed the manner of his clothing because of the weakness of his body, nor even bathed his feet with water. Yet, he remained quite healthy, for he saw well because his eyes were undimmed and sound, and not one of his teeth had fallen out; only, near the gums they had become worn because of the old man's great age. He remained strong both in hands and feet, and altogether he seemed brighter and appeared to have greater physical strength than all those who use various foods, and baths, and different garments.

The fact that he was everywhere spoken of and admired by all, and sought after even by those who had not seen him, is proof of his virtue and of a soul dear to God. For, Anthony was not known for his writings nor for his worldly wisdom, nor for any art, but simply for his reverence toward God. That this was the gift of God no one could deny. For, how was he heard of in Spain and in Gaul, how in Rome and in Africa—he sitting on the mountain—if it were not God who everywhere makes known. His own people, and who in the beginning had promised this to Anthony, also? For, though they themselves act in secret and though they wish to be hidden, the Lord, however, shows them as lamps to all, that even those who thus hear of them may know that the Commandments can be fulfilled and that they may acquire zeal for the path of virtue.

Chapter 94

Read this, therefore, to the other brethren that they may learn what the life of monks should be, and that they may believe that our Lord and Saviour Jesus Christ glorifies those who glorify Him and not only leads to the kingdom of heaven those who serve Him to the end, but even here, though they hide themselves and seek to withdraw, He makes them known and spoken of everywhere because of their virtue and the help they gave others. And if there be need, read this to the pagans, also, so that perhaps in this manner they, too, may acknowledge that our Lord Jesus Christ is God and the Son of God that they may learn also that the Christians, who sincerely worship Him and piously believe in Him, not only prove that the demons whom the Greeks look upon as gods are not gods, but also trample on them and drive them out as deceivers and corrupters of men, through Christ Jesus our Lord, to whom be glory for ever and ever. Amen.

LIFE OF ST. PAUL
THE FIRST HERMIT

BY ST. JEROME

Translated by

SISTER MARIE LIGUORI EWALD, I.H.M. Ph.D.

Marygrove College

INTRODUCTION

NEXT TO St. Augustine, St. Jerome was the most learned of the church writers. To this end he was aided by a good dialectic and rhetorical schooling, an extensive knowledge of language, familiarity with classical writing, a rich library, travels for study and a personal acquaintance with many contemporary learned persons.[1]

St. Jerome's Scriptural commentaries, revisions, and translations, culminating in the Vulgate, are his greatest literary achievement. His letters, gems of rhetoric and Ciceronian prose, are of perennial interest because they portray so vividly Jerome the man, the great humanist,[2] and they throw additional light on the life and times of the Christians of his day. The biographies, a significant part of his historical writings, hold a unique place of their own, for 'it was largely through him and his labors on the lives of the hermit saints, Paul of Thebes, Hilarion of Gaza, and the Syrian Malchus, that the Western world became intimately acquainted with the principles and practices of the ascetic life, whose organized form, monasticism, an institution of Eastern origin . . . [was] introduced at Rome only shortly before Jerome's lifetime.'[3]

---

1 L. Schade, 'Hieronymus,' *LTK* 5 (1933) 17.
2 *Ibid.*
3 R. F. Strout, 'The Greek Versions of Jerome's *Vita Sancti Hilarionis,*' *Studies in the Text Tradition of St. Jerome's Vitae Patrum,* ed. W. A. Oldfather (Urbana 1943) 306.

The popularity of Jerome's biographies is well attested by the fact that, in the 523 extant codices of the *Vitae* in Latin alone, there are 395 copies of the *Life of Paul,* 250 of the *Life of Hilarion,* and 302 of the *Life of Malchus.*[4] In addition, manuscripts in Greek, Coptic, Syriac, Old Slavic, Armenian, Ethiopic, and Arabic have been located.[5]

The *Lives* are important, too, for the new direction they have given to hagiographical writings.[6] With them, the era of bloodshed in the Acta and passions of the martyrs closes and there opens the age of the new ascetic hero, who abandons the world for the desert, where he fights and wins conquest over self and, in the words of Malchus, becomes virtually his own persecutor and martyr.[7] Rich, too, in intimate touches and personal insight, the *Lives* constitute legitimate and important history.[8] In them, Cavallera finds the brilliant pupil of the Roman rhetoricians at his best in the role of the pleasing story-teller, excelling in descriptive and narrative power[9] and drawing freely upon his classical heritage.

We know from St. Jerome's introduction to the *Life of Malchus* that he had once intended to write a Church History. The biographies of the monks, however, are all that remain of the project. 'Formerly legends had grown up about the martyrs, now they abounded about the hermits. Accounts of their lives went from mouth to mouth in the desert. Poetical fancy united fact with fiction in the oral tradition. Jer-

---

4 Oldfather, 'Introduction,' *Studies* 4.

5 *Ibid.* 5

6 P. de Labriolle, *Histoire de la littérature latine chrétienne* (Paris 1920) 457-458; cf. G. Grützmacher, *Hieronymus,* (Studien zur Geschichte de Theologie und der Kirche 6.3, Leipzig 1901) II 85.

7 *Life of Malchus* 6.

8 O. Bardenhewer, *Geschichte der altkirchlichen Literatur* (Freiburg 1923) III 638; cf. Grützmacher, *op. cit.* II 85.

9 F. Cavallera, *Saint Jerome, sa vie et son oeuvre* (Louvain 1922) I 44-45.

ome's great zeal and enthusiasm for the ascetic life naturally directed his talents to this province of literature.'[10] No one, in the opinion of Leclercq and de Labriolle, has succeeded better than St. Jerome in writing ecclesiastical tales, really historical novels, profitable to the conscience for the moral lesson they convey.[11]

The *Life of Paul* was probably written about 376 while St. Jerome was still in the desert of Chalcis,[12] that is, before 380 or 381.[13] About this time, he sent a copy of the *Life* to Paul of Concordia, a remarkably alert centenarian and book-collector, as an expression of gratitude for the books he had borrowed from him. In a letter announcing the gift, he wrote: 'To Paul the old, a Paul yet more old . . . If this little present is to your taste, I have others in reserve with various oriental wares that will come to you if the Holy Spirit will lend them wings.'[14]

It was natural for St. Jerome to be interested in the origins of the hermit life which he had just embraced. Paul of Thebes was his answer to the controversy over who was the first hermit to take up his abode in the desert. St. Anthony had been the long accepted initiator of monachism. His position, apparently, had been reaffirmed a few years before by the translation into Latin of St. Athanasius' Greek *Life of St. Anthony*.[15] The priest Evagrius, who had made the translation, was the intimate friend and host of St. Jerome dur-

10 M. Schanz, *Geschichte der römischen Literatur* (I. von Müller's Handbuch der Klassischen Altertumswissenschaft, 2nd ser. 8.4.1, 2nd ed., Munich 1914) IV 1.435.

11 Labriolle, *op. cit.* 456; cf. H. Leclercq, 'Jerome,' *DACL* VII.2 (1927) 2262.

12 P. Monceaux, *St. Jerome, the Early Years*, trans. F. J. Sheed, (London 1933) 148; cf. Cavallera, *op. cit.* II 154; Bardenhewer, *op. cit.* III 636; Grützmacher, *op. cit.* I 101.

13 Cavallera, *op. cit.* II 155.

14 *Ep.* 10.3; Cavallera, *op. cit.* I 44-45; Monceaux, *op. cit.* 72.

15 Cavallera, *op. cit.* I 43.

ing his long illness at Antioch[16] just previous to his entrance
into the Syrian desert. Some scholars[17] reasonably see a reference to Evagrius' work in Jerome's statement that, since
the life of Anthony had been carefully handed down to posterity in both Greek and Latin, he had decided to write
a few words about the beginning of Paul's hermit life and
about his death.[18] In Egypt, there was the tradition that, before Anthony, a certain Paul of Thebes had lived in the
desert and that Anthony had visited and honored him as his
master.[19] Witnesses to these facts were two of Anthony's own
disciples, Amathus and Macarius, whom Jerome names as
his authorities.[20] The *Life* itself is a fanciful blending of legend and fact. Wonderful and unbelievable events are reported, but the author reminds his readers that 'all things
are possible to them that believe.'[21] Jerome may have received his information from the Egyptian confessors exiled
not far from Chalcis or from monks who came to visit him.[22]

Jerome intended the style of the first biography to be
simple enough to reach all people with its moral teaching.
That he did not succeed in divesting himself of his rhetorical
training, he knew, for, in confiding his aim to Paul of Concordia, he says, 'fill a bottle with water, it still retains the
perfume with which it was impregnated when it was new.'[23]
The story, an original writing of St. Jerome,[24] pleased the

---

16 Monceaux, *op. cit.* 86; Cavallera, *op. cit.* I 27-31.
17 K. S. Tubbs, 'The Greek Versions of Jerome's *Vita Sancti Pauli,*'
   Studies 144.
18 *Life of Paul,* Prologue.
19 Monceaux, *op. cit.* 147.
20 *Life of Paul,* Prologue.
21 Schanz, *op. cit.* IV 1.436.
22 Monceaux, *op. cit.* 147; Cavallera, *op. cit.* I 44.
23 Monceaux, *op. cit.* 158; Cavallera, *op. cit.* I 44.
24 Schanz, op. cit. IV 1.437; Bardenhewer, op. cit. III 637; Tubbs, op:
   cit. 144.

literary public; nevertheless, it aroused a storm of criticism.
Jerome was accused of having fabricated the facts, legend,
and Paul himself. An echo of his protest appears in the prologue to his *Life of Hilarion*, in the preface of his *Chronicle,*
and in several of his letters.[25] Monceaux, however, basing
his conclusion on the investigation of Delehaye, affirms that:
'we have proof that Paul of Thebes did really exist; as early
as the fourth century, he was the object of a cultus in Egypt,
at Oxyrhyncus; this we know from a document of the time,
a petition addressed to the emperors Valentinian, Theodosius, and Arcadius by the Luciferian priests Marcellinus and
Faustinus.'[26]

The *Life of Paul,* then, is important for its presentation
of the eremetical concept and as an established historical
document.

The translation of this, and of the subsequent *Life of
Hilarion* and *Life of Malchus,* have been translated from the
H. Hurter text as reprinted by William A. Oldfather, *Studies
in the Text Tradition of St. Jerome's Vitae Patrum* (Urbana,
Ill. 1868-1943), and the D. Vallarsi text in Migne, *PL* 23.
The present translations, however, have had the distinct ad-
vantage of the perusal, criticism, and corrections of Professor
Kenneth M. Abbott of The Ohio State University. Professor
Abbott has brought to completion the textual studies begun
by the late Professor Oldfather and, with the collaboration
of Dr. Leo M. Kaiser of St. Louis University, is about to release a much-needed definitive text of St. Jerome's *Vitae
Patrum* for the *CSEL.*

25 *Ep.* 22.36; 58.5; 108.6; cf. Monceaux, *op. cit.* 155-156; Cavallera,
   op. cit. I 44 n.2.
26 Monceaux, *op. cit.* 156-157.

THE LIFE OF PAUL THE HERMIT

ANY HAVE often questioned exactly who was the first monk to take up his abode in the desert. Some, indeed, searching quite deep, have gone back as far as blessed Elias and John to find the beginning of monastic life. Elias, however, seems to me to have been more than a monk,[1] and John began to prophesy before he was born. Others, on the contrary, claim that Anthony was the founder of this mode of life—an opinion in which the generality of mankind agrees. They are right in part; not so much that he holds precedence in time as that all others were inspired by him. In truth, Amathas and Macarius, disciples of Anthony, the former of whom buried his master, affirm even to this day that a certain Paul of Thebes was the originator of the practice—though not of the name—of solitary living. I, too, hold this opinion. Some, according to their whims, toss out one absurdity after the other: in an underground cave, for instance, there was a man with hair hanging down to his heels; and they go on to invent many incredible tales which it is useless to recount. Because theirs is an impudent lie, their opinon does not seem worth refuting. The story of Anthony has been diligently handed down to posterity in both Greek and Latin. I have therefore determined to write a few words about the beginning of Paul's eremetical life and about his death, more because

---

1 Abbott: *Helias plus nobis videtur fuisse quam monachus.*

the account has never been written than because of any confidence in my ability. As a matter of fact, no one has yet discovered[2] how he lived during his middle life and what snares of Satan he endured.

(2) Under the persecutors, Decius and Valerian, at the time when Cornelius at Rome and Cyprian at Carthage suffered martyrdom with joyful hearts, a savage tempest ravaged[3] many churches in Egypt and The Thebes. At that time, the Christians were vowed to fall by the sword in the name of Christ; but the wily enemy,[4] eager to strangle souls, not bodies, sought out lingering tortures. Cyprian himself, who suffered at his hands, said those who wanted to die were not permitted to be killed.[5] That his cruelty may be better known, I add two examples for remembrance sake.

(3) The persecutor commanded one martyr who had persevered in his faith, and had survived being roasted on hot metal plates, to be anointed with honey and prostrated under the burning sun with his hands bound behind his back, in the hope that the victor over the glowing gridiron would yield to the agony of the stings of insect hordes. Another youth, in the first bloom of manhood, was carried off into a most beautiful garden. There, among white lilies and red roses, with the soft murmuring waters of a winding stream nearby,[6] and the wind gently rustling the leaves of the trees in lulled whispers, the persecutor bade him recline on a bed of down. To prevent his escape, an alluringly scented snare of garlands held him captive with entangling coils. When all others had withdrawn, a beautiful harlot came to him,

---

2 Cf. Cicero, *Pro Cluentio* 47.131; *Pro Fonteio* 7.29; Sallust, *Catilina* 29.1.

3 Cf. Florus 2.8.5-6; 9.22.

4 Cf. Florus 1.22.26.

5 Cyprian, *Ep.* 56.2.20 (ed G. Hartel, *CSEL* 3.2) ; Seneca, *Phoenissae* (*Thebaïs*) 100; cf. Cicero, *Pro Scauro* 4.5.

6 Abbott: *juxta murmure serperet rivus.*

entwined her arms around his neck in tender embraces, and then—oh, sinful even to relate—began to caress him wantonly, in order that she might force him to yield to her shameless advances. What should a soldier of Christ do? Where could he turn? Lust was on the point of overcoming him whom torture could not conquer. At last, inspired from heaven, he bit off a piece of his tongue and spat it into her face as she kissed him. Ensuing pain prevailed over lustful passion.[7]

(4) At the time that such outrages were being prepetrated in the lower Thebaid, Paul, at about the age of sixteen, came into a rich inheritance, upon[8] the death of his parents. His sister was already married. Highly educated not only in Greek but also in Egyptian letters,[9] he was a gentle lad who loved God exceedingly. Until the storm of persecution should cease thundering,[10] [he lived][11] in seclusion in a more distant villa. But, alas, 'to what dost thou not drive the hearts of men, O accursed hunger for gold!'[12] His own brother-in-law, instead of concealing him, plotted to betray the boy. He heeded not the ears of his wife, not the ties of consanguinity,[13] not God beholding all things from heaven; nothing could deter him from his criminal intent.[14] He came; he threatened; he employed curelty as if it were piety.[15]

(5) When the prudent young man realized what was hap-

---

7 Cf. Cicero, *Pro Cluentio* 6.15; Ovid, *Metamorphoses* 9.164.
8 Abbott: *mortem amborum parentum*, not *post mortem*.
9 Cf. Sallust, *Jugurtha* 95.3.
10 Cf. Florus 2.13.2-3; 2.9.18.
11 Abbott: *dum persecutionis detonaret procella in villa remotiore secretior*, not *in villam remotiorem et secretiorem*:
12 Virgil, *Aeneid* 3.56-57 (trans. H. R. Fairclough, Loeb Classical Library); cf. 4.412; 1.349.
13 Abbott: *non illum uxoris lacrymae non communio sanguinis*.
14 Cf. Cicero, *Pro Clutenio* 5.12-13.
15 Florus 1.40.7; cf. Cicero, *In C. Verrem* 2.1.30.75.

pening, he fled into the fastnesses of the mountains, where, awaiting the end of the persecution, he made a virtue of necessity. After careful examination of his surroundings, he found a rocky ridge,[16] at the foot of which there was a cave, its opening shut off by a stone of no great size.[17] Eagerly removing the stone—curiosity is human—he came upon a large chamber open to the sky. The spreading branches of an ancient palm tree protected the vestibule.[18] He discovered, too, a clear spring whose gushing waters were almost immediately swallowed up again by the earth which had given them birth.[19] Throughout the hollowed mountain,[20] there were many smaller chambers in which Paul saw rusty forges and mallets of the kind used in coining money. The place, according to Egyptian accounts, was a secret mint during Anthony's stay with Cleopatra.

(6) There in this humble dwelling which he grew to love (just as if God Himself had given it to him), he passed the rest of his life in prayer and solitude. The palm tree supplied his few needs of food and clothing. Lest anyone should question the possibility of such an existence, I call upon Christ[21] and His holy angels to witness that I have seen, and still see, monks living in that part of the desert which lies between Syria and the land of the Saracens. One monk, in fact, lived in seclusion in that wilderness for thirty years, subsisting on barley bread and muddy water, while another, sustained by five dry figs a day, inhabited an old cistern (which they call

---

16 Cf. Seneca, *Phoenissae* 14; Florus 1.36.14.
17 Abbott: *ac paulatim procedens rursusque tantumdem, atque idem saepius faciens, repperit saxeum montem ad cuius radices haud grandi spelunca lapide claudebatur.*
18 Cf. Sallust, *Jugurtha* 93.2-5; 92.5-7.
19 Abbott. *tantummodo foras eadem quae genuerat terra sorbebat.*
20 Cf. Seneca, *Phoenissae* 72.
21 Cf. Virgil, *Aeneid* 2.155; 12.581.

kubba in the Gentile language of Syria). I know, of course, that all this will seem incredible to those who will not admit that 'all things are possible to them that believeth.'[22]

(7) But, to return[23] from my digression. When blessed Paul, already one hundred and thirteen years old, was leading a heavenly life on earth, and Anthony, a nonogenarian, was tarrying in another solitude (as he was wont to say), the thought occurred to Anthony that no other monk had gone to live in the desert.[24] It was revealed to him in sleep,[25] however, that another more worthy than he dwelt in the deeper recesses of the desert and that it was his duty to seek him out. At the break of dawn, the venerable old man, supporting his weak legs with a sturdy staff, without delay set out on his quest—whither he did not know. Soon, the midday sun was beating down its scorching rays; nevertheless, nothing could hold him back from the journey he had undertaken. 'I believe in my God,' he prayed, 'I believe that He will guide me to His servant,[26] the sight of whom He has promised me.' His prayer barely finished, he became aware of a creature, half man and half horse, which the poets call a centaur.[27] Arming himself with the sign of the Cross on his forehead, Anthony cried: 'Ho, there, where does the servant of God live?' The creature, barbarously gnashing its teeth, and mouthing rather than uttering words with its shaggy lips, attempted to answer him respectfully.[28] Then, indicating the proper direction with is right hand, it stretched over the open fields in swift flight and vanished[29] from the

---

22 Mark 9.22.
23 Cf. Sallust, *Jugurtha* 79.10.
24 Abbott: *nullam ultra se monachorum in heremo consedisse.*
25 Cf. Florus 2.17.8.
26 Abbott: *quod servum,* not *quod olim servum.*
27 Abbott: *centauro,* not *hippocentauro.*
28 Abbott: *satis blandum,* not *setis.*
29 Florus 2.17.8; cf. Virgil, *Aeneid* 4.278.

sight of the astonished hermit. Whether, indeed, it was the Devil who assumed this form to frighten him or whether the desert productive of monstrous animals, brought forth this beast, too, we do not know for certain.[30]

(8) Mystified, Anthony hastened on his way, pondering over the strange event. He had not advanced very far when, in the midst of a little[31] rocky valley, he met a manikin with a hooked nose and a forehead pointed with budding horns, the lower part of his body shaped[32] like a goat. At this startling encounter, Anthony, like a good warrior, seized the 'shield of faith'[33] and the breastplate of hope.[34] As if to reassure him, the beast, as a pledge of peace,[35] offered him fruit from a palm tree for refreshment on his journey. Anthony recognized the overtures of peace, stopped and asked him who he was, receiving the answer: 'I am a mortal and one of the inhabitants of the desert whom the pagans, deluded by all manner of error, worship under the names of fauns, satyrs, and incubi. I serve as the ambassador of my flock. We beseech you to intercede for us with Him who is "Lord over all,"[36] for we know that He came at one time[37] for the salvation of the world and that His "sound hath gone forth into all the earth." '[38] The aged traveler wept many tears over these words, tears that told of the great overflowing joy of his heart. He rejoiced over the glory of Christ and the defeat of Satan. At the same time, he marveled that he could understand the creature's speech and, striking the

---

30 Sallust, *Jugurtha* 95.4; 46.8. Compare this account with that in *Life of St. Anthony* 63, above.
31 Cf. Cicero, *Pro Cluentio* 63.180.
32 Cf. Virgil, *Aeneid* 10.211; Ovid, *Metamorphoses* 4.727.
33 Eph. 6.16; cf. 1 Thess. 5.8.
34 Cf. Eph. 6.14; 1 Thess. 5.8.
35 Cf. Cicero, *Philippic* 1.13.32.
36 Rom. 10.12.
37 Abbott: *depreceris. Salutem mundi olim venisse cognovimus.*
38 Rom. 10.18.

ground with his staff, cried out: 'Woe to you, Alexandria, because you worship monsters for God! Woe to you, meretricious city, in which all the demons of the world find refuge.[39] What now will you answer? Beasts speak the name of Christ.'[40] He had not yet finished his lamentation when the horned animal fled away as if borne on wings. If anyone should find it difficult to believe this incident, let him heed the testimony of the whole world under the rule of Constantine, for just such a creature was brought to Alexandria alive and exposed to public view as a great spectacle. Later, they preserved the dead body of the brute from decaying in the summer heat by salting it, and then sent it on to Antioch for the emperor to see.

(9) I must return to my story. Anthony continued his anxious wandering through the region, intent only on the tracks of wild beasts through the vast waters of the desert.[41] What should he do? Where should he turn his steps?[42] Another day slipped by. Sure of only one thing, that Christ would not abandon him, he prayed without ceasing throughout that second night.[43] In the dim light of early dawn, he discerned not far away a wolf, panting with burning thirst, which crawled to the foot of the mountain. He followed it with his eyes and, when the beast had disappeared from view, he approached closer to the spot and tried to peer within the cave which it had entered. His effort availed him nothing; he could see nothing in the darkness. But, as the Scripture says, 'perfect love casteth out fear,'[44] cautiously and with bated breath, the wary[45] explorer made his way

---

39 Cf. Tacitus, *Annales* 15.44.
40 Abbott: *Bestiae Christum loquuntur. Necdum.*
41 Abbott: *ferarum tantum vestigia intuens et heremi latam vastitatem.*
42 Abbott: *quid ageret, quo verteret gradum. Jam altera.*
43 Cf. Luke 6.12.
44 1 John 4.18.
45 Cf. Florus 1.22.16.

slowly and carefully into the cave, stopping frequently to catch every sound. Finally, through the terrifying darkness, he saw a light in the distance. Eagerly, he hurried toward it and in his haste his foot struck against a stone which made a rattling noise.[46] At the first sound of an intruder, blessed Paul [for this was Paul's hiding-place] quickly closed and firmly barred the entrance to his retreat. Then, indeed, Anthony fell in a heap on the ground in front of the door and lay there until the sixth hour and longer, begging and imploring for admision: 'Who I am, whence I came, why I came, you know. I know that I am not worthy to behold you; nevertheless, I shall not go away until I have seen you. You who receive beasts, why do you refuse man? I have sought, and I have found; I knock that it may be opened to me.[47] If you do not grant my request, I shall die right here before your very door. Certainly, then, you will bury my body.'

'So he continued in his speech and remained unshaken.[48] . . . To whom the hero thus made brief reply:'[49]

'No one who pleads so earnestly means to threaten. No one with such tears plans mischief. You come when you are about to die and then you wonder why I do not open to you?' Paul laughingly opened wide the entrance. Immediately, they embraced each other, called one another by name, and together offered their thanks to God.

(10) After the holy kiss, Paul seated himself beside An-

---

46 Cf. Sallust, *Jugurtha* 53.7.
47 Cf. Matt. 7.7-8; Luke 11.10-11.
48 Virgil, *Aeneid* 2.650.
49 *Ibid.* 6.672.

thony and spoke thus: 'Behold whom you have sought with so much fatigue; tangled gray hair covers an old man with wasted limbs. Behold, you see a man soon to return to dust. But, truly as "Charity . . . endureth all things"[50] tell me, I beg of you, how is man faring in the world? Are there new roofs rising in the ancients cities? What power rules the world? Are there still some who are ensnared by the horror of demons?' While they were discoursing about such matters, they noticed a fleet raven alight upon a branch of a tree. Gently swooping down, to their amazement, it deposited a whole loaf of bread between them. 'Ah,' said Paul when the bird had flown away, 'God has sent us our dinner, God truly good, truly merciful. For sixty years now, I have received a piece of bread every noon. Today, in honor of your arrival, Christ has doubled the rations of His soldiers.'

(11) Giving thanks to God, they said their grace and sat down at the edge of the clear spring. Here arose a dispute, which lasted almost until evening, over who should break the bread. Paul, as host, urged Anthony, while Anthony felt that, by right of his seniority, the privilege belonged to Paul. Finally it was decided that each would pick up one end of the bread and pull it toward himself; his own portion would remain in his hand. Afterwards, prone on the ground, they sipped a little water. Then, offering God a sacrifice of praise, they spent the rest of the night in prayerful vigils. When day had already returned to earth, blessed Paul spoke thus to Anthony: 'For a long time now, brother, I have known that you dwelled in these regions; for a long time, God had promised you to me for a companion. Since my hour of eternal sleep has arrived, and because I have always desired "to be dissolved and to be with Christ,"[51] having

50 1 Cor. 13.7.
51 Phil. 1.23.

"finished the course, . . . a crown of justice"[52] remains for me. You have been sent by God to bury my miserable body, [rather,][53] to return earth to earth.'

(12) Anthony listened to these words with tears and groans, imploring Paul not to forsake him, but to accept him as a companion on that journey. Paul answered: 'You ought not seek your own interests[54] but those of another. It is indeed profitable for you to cast off the burden[55] of the flesh, to follow the Lamb,[56] but it is also profitable for the rest of your brethren that they may be the more instructed by your example. I beg of you, hasten, if it is not too much to ask, and bring back the cloak which Athanasius the bishop gave you, to wrap about my wretched body.' Now, blessed Paul made this request, not because he cared at all whether or not his body decayed covered up or naked, since for a long time now he had been wearing garments woven from palm leaves, but because he wanted to spare Anthony the grief of witnessing his death. Anthony was amazed that he had heard about Athanasius and his cloak and, as if he saw Christ in Paul, worshiping God in his heart, dared make no reply. Weeping, he silently kissed Paul's eyes and hands and returned to his monastery, which was later seized by the Saracens. His steps could scarcely keep pace with the ardor of his soul, but although his body was wasted from fasting and broken by the years of great age, his spirit triumphed over infirmity.

(13) At last, worn out and breathless, his journey ended, he reached his dwelling place. Two disciples who had been serving him for some time hurried out to meet him and in-

---

52 2 Tim. 4.7-8.
53 Abbott: *immo,* not *imo.*
54 Cf. Phil. 2.21; John 5.30.
55 Cf. Sallust, *Jugurtha* 91.2.
56 Cf. Apoc. 14.4.

quired: 'Where have you delayed so long, father?' 'Woe to me a sinner,' he replied, 'who falsely bear the name of monk! I have seen Elias, I have seen John in the desert, and, in truth, I have seen Paul in paradise!' Then, with sealed lips and striking his breast, he brought out the cloak from his cell. To his disciples begging for more detail, he said: 'There is a "time to keep silence and a time to speak." '[57]

(14) Without taking even a little food, Anthony set out again on the same road by which he had returned. Longing after Paul, ardently desiring to see him, he was absorbed[58] in thinking about him, for he feared what actually did happen, that during his absence Paul would give his soul back to Christ. When another day had dawned and he still had a three-hour journey to go, he saw Paul, shining in snowy whiteness,[59] ascend into heaven amid a host of angels and the choirs of Prophets and Apostles. Anthony immediately fell prostrate, threw sand upon his head, groaned and wept: 'Why do you dismiss[60] me, Paul? Why do you go without a farewell? I have known you so late; why do you depart so quickly from me?'

(15) In relating the event later, blessed Anthony recalled that he ran the rest of the way with such great speed that he seemed like a bird flying. Justly so, for, when he entered the cave, he found Paul kneeling, his head erect and his hands raised toward heaven, his body lifeless. At first, thinking that he was alive, he began to pray with him. When he did not hear the habitual sighing of the praying monk, he fell upon his face, weeping, for he realized that even the lifeless body of the saint rendered by its attitude dutiful homage to God unto whom all creatures live.[61]

---

57 Eccle. 3.7.
58 Abbott: *ac mente,* not *ac tota mente.*
59 Cf. Matt. 17.2; Mark 9.2; Luke 9.29.
60 Cf. Luke 2.29.
61 Cf. Rom. 14.8.

(16) Thereupon, Anthony wrapped up the body and carried it out beyond the entrance, chanting hymns and psalms
in the Christian manner. He grieved that he did not have
an implement to dig a grave. His mind in a turmoil, he
pondered: 'If I return to the monastery, it will mean a journey of four days; if I remain here, I shall accomplish nothing. Let me die, as it is fitting, alongside of your warrior,
O Christ; falling, let me pour forth my last breath.' While
he was entertaining such thoughts, behold, there came rushing
from the interior of the wilderness two lions with their manes
flowing about their necks. At the first sight of them, he was
thoroughly frightened, but, turning his thoughts back to God,
he remained as undaunted as if he were looking at doves.
They dashed directly to the body of the blessed old man,
stopped short, wagging their tails, and dropped down at his
feet, roaring with mighty roars to communicate their grief
in the only way they could. Then, not far from the corpse,
they began to scratch the ground with their paws; vigorously
scooping away the sand, they dug out a space that would
hold the body of a man. Straightway, as if demanding a reward for their work, with heads hanging but ears twitching,
they made for Anthony and began to lick his hands and
feet. He understood that they were merely begging a blessing from him. His joy burst forth in praise of Christ, that
even dumb animals sensed Him to be God: 'O God, without
whose permission not even a leaf flutters, nor a single sparrow
falls to the ground,[62] grant unto them as Thou knowest how
to give';[63] and, making a sign with his hand, he commanded
them to go away. After they had gone, he lifted the saint's

62 Cf. Matt. 10.29; 2 Kings 14.11.
63 Cf. Matt. 7.11; Luke 11.13.

body, his aged shoulders bending under the burden, deposited it in the grave, and covered it over with the customary mound of earth. On the next day, lest the devoted heir[64] go without something from his possessions who had died without a will, Anthony claimed for himself the tunic which, in the manner of a plaited basket, the holy man had woven for himself from the leaves of the palm. He returned to his monastery with his relic and related to his disciples all that had happened. From that time, he always wore Paul's tunic on the solemn feasts of Easter and Pentecost.

(17) I should like to close this little work by asking those whose heritage is so vast that they cannot keep account of it, who veneer their houses with marble, who string upon one thread the value of whole estates,[65] if there was anything wanting to this naked old man? You drink from jeweled goblets; he satisfied nature with the hollow of his hands. You wear tunics interwoven with gold;[66] he did not possess even the covering of the meanest of your slaves. On the contrary, paradise opens to him, a pauper; hell awaits you, robed in luxury. He, naked, has preserved the garment of Christ;[67] you, clothed in silks, have cast off the vestment of Christ. Paul, who lies covered with the lowliest dust, will rise again in glory; you, pressed down by mighty sepulchres of stone, will burn with your riches. Have mercy, I beseech you; at least, spare the riches which you love so much. Why do you shroud your dead in vestments of gold? Why does not your ambition cease with grief and tears? Or is it true, perhaps,

---

64 Cf. Virgil, *Aeneid* 7.5-6.
65 Abbott: *qui uno lino villarum insuunt pretia.*
66 Cf. Luke 16.19.
67 Cf. Rom. 13.14; Gal. 3.27.

that the corpses of the rich do not decay unless wrapped in silk?

(18) I beg of you, whoever read this, that you remember the sinner Jerome, who, if God should grant him his greatest desire, would much rather choose the tunic of Paul with his merits than the purple of kings with their kingdoms.[68]

---

68 Abbott: *regnis,* not *poenis.*

LIFE OF ST. HILARION

BY ST. JEROME

Translated by

SISTER MARIE LIGUORI EWALD, I.H.M. Ph.D.

Marygrove College

INTRODUCTION

WHILE THE PROTAGONISTS of two of the *Lives*, Paul of Thebes and the Syrian Malchus, were essentially solitaries (dwellers apart from the world activity), the central figure in the *Life of Hilarion* was a man eager for solitude which an adoring populace would never grant him, a man of the world yet apart from it, in reality a monastic, by necessity if not by choice. As a result, the *Vita Sancti Hilarionis* was . . . a handbook of asceticism, relating in some detail not only the ascetic practices of the *Einsiedler*, the solitaries, but also the routine life of groups of ascetics, which constituted then, as later, what is now termed the 'monastic life.'[1] The great number of manuscripts found by the careful contributors to the *Studies in the Text Tradition of St. Jerome's Vitae Patrum* would seem to indicate that the *Life of Hilarion* was read in almost every monastery.

The *Life of Hilarion* appears to have been written about 391,[2] shortly after the *Life of Malchus*, which it directly follows in St. Jerome's catalogue of his own contributions to ecclesiastical literature recorded in the *De viris illustribus*.[3] Already acquainted with St. Epiphanius' short biography,[4]

---

1 Strout, *op. cit.* 306-307.
2 Cavallera, *op. cit.* II 157.
3 Migne, *PL* 23.717.
4 He was the Bishop of Salamis in Cyprus whom Jerome had accompanied to the Synod in Rome in 382. Cf. Jerome, *Ep.* 127.7.

St. Jerome, in his travels, became familiar with the oral account of the life of St. Hilarion and many of his famous miracles. He must have been fascinated by this patriarch and
founder of monasticism in Palestine, charmed by this holy
man whose early struggles and experiences in the desert were
so akin to his own, whose noble scorn for the applause of
the world he longed to emulate, whose constant yearning for
solitude found an enviable response in his heart that craved
for solitude but could not give up friends, whose miracles
and wondrous works were so similar to those of his ideal,
Jesus Christ.

In his preface, Jerome speaks bitterly of the censure of
his *Life of Paul* and anticipates a similar fate for the *Life of
Hilarion*. There seems to have been no questioning this time,
however, of his historical trustworthiness and the historicity
of the person of Hilarion.[5]

What strikes the reader most in contrast to the two other
Lives is Jerome's more frequent use of Scripture and Scriptural language. Both phenomena are quite understandable
in view of his intense preoccupation with Scriptural studies
during the Bethlehem period of his life. The narrative tone
echoes the Acts of the Apostles, especially the series of Hilarion's travels, whereas the account of Hilarion's miracles
is strongly reminiscent of the Gospel. Many of the miracles
related contain one or two features of the works of our Lord.
Sometimes, the details of one episode are borrowed from two
or even three different occasions[6] in the life of Christ. Interesting parallels, too, may be drawn between Jerome's own
life history, as gleaned from his letters,[7] and that of Hilarion:

---

5 Bardenhewer, *op. cit.* III 639; Grützmacher, *op. cit.* II 87-88,90.
6 Cf. *Life of Hilarion* 15.
7 Cf. *Ep.* 17.2,3; 22.7; 5.1; 7.1; 14.10; 6.

for example, his youthful enthusiasm, the similarity in intellectual endowments, education, attraction for friends; then, the details of his life in the desert, his struggles and temptations; his program of the day, diet, care or lack of care for the body, his health, delicacy of body and infirmities from prolonged fasting; the loving admiration and attachments of friends and followers; finally, the devoted affection and attention of the holy noble women.

In this work, the style differs from that of the other two *Lives*. In the *Life of Paul,* he worked hard to please; in the *Life of Malchus,* he exercised and sharpened his pen. In the *Life of Hilarion,* however, the presentation, once under way, seems much less self-conscious[8] and less studied, partly, perhaps, because his style was less deliberate than that of the others; and partly because he was dealing with so much that that he had personally experienced or meditated upon.

A special edition of the *Life of Hilarion* appears to have been dedicated quite fittingly by St. Jerome to the virgin Asella,[9] a companion of the famous Roman matron, Marcella, and one who would have sympathetically welcomed the tribute.

---

8 Cf. Grützmacher, *op. cit.* II 89.
9 Sister Mary Donald McNeil, 'The Latin Manuscript Tradition of the *Vita Sancti Hilarionis,'* *Studies* 254,259. Cf. Jerome, *Ep.* 45.

THE LIFE OF HILARION OF GAZA

EFORE BEGINNING to write the life of blessed Hilarion, I call upon the Holy Spirit dwelling within him that He who has bestowed upon him such abundant virtues may grant me the power to describe these virtues, so that my words may equal his deeds.[1] As Crispus says: 'The merit of those who did the deeds is rated as high as brilliant minds have been able to exalt the deeds themselves by words of praise.'[2] Alexander the Great of Macedon, whom Daniel refers to as a kingdom of brass,[3] a leopard,[4] or a buck goat,[5] on reaching the tomb of Achilles, exclaimed: 'Happy youth, to enjoy a great herald of your merits!'[6]—meaning Homer, of course.

Now I must tell the story of the conversation and life of a man so great and so unusual[7] that Homer himself, were he present, would envy the subject or be overcome by it. Although St. Epiphanius, Bishop of Salamis in Cyprus, who knew Hilarion intimately, has written his praise in a brief letter that is commonly read, it is nevertheless one thing to praise in generalities a man who is dead, and quite another

---

1 Sallust, *Catilina* 3.2; cf. Cicero, *Pro Archia* 10.24.
2 Sallust, *Catilina* 8.4 (trans. J. C. Rolfe, Loeb Classical Library).
3 Abbott: *aes,* not *aries;* cf. Dan. 2.39.
4 Cf. Dan. 7.6.
5 Cf. Dan. 8.5,21.
6 Cicero, *Pro Archia* 10.24.
7 Cf. Sallust, *Jugurtha* 95.2-3.

to portray his specific virtues. With all good will, therefore,
and with no intention of disrespect toward the bishop, we
undertaken to carry forward the task he began. We scorn,
moreover, and ignore the voices of slanderers, who, formerly
depreciating my Paul, will probably disparage Hilarion also.
They misrepresented Paul's solitude; now, I suppose, they
will object to Hilarion's frequent appearance among men.
He who always lived unknown for that very reason did not
exist at all; on the other hand, he who was seen by many
will very likely be deemed vile and cheap. Their ancestors,
the Pharisees, were guilty of this same calumny when they
found fault with the desert and fasting of John, criticized
the crowds that gathered about our Lord and Saviour, and
were displeased with His eating and drinking.[8] Nevertheless,
I shall begin my work as I planned it, passing by the Scyllaean
hounds and refusing to heed them.

(2) Hilarion was born in Tabatha, a village in southern
Palestine, about five miles from Gaza. His parents were
dedicated to the worship of idols and the boy grew up, as
the saying goes, a rose among thorns. He was sent to Alexandria to be educated in the school of a grammarian. There,
so far as his youth allowed, he gave, in a short time, extraordinary proofs of talent[9] and character; he was beloved[10] by
all and skilled in the art of oratory. Greater than all these
accomplishments, however, was his belief in our Lord Jesus.
The mad excitement of the circus, the bloody contests of the
arena, the extravagance of the theatre did not thrill him, for
his sole pleasure was in the congregation of the Church.

(3) Then Hilarion heard of the celebrated Anthony, whose

---

8 Cf. Matt. 11.8, 18-19; Mark 2.16-18; Luke 5.30,33; 7.25,33-34.
9 Cf. Sallust, *Jugurtha* 6.1.
10 *Ibid.*

name was on the lips of all Egypt, and was seized with so
ardent a longing to see him that he set out to find him in the
wilderness. Upon meeting him, he changed his whole mode
of life and remained close by him for almost two months, intently observing his way of living, the gravity of his conduct,
his frequent prayer, his meekness and humility in dealing
with the brothers, his severity in correcting them, his eagerness to exhort them, and finally, his stern continency and
mortification in eating, which no infirmity ever interrupted.
Then, no longer able to bear the crowds who flocked to
Anthony because of some affliction or other or because of
the assaults of evil spirits, he said[11] that it was incongruous
to have to endure in the desert the people from the cities,
and that he was convinced that he ought, like Anthony, to
begin his life as a hermit. Anthony, the brave hero, was receiving the reward of victory; he was as one who had not
yet begun to fight.[12]

Thereupon, Hilarion went back to his own country, taking
with him a few monks. As his parents had died while he was
away, he gave a part of his possessions to his brothers and
the rest to the poor, reserving nothing at all for himself, because he feared either the example or the punishment of
Ananias and Saphira recorded in the Acts of the Apostles.[13]
He was, moreover, especially mindful of the words of our
Lord: 'Every one of you that doth not renounce all that he
possesseth, cannot be My disciple.'[14] At that time he was only
fifteen years old. Thus stripped of all his possessions, but
armed in Christ, he entered the wilderness seven miles from
Maiuma, the port of Gaza, in that part of the desert which
curves to the left as one goes along the coast to Egypt. Al-

11 Abbott: *dicens*, not *ducens*.
12 Cf. 2 Tim. 4.7-8.
13 Cf. Acts 5.1-10.
14 Luke 14.33.

though the place was stained with the blood of the victims of brigands, and friends and relatives strongly warned him of the menacing danger, he despised death in order to escape death.

(4) Everybody marveled at his spirit; they marveled at his age until [they saw] that in his eyes[15] there gleamed a flame of spirit and the sparks of faith. His cheeks were smooth; his body, delicate, slender and susceptible[16] to all inclemencies of the weather, suffered from the slightest excess of cold or heat. Despite his frailty, he covered his body with only a sackcloth. Besides this, he had only an outer garment made of skins which blessed Anthony had given him on his departure, and a coarse mantle. Between the sea and the marshes, he enjoyed a vast and terrible solitude, eating only fifteen dry figs a day and that after sunset, and never twice spending[17] the night in the same place because the region was notorious for robbers. What could the Devil do? Where should he turn? He who used to glory in saying: 'I will ascend above the height of the clouds,' 'I will exalt my throne above the stars of heaven,' 'I will be like the most High,'[18] beheld himself vanquished by a boy and trodden under foot by him before he was old enough to commit sin.

(5) The Devil, consequently, tickled the boy's senses and excited the fires of passion usual in puberty. Christ's young novice was compelled to reflect upon what he knew not and to revolve in his mind processions of seductive images and scenes which he had never experienced. Enraged with himself, he beat blows upon his heart as if he could destroy the disturbing thoughts by the sheer violence of his attack. 'You ass,' he said to his body, 'I'll see that you don't kick against

---

15 Cf. Livy 21.4.2.
16 Cf. Livy 21.4.6; Sallust, *Catilina* 5.3.
17 Abbott: *mansitans*, not *habitare consueverat*.
18 Isa. 14.14, 13,14.

the goad;[19] I'll fill you not with barley, but with chaff. I shall wear you out with hunger and thirst; I shall weigh you down with a heavy burden; through the heat and cold I shall drive you, so that you will think of food rather than lust.' Then he would revive his weakened spirit with the juice of grass and a few figs, but only after a period of three or four days, praying frequently, singing the psalms of David, and digging the ground with a hoe that the labor of work might double the labors of fast. He also used to weave baskets from rushes, imitating the example of the Egyptian monks and following the teaching of the Apostle: 'if any man will not work, neither let him eat.[20] Under such a regimen, he soon became very weak; he lost so much weight that his flesh scarcely covered his bones.

(6) One night, he began to hear the crying of infants, the bleating of sheep, the lowing of cattle, the sobbing of women, the roaring of lions, the rumbling of an army, and one after another the portens of various voices. He was frightened to the point of yielding, but realized that it must be the mockery of the evil spirits. Falling on his knees, he signed his forehead with the Cross of Christ. Thus armed with a helmet and the breastplate of faith,[21] prostrate, in prayer, he joined battle more bravely, anxiously looking about everywhere, in some way[22] desiring to see what he shuddered to descry. Meanwhile, in the glow of the moonlight, he suddenly beheld a chariot drawn by spirited horses rushing to attack him. He called upon Jesus, and there before his very eyes the whole equipage was swallowed up in a sudden gaping of the earth. He cried out triumphantly: ' "The horse and rider he hath

---

19 Cf. Acts 9.5; 26.14.
20 2 Thess. 3.10.
21 Cf. Eph. 6.13-17.
22 Abbott: *quodammodo,* not *amodo.*

thrown into the sea."[23] Some trust in chariots, and some in horses: but we shall be magnified in the name of the Lord our God." '[24]

(7) Many were his trials and temptations; the deceits[25] of the evil spirits, day and night, were so varied that, if I tried to relate them all, I would exceed the measure of this book. How many times naked women appeared to him as he lay on his cot; how many lavish feasts appeared to him when he was hungry. Once, while he was praying, a howling wolf and snarling fox leaped over him. At another time, while he was singing the psalms, gladiators performed a battle for him in a spectacle; one of them, as if dying and collapsing before his feet, implored him for burial.

(8) Once, when he was praying with his head almost buried in the ground and, as is natural for man, his mind was distracted from prayer by some thought or other, the tormentor suddenly leaped upon his back and, digging with his heels into his sides and flogging his neck with a whip, cried out: 'Ho, why do you sleep?' and, laughing derisively, inquired whether he were tired or would like a little barley.

(9) From his sixteenth to his twenty-fifth year, Hilarion protected himself from the heat and rain in a tiny hut which he had woven from rushes. Later on, he constructed a small cell, which remains to this day, four feet wide and five feet hight, that is, a little lower than his height, but a little more in length. It barely admitted his poor body, so that when he lay asleep you might think it a sepulchre rather than a house.

(10) He clipped his hair once a year, at Easter, and until his death slept on rushes strewn on the bare ground.[26] He

---

23 Exod. 15.1.
24 Ps. 19.8.
25 Eph. 6.11
26 Cf. Livy 21.4.7.

never washed a sackcloth he once donned, saying that it was superfluous to seek cleanliness in Cilician goat skins, nor did he change to another tunic until the old was was worn to shreds. After he said his prayers and sang his usual psalms, he used to recite Sacred Scripture, which he knew from memory, as if he were face to face with God. Because it would take too long to describe his progress in asceticism through its various stages, I shall briefly summarize[27] his life for my reader, outlining each period, and then I shall return to the historical sequence of my narrative.

(11) For the first half of the time between his twenty-first to his twenty-sixth year, he lived on a half a pint of lentils a day, soaked in cold water; for the last half, on dry bread with salt and water. Then, from his twenty-seventh to his thirtieth year, he kept himself alive on wild herbs and the raw roots of some shrubs. From thirty-one to thirty-five, he had for his daily food six ounces of barley bread and a slightly cooked green vegetable without oil. Perceiving after a while that his eyes were weakening and that his whole body was shrinking from a scabby eruption of the skin and a kind of mange, he added olive oil to his slender diet and maintained this rigid degree of abstinence until his sixty-third year, tasting nothing beyond that, either of fruit, or legumes, or anythng else. Then, when he realized that he was exhausted and felt that he was very close to death, from sixty-four to eighty, he abstained from bread with unbelievable fervor and was serving God as a novice at an age when others are inclined to live a little less strenuously. A small mess[28] of meal and crushed vegetables was made for him; his food and drink together weighed scarcely five ounces. We may note, finally, that he never broke his fast before sunset, not even

---

27 Cf. Sallust, *Jugurtha* 17.1-3.
28 Cf. 2 Kings 13.6.

on feast days or because of serious illness. But now it is time[29] for us to return to the proper order of events.

(12) Once, during the time that he was living in his tiny hut, when he was eighteen years old, brigands tried to find him by night, either because they believed that he had something that they might steal or because they thought the solitary boy would hold them in contempt if they did not intimidate him. Between the sea and the swamp, from evening until dawn, they hunted in all directions but did not succeed in finding his place of rest. In the broad daylight, however, they came upon him and in apparent jest asked him: 'What would you do if robbers attacked you?' He answered: 'One who is naked does not fear robbers.' And they: 'You could certainly be killed.' 'Certainly I could,' he said. 'I could, but I am not afraid of robbers because I am ready to die.' In utter admiration of the steadfastness of his faith, they confessed their folly of the night and their blindness, and promised to reform their lives.

(13) By the time he had spent twenty-two years in the desert, he was widely known by reputation throughout the cities of Palestine. A certain woman of Eleutheropolis, finding herself despised by her husband because of her sterility —after fifteen years of married life she had brought forth no children—was the first who dared to intrude upon blessed Hilarion's solitude. While he was still unconscious of her approach, she suddenly threw herself at his knees saying: 'Forgive my boldness, forgive my importunity. Why do you turn away your eyes? Why do you shun my pleas? Do not look upon me as a woman, but as a creature to be pitied, as one of the sex that brought forth the Redeemer, for 'they that are whole need not the physician: but they that are sick.'' [30]

---

29 Cf. Sallust, *Jugurtha* 19.2,8.
30 Luke 5.31; Matt. 9.12; Mark 2.17; Luke 5.31.

He stood still, and, finally aware of the woman, asked her why she had come and why she was weeping. When he learned the cause of her grief, raising his eyes to heaven, he commanded her to have faith and to believe. He followed[31] her departure with tears. When a year had gone by, he saw[32] her with her son.

(14) This, the beginning of his miraculous works,[33] was followed by another and greater miracle. Aristaenete, the wife of Elpidius, who later became praetorian prefect, a woman well known among her own people and even more renowned among the Christians, returning with her husband and their children from blessed Anthony, was detained at Gaza by the illness of her sons. There, either because of the infected atmosphere or (as it later appeared) for the glory of Hilarion, servant of God, they were seized with a semi-tertian ague which the physicians pronounced incurable. The distraught mother was crushed with grief and ran from one to the other of what seemed to be the corpses of her three children, not knowing which one to mourn for first. Then, hearing that there was a certain monk in the desert nearby [who might help her], she laid aside her matronly dignity and, remembering only that she was a mother, set out [on foot] to find him, accompanied by maid-servants and eunuchs. With difficulty, her husband finally persuaded her to ride on an ass. When she found Hilarion, pleading for his intercession, she said: 'I beseech you through the most merciful Jesus our Lord, through His Cross and His Blood, that you restore to me my three sons, that the name of the Lord our Saviour may be glorified in the city of the Gentiles, and that His servant may enter Gaza and overthrow the idol, Marnas.'

31 Cf. Virgil, *Aeneid* 1.406.
32 Abbott: *vidit,* not *venit.*
33 Cf. John 2.11.

He refused, saying that he had never left his cell and that it
was not his custom to enter even a small village, much less
the city. The desperate woman prostrated herself before him,
crying out again and again: 'Hilarion, servant of Christ, give
me back my children; Anthony watched over them in Egypt,
you must save them in Syria.' All who were present wept,
and Hilarion himself wept, too, in pity, but he continued to
refuse to go. To make a long story short,[34] the woman would
not leave until he promised her that he would enter Gaza
after sundown. In Gaza, he stopped at the bedside of each
child and, gazing sorrowfully at the feverish body, he invoked Jesus. O wonderful virtue! As from three fountains,
perspiration burst forth from each one. In the same hour,
the children took food, recognized their moaning mother and,
blessing God, they covered the hands of the saint with kisses.
When word of this miracle spread far and wide, people from
Syria and Egypt flocked to him eagerly, with the result that
many believed in Christ and decided to become monks. Up
to that time, there had been no monasteries in Palestine nor
had anyone known of any monk in Syria before St. Hilarion.
He was the founder, inspiration, and teacher there of monastic life and service to God. Our Lord Jesus had His senior
servant Anthony in Egypt and His junior, Hilarion, in Palestine.

(15) Facidia is a small suburb of Rhinocorura, a city of
Egypt. From this village, a woman who had been blind for
ten years was brought to blessed Hilarion. On being presented
to him by the brothers (already there were many monks
with him), she told him that she had bestowed all her substance on physicians.[35] To her the saint replied: 'If what
you lost on physicians you had given to the poor, Jesus the

34 Cf. Cicero, *De oratore* 1.20.93; *Orator* 27.95.
35 Cf. Luke 8.43.

true Physician would have healed you.' Whereupon she cried aloud and implored him to have mercy on her.[36] Then, following the example of the Saviour,[37] he rubbed spittle upon her eyes and she was immediately cured.

(16) A charioteer, from Gaza also, was struck by a demon while in his chariot and his whole body so completely stiffened that he could neither move his hand nor bend his neck. He was carried on a stretcher to the saint, able to move only his tongue to indicate his petition, but he heard and understood that he could not be healed until he believed in Jesus and renounced his former occupation. He believed, he promised, he was cured, rejoicing more in the salvation of his soul than in the cure of his body.

(17) Then there was the very powerful young man named[38] Messicas[39] from the district of Jerusalem, who was very proud of his strength. He boasted that he could carry fifteen pecks of grain for a long time and a great distance. He considered it the peak of his prowess that he could surpass the asses in endurance. He became afflicted by the worst kind of demon, so that nothing could hold him, not chains, not fetters,[40] nor bolted doors. He had even bitten off the noses and ears of many people; of some he had broken the legs; others he had strangled. He had, in fact, aroused such great terror in everybody that, covered with chains and pulled by ropes from all sides, he was dragged to the monastery like a raging bull. When the brothers caught sight of him, they were thoroughly frightened (for he was of towering size) and reported him at once to the father. Right from where he was sitting, the saint ordered the poor creature to be brought to

36 Cf. Luke 17.13; 8.28.
37 Cf. John 9.1-7.
38 Cf. Sallust, *Jugurtha* 65.1.
39 Abbott: *Messicas,* not *Marsitas.*
40 Cf. Mark. 5.4.

him and released. When he was set free, he said to him:
'Bow your head and come.' The youth, trembling and twisting his neck, did not dare to look him in the face and then,
all of a sudden, laying aside his ferocity, began to lick the
feet of the man seated before him. Finally, the demon that
had possessed the youth was wrenched[41] out of him by ex-
orcism on the seventh day.

(18) Then, there is the story of Orion, a prominent and
very wealthy citizen of the city of Haila,[42] situated on the
coast of the Red Sea. Having been possessed by a legion of
devils,[43] he was led to Hilarion. His hands, neck, sides, and
feet were loaded with iron; his wild eyes were menacing with
the savagery of madness. While the saint was walking along
with the brothers, interpreting for them some passage from
Scripture, the mad man broke away from those who were
holding him, caught up the saint from behind, and raised
him high into the air. A cry[44] rose up from everybody, for
they feared that he would crush that body so consumed from
fasting. The saint laughed, however, and said: 'Silence, and
leave my wrestler to me.' Reaching his hand back over his
shoulder, he seized the madman by the hair and pulled him
[over his shoulders and flung him] before his feet. Then,
spreading out both arms from his sides, he stood upon his
hands [and prevented him from moving], at the same time
repeating: 'Be tortured, you band of demons, be tortured.'[45]
With this, the maniac howled and arched his head against
the ground. 'Lord Jesus,' prayed the saint, 'release this miserable creature, release this captive. As You have the power

---

41 Abbott: *et extortus daemon,* not *daemon et tortus.*
42 Abbott: *Haila,* not *Alia.*
43 Cf. Mark 5.2-9; Luke 8.27-31.
44 Cf. Sallust, *Jugurtha* 57.3.
45 Cf. Mark. 5.7.

to conquer one, You have the power to conquer many.' I shall now mention a thing unheard of: from the mouth of one man there actually came forth many different voices, that resounded like the confused shouts of a populace.[46] He, too, was cured, and not long after returned to the monastery with his wife and children, bringing ever so many gifts as if to pay his thanks. The saint said to him: 'Have you not read what happened to Giezi and to Simon? Giezi[47] accepted a reward; Simon[48] offered one; the former in order to sell the grace of the Holy Spirit, the latter to buy it.' Orion, weeping, said: 'Take these gifts and give them to the poor.' He replied: 'You yourself are better able to distribute them, you who go about the cities and know the poor. I who have renounced all my possessions, why should I seek those of another? To many, the name of the poor is an occasion of avarice. True compassion is without guile. No one spends better than he who reserves nothing for himself.' When the man lay down sadly upon the sand,[49] he said: 'Do not be sad, my son. What I do, I do for myself and for you. If I were to accept these gifts, I would offend God and you would be plagued again by the legion of devils.'

(19) Who, indeed, could pass over in silence the case of Zananus of Maiuma? While he was hewing stones[50] for building purposes along the sea coast not far from the monastery, he was stricken with a total paralysis. His fellow laborers carried him to the saint, and immediately he was able to return to his work. The shore line which spreads out before Palestine and Egypt is naturally soft, but as the sand hardens

46 Cf. Sallust, *Jugurtha* 60.2.
47 4 Kings 5.20-27.
48 Acts 8.18-24.
49 Abbott: *in harenis,* not *in terra.*
50 Cf. 1 Par. 22.2.

into rock it grows rough, and as it forms concretions with gravel it loses the texture, although not the appearance [of sand].

(20) Italicus, also a citizen of the same city and a Christian, was training horses for the chariot races against the duumvir, a worshiper of the idol Marnas. This contest had been held, at least in all the Roman cities, ever since the time of Romulus, when it was inaugurated to celebrate the happy capture of the Sabine women. In honor of Consus, as being the god of counsel, chariots ran seven times around the circus and victory went to that side which succeeded in breaking down the horses of their opponent. Now, as Italicus' rival had a magician who by certain demoniacal imprecations could impede his opponent's horses and at the same time spur on his own to the race, Italicus went to blessed Hilarion and begged for help, not so much to injure his adversary as to protect himself. It seemed foolish to the venerable old man to waste prayer on this kind of nonsense. He smiled and said: 'Why don't you rather spend the price of horses on the poor for the salvation of your soul?' He answered that the contest was his public duty and it was not that he wanted to do it but that he was forced to; he urged, furthermore, that a Christian could not employ magical arts, but that he could petition help from the servant of God, especially against the people of Gaza, who were enemies of God and were not so much insulting him as they were insulting the Church of Christ. At the request of the brothers who were present, Hilarion ordered the cup from which he usually drank to be filled with water and given to Italicus, who took it and sprinkled his stable, horses, charioteers, carriage and even the bars of the starting stalls. On the day of the contest, the expectation of the mob was at high tension, for Italicus' opponent had mocked and belittled him. On the other hand,

his own partisans were in high spirits, promising themselves certain victory. The signal was given. His horses flew, his opponent's horses became entangled and hindered each other. The wheels of his chariot glowed and his opponents scarcely caught sight of the horses' backs as they flew by. The clamor of the crowd was so great that the heathens themselves joined in the shout of triumph with: 'Marnas is conquered by Christ!' Furious, Italicus' adversaries demanded that Hilarion, the magician of the Christians, be punished, but the victory was incontestable and became the occasion of faith for a great many at this and subsequent contests.

(21) In this same port town of Gaza, a Christian virgin was desperately loved by a youth of the neighborhood. When he had made no progress with his frequent attempts at caresses, his beckonings, jests, whisperings, and similar advances that are usually the first steps toward seduction, he went to Memphis in order to reveal the wound [of his love] to the seer, to arm himself with magical arts, for his return to the girl. One year later, trained by the seers of Aesculapius, not the healer but the destroyer of souls, he came back, nursing in his thoughts a passionate determination to carry out his evil intentions. Under the threshold of the girl's home, he concealed certain revolting words of magic and hideous figures engraved on thin sheets of Cyprian copper. From that moment, the virgin went mad, threw aside her veil, tore her hair, gnashed her teeth, and shouted the name of the young man. The intensity of passion had turned to madness. Her parents led her to the monastery and entrusted her to Hilarion. At once, the demon that possessed her howled and confessed: 'I have resisted this power; I have been carried off against my will. How well I used to delude people at Memphis with dreams! O crucifixions, O torments that I suffer! You compel me to go and I am here bound under the threshold. I am

not going unless the young man who holds me here dis-
misses me.' The old man said: 'Great, indeed, is your strength,
you who are held bound by thread and thin sheets of copper!
Tell me, why did you dare enter a girl who belongs to God.'
'To preserve this virgin,' was the answer. 'You preserve virginity, you betrayer of chastity? Why didn't you rather enter
into him who sent you?' 'Why should I enter him who is
already possessed by my colleague, the demon of love?' Not
until he had exorcised the virgin did the saint want to command a diligent search for the charms or even for the youth,
lest it appear either that the demon had withdrawn by magic
or that he himself put faith in what the demon said, affirm-
ing that demons are deceitful and clever in lying. Furthermore, he reproved the girl, when her health returned, for
having, by her imprudent conduct, permitted the devil to gain
control over her.

(22) Hilarion's fame extended not only throughout Palestine and the neighboring cities of Egypt and Syria, but also
to the distant provinces. There was an officer in the body-
guard of Emperor Constantine whose red hair and fair skin
indicated his origin. (His country, which lay between the
Saxons and the Alemanni, not great in size but powerful, was
referred to as Germany by the historians, but is now called
Francia.) For a long time, that is, from his infancy,[51] this
military official had been possessed by a demon that caused
him to scream, groan, and gnash his teeth during the night.
He secretly petitioned the emperor for a post-warrant, stating his reason for the request with frank simplicity. His petition was granted and he also procured a letter to the governor
of Palestine. He was, therefore, conducted to Gaza with great
honor by the imperial escort. When he inquired there of
the municipal senators where the monk Hilarion dwelt, the

---

51 Cf. Mark 9.16-21.

people of Gaza became quite disturbed and, thinking that
he had been sent by the emperor, led him directly to the
monastery. They extended this courtesy both as a gesture of
respect to so distinguished a person and as an act of homage
to Hilarion in satisfaction for their past offenses against him.
It happened that, at the moment, the old man was strolling
along on the soft sands, murmuring to himself one of the
psalms. Becoming aware of the great throng approaching, he
stopped, waited, and greeted them all with a blessing. An
hour later, he asked the others to withdraw and the possessed
man to remain with his servants and public attendants, for,
from the look in his eyes and the expression on his face, he
knew his reason for coming. As soon as the servant of God
began to question him, he rose in the air, suspended, with
his toes scarcely touching the ground, and, roaring loudly,
answered in Syriac, the same language in which he was being interrogated. From the lips of a barbarian who knew only
Frankish and Latin came such pure Syriac that not a sibilant,
not an aspirate, not a Palestinian idiom was lacking. He confessed by what order of events the demon had entered him.
Then, that the interpreters who knew only Greek and Latin
might understand what was going on, Hilarion questioned
him again in Greek. The man gave the same answers in
Greek, excusing the many occasions on which he had taken
part in wizardry and the many times that he had found it
necessary to use magical arts. 'I don't care,' Hilarion said,
'how you gained entrance, but in the name of Jesus Christ, I
command you to depart.' And the demon departed. With
homely simplicity, the officer offered the saint ten pounds of
gold. Hilarion refused the gift and gave him a barley loaf
instead, with the admonition that they who are nourished
by such food look upon gold as mere clay.

(23) Not only human beings, but brute animals also,

foaming with rage, were brought to Hilarion daily. Among these was a Bactrian camel of enormous size which had trampled many people to death. More than thirty men, amid a great clamor, dragged the beast along by strong ropes. Its eyes were bloody, its mouth was foaming, its rolling tongue was swollen, but terrible above all were the mighty roars that it let out. The old man ordered the animal to be released. Immediately, those who had been pulling it, as well as those who were with Hilarion, fled away in all directions. He alone stood fearless in its path and said in Syriac: 'You do not frighten me, demon, with your huge bulk of body; whether in a little fox or in a camel, you are one and the same.' All this time he was standing with his hand stretched forth before him. The beast that had come to him, raging, as if about to devour him, suddenly crouched down and placed its head submissively on the ground. To the amazement of everyone, its savage wildness suddenly changed to tame gentleness.[52] The old man used this opportunity to teach how the Devil even took possession of beasts of burden, for so burning, indeed, is his hatred of man that he longs not only to destroy him but also his possessions. To illustrate this point he set before them the example of blessed Job[53] whom the Devil was not permitted to tempt until he had destroyed all his substance. Nor ought it upset anyone, he added, that by the Lord's command two thousand swine[54] were destroyed by demons, for those who had witnessed the miracle could not have believed that so many devils went out of one man unless a vast number of swine, driven by almost a legion, perished at the same time.

(24) There would not be time if I wished to tell of all

52 Cf. Mark 5.3-4,15.
53 Cf. Job 1; 2.
54 Cf. Mark 5.8-16; Matt. 8.28-33.

the signs and wonders[55] performed by Hilarion, for he had
been raised by God to such glory that blessed Anthony, hearing about the ascetic and holy routine of his life, wrote to
him and with pleasure received letters in return. Whenever
the sick and infirm came to Anthony from any part of Syria,
he would say to them: 'Why did you weary yourselves with
so long a journey when you have right there in Syria my
son Hilarion?' Because of Hilarion's example, monasteries
began to appear throughout all of Palestine and all the
monks eagerly hastened over to him. Anthony, seeing this,
praised the grace of the Lord and encouraged individuals
to strive after the perfection of their souls, saying: ' " the
fashion of this world passeth away"[56] and that is the true
life which is purchased by the discomfort of the present life.'

(25) Intending to give the monks an example of humility
and devotion to duty, Hilarion visited and blessed their cells
on stated days before the vintage. As soon as they learned
of his intention, all the monks flocked to him and escorted
their revered leader from monastery to monastery, taking
with them their own provisions, because sometimes as many
as two thousand men congregated for the visitation. As time
went on, however, it became the custom for each farm to
provide food for the neighboring monks, rejoicing at the opportunity to receive the holy brethren. The fervor of Hilarion's zeal and devotion in not slighting a single brother, no
matter how humble or poor he might be, is shown in his
going even to the desert of Cades to visit one of his disciples.

On this occasion, it happened that, accompanied by a
great procession of monks, he arrived at Elusa on the very day
that all the townspeople had assembled in the temple of Venus
to celebrate a solemn festival in her honor. Now, the Sara-

55 Dan. 3.99; Matt. 24.24; John 2.11.
56 1 Cor. 7.31.

cens worship this goddess as the morning star and to her
cult their nation is dedicated. The town itself is, for the most
part, semi-barbarian because of its location. When it was
heard that St. Hilarion was passing through (for, frequently,
he had healed many Saracens by snatching them away from
the Devil), the men swarmed out with their wives and children to meet him and, with their heads reverently bowed,
cried out in Syriac: 'Barech,' that is, 'Bless us!' He received
them graciously and humbly and besought them to worship
God rather than idols. Weeping and looking up to heaven,
he promised them that, if they would believe in Christ, he
would come to them frequently. Oh, wonderful is the grace
of God! They did not allow him to go away until he had
planned[57] a church for them, and the priest of Venus,
wreathed as he was, was marked with the sign of Christ.

(26) Another year, when Hilarion was about to set out
on his visitation, he drew up a schedule of the monks with
whom he would spend[58] the night and those whom he ought
to visit in passing. His followers, knowing that a certain
brother was quite miserly and desiring to cure him of this
vice, urged Hilarion to stay a night with him. But he said:
'What! Do you want me to do you an injury and vex your
brother?' Later, however, when the illiberal brother heard of
this, he was ashamed and, with all the other brothers supporting his plea, he finally obtained the father's unwilling
consent to include his monastery in the list of those where he
would pass the night. Accordingly, they came to his monastery in the evening of the tenth day, only to find that, in the
farmlike[59] vineyard through which they had to pass, he had
stationed guards who with stones, clods of earth, and slings

---

57 Cf. Plautus, *Mostellaria* 1070.
58 Abbott: *maneret,* not *manere.*
59 Abbott: *quasi villa esset.*

were to frighten away the oncomers. Early the next morning, they all went away without tasting a single grape, but with the old man smiling and pretending not to have observed what had happened.

(27) Again, he was received by another monk named Sabas. (We ought certainly refrain from giving the name of the miserly monk; we should, however, make known the generous one.) Because it was the day of the Lord, they were all invited into the vineyard before it was time for supper to refresh themselves from the fatigue of the journey with a repast of grapes. The saint remonstrated: 'Cursed be he who seeks to refresh his body before he refreshes his soul. Let us pray, let us sing the psalms, let us give the Lord His due, and then we shall hasten into the vineyard.' When the prayers were over, standing on an elevation he blessed the vineyard and sent his sheep to pasture. Now, of those who did eat[60] there were no less than three thousand. Although up to that time the yield of the entire vineyard had been estimated at a hundred flagons, after twenty days it rendered three hundred. On the other hand, the miserly brother gathered much less than usual, and, when the wine which his grapes yielded turned to vinegar, he regretted too late his niggardliness. Hilarion had predicted this turn of events to many of the brothers before it actually came to pass.

(28) He particularly detested monks who, with a certain lack of faith, stored away supplies for the future and who were very solicitous[61] in looking after their expenses, clothing, or any of the things that pass away with the world.[62] He even banished from his sight one of the brothers who lived only five miles away from him, because he noticed that he

---

60 Cf. Matt. 14.21; 15.38; Mark 6.44; 8.9.
61 Cf. Matt. 6.31-33.
62 Cf. 1 John 2.17; 1 Cor. 7.31.

was too cautious and fearful a custodian of his tiny garden
and that he kept on hand a small amount of money. This
monk wanted to be reconciled to Hilarion, and he frequently came to see the brothers, especially Hesychius, who was
dearly loved by the old monk. One day, he brought with him
a bundle of green pulse, just as it had been gathered on
the stalk. When Hesychius served it in the evening, Hilarion
exclaimed that he was not able to bear its foul odor and
asked him where it had come from. Hesychius answered that
a certain monk, wishing to give the first fruits of his little
field to the brothers, had brought it. 'Don't you notice a
most loathsome stench, the stench of avarice in the foul
pulse? Give it to the cattle, give it to the brute animals and
see if they will eat it.' No sooner did he place it in the stalls
as he had been bidden than the cattle bellowed in fear and,
bursting their bonds, fled in all directions. The old man had
extraordinary grace to know from the odor of the body, the
clothing, and the things that anyone had touched what devil
or what vice had predominance over him.

(29) When Hilarion, in the sixty-third year of his life,
reviewed his grand monastery and the multitude of brothers
dwelling with him, and the crowds of those who came to him
suffering from divers diseases[63] and possessed by unclean
spirits,[64] and when he saw the desert for miles around filled
with all kinds of men, he wept daily, recalling with an incredible longing his old manner of living. When the brothers
asked what the trouble was and why he was consuming himself with grief, he said: 'I have returned to the world and
I have received my reward[65] in my lifetime. See how the men
of Palestine and the neighboring provinces think me a per-

---

63 Matt. 4.24; 10.1; Mark 1.34; Luke 4.40.
64 Matt. 10.1; Mark 6.7; 1.27; 3.11; 5.13; Luke 4.36; Acts 5.16; 8.7.
65 Cf. Matt. 6.2,5,16.

son of importance, and I, under the pretext of a monastery
for the ministration of brothers, possess all the cheap goods
of the world.' He was carefully watched over by the brothers,
especially Hesychius, who was devoted to the old man with
a wonderful love and veneration. After he had passed two
years grieving in this way, that Aristaenete whom we mentioned above, who was then the wife of the prefect but without any of his pretensions, came to see him, with the intention
also of visiting Anthony. Weeping, he said to her: 'I would
want to go myself if I were not held imprisoned in this monastery, and if, too, it were worth while going, for it is two days
now since the whole world has been bereft of a greater father.'
She believed him and did not go. After a few days, word
came to her that Anthony had died.

(30) Some may wonder at Hilarion's miraculous works,
his extraordinary fasting, his knowledge, his humility. What
amazes me most, however, is how he could trample under
foot all glory and honor. Everybody came to him—bishops,
priests, flocks of clerics and monks, and of Christian matrons,
too (a great temptation); the common people from all parts
of the cities and country; likewise, men of power, and judges
—that they might receive from him bread or oil that he had
blessed. He however, could think of nothing but his solitude,
to the point that one day he decided to return to it. He prepared an ass, therefore (for he could scarcely go otherwise,
consumed and worn out from fasting as he was), and attempted to make his flight. When the news leaked out, it was
as if a public day of mourning had been appointed for the
desolation of Palestine; more than ten thousand people of
all ages and both sexes assembled to prevent him from going.
Unmoved by their prayers, however, and striking the sands
with his staff, he said half aloud: 'I shall not make my Lord
deceitful; I cannot see the churches overthrown, the altars of

Christ trodden upon, the blood of my sons spilt.' From this, all present understood that some secret had been revealed to him which he did not want to make known. Nevertheless, they continued to guard him and prevent his departure. He then announced publicly that he would take neither food nor drink until he was released. Finally, after he had fasted seven days, the vigil was relaxed, and, bidding farewell to many, with a great throng of followers he went to Betilium. There he persuaded the crowds to return, keeping with him forty monks, who had provisions with them and who could continue the journey fasting, that is, without taking food until after sundown. On the fifth day[66] he came to Pelusium and, after visiting the brothers who were staying in the desert nearby at a place called Lychnos, he arrived three days later at Fort Thaubastus to see the bishop and confessor, Dracontius, who had been exiled there. The outcast was incredibly consoled by the presence of the great saint. After another three days, with much difficulty, he reached Babylon to visit the bishop and confessor, Philo. Constantius, the ruler, who favored the Arian heresy, had deported the bishops to these places. Moving on from there, in three days journey he came to the town of Aphroditon, where he became acquainted with the deacon Baisane who, because of the scarcity of water in the desert, used to hire out dromedaries and serve as a guide for those going to visit Anthony. He informed the brothers that it was the anniversary of blessed Anthony's death and that they ought to celebrate a vigil in the very place where he had died. At last, at the end of three days in the vast and terrible solitude, they arrived at a very high mountain where they found two monks: Pelusianus, and Isaac, Anthony's interpreter.

(31) It seems fitting at this point in our story, since the

---

66 Cf. Sallust, *Jugurtha* 105.3.

opportunity presents itself, to describe briefly the dwelling place of this eminent man.[67] There was a high rocky mountain about a mile in length. Water sprang forth from the crevices and flowed down to its base, where some of it was absorbed by the sand and the rest, falling deeper, gradually formed a river shaded by numerous palm trees overhanging from both shores, making the location very pleasant and comfortable. You might see the old man strolling back and forth, chatting with blessed Anthony's disciples. Here,[68] they would tell him, Anthony used to sing the psalms; here, he used to pray; here, work; and here, rest when wearied. These vines, these shrubs, he himself planted. That little garden he prepared and arranged with his own hands. This pond he laboriously dug to irrigate his garden. Many years he used this hoe to work the soil. Hilarion would then lie on his pallet and kiss it as if it were still warm from his body. His cell, moreover, was no more than a square box that could only hold a man sleeping stretched out. On the very top of the mountain there were two more cells of about the same size, accessible only after a difficult spiral climb. Here, Anthony had sought refuge from the multitudes who came to him and from the companionship of his disciples. The cells were actually hollowed out of the living rock, so that only doors had had to be added to them. Later, when they had come to the garden, Isaac said: 'Do you see this fruit garden, planted with shrubs and verdant with vegetables? Almost three years ago, when a herd of wild asses was devastating it, he commanded one of the leaders to stand still and, beating its sides with his staff, said: "Why do you eat up what you have not sown"?[69] From that time on, they continued

---

67 Cf. Sallust, *Jugurtha* 95.2; 17.1.
68 Cf. Virgil, *Aeneid* 7.170-176,150-151; 2.29-30.
69 Cf. Matt. 25.24,26; Luke 19.21-22.

to come here for drinking water, but never touched a bush or a vegetable.' Hilarion especially requested that they show him where they had buried Anthony. They took him aside, but whether or not they pointed out the grave is not known. The reason for the secrecy was, they said, that Anthony himself had given orders for it, because he was afraid that Pergamius, the wealthiest man of the district, would remove his body to his villa and erect a martyr's shrine there.

(32) Hilarion, retaining with him only two of the brothers, returned to Aphroditon, where he stayed in a nearby desert, observing such strict silence and abstinence that he said he was just beginning to serve God for the first time. Now, it was the third year that heaven was shut up[70] and the earth was parched with drought; the people were saying that even the elements were mourning the death of Anthony. Hilarion could not long conceal his fame. Men and women earnestly sought him with their ghastly faces and bodies weakened by hunger, beseeching rain from the servant of Christ, blessed Anthony's successor. Looking upon them sadly, he grieved exceedingly and, raising his eyes to heaven and stretching forth[71] both arms, immediately obtained what he petitioned for them.[72] Behold, however, the thirsty sand region, upon being watered by the rain, suddenly brought forth an abundance[73] of serpents and venomous creatures that attacked numberless persons who would have died immediately if they had not gone directly to Hilarion. All the farmers and shepherds anointed their wounds with blessed oil at his bidding and were completely healed.

(33) Seeing that extraordinary honors were inflicted upon him even there, he went to Alexandria, intending to cross

---

70 Cf. Luke 4.25; Eccli. 48.3; 2 Par. 6.26; 7.13; Deut. 11.17.
71 Cf. Exod. 3.20; 8.6.
72 Abbott: *his rogaverat,* not *rogaverant.*
73 Cf. Exod. 8.3.

over into the interior oasis of the desert. Because he had never passed the night in a city from the time he had first become a monk, he stopped with certain brothers known to him who dwelt in Bruchium, not far from Alexandria. They received the old man with great joy but, when it was close to nightfall, they suddenly heard his disciples saddle an ass and prepare for Hilarion's departure. Throwing themselves at his feet, they begged him not to go and, prostrating before the threshold, protested that they would rather die than be so wanting in hospitality. But he said to them: 'I hasten to go because I fear to cause trouble for you. From past experience you certainly know that I would not suddenly leave without reason.' On the very next day, the prefects of Gaza with their lictors (for they had learned the day before that he had arrived) entered the monastery and, when they did not find him after a thorough search, said among themselves: 'Isn't it true what we have heard? He is a magician and knows the future.' After the departure of Hilarion from Palestine, on the succession of Julian to the emperorship and the destruction of Hilarion's monastery, the city of Gaza had petitioned the emperor for the death of Hilarion and Hesychius. The request was granted and a thorough search for both had been proclaimed.

(34) Going out from Bruchium and making his way through the trackless desert, he entered the oasis. After he had been there for a year, more or less, his fame caught up with him; it seemed he could no longer hide in the Orient where many knew him either from report or by sight. He thought, therefore, of sailing to the lonely islands, so that him whom land had made known the sea might conceal. Almost simultaneously, his disciple Hadrian arrived from Palestine, announcing that Julian had been slain, and that a Christian emperor was reigning in his place, and urging that

he return to what was left of his monastery. Hilarion, solemnly disregarding Hadrian's admonition, procured a camel, and traveled through the vast wilderness to Paraetonium, a city on the coast of Libya. There, the unhappy Hadrian, wishing to return to Palestine and recapture former glory under the aegis of the master, committed many outrages against him. Finally, he packed up the presents which the brothers had sent to Hilarion by him and departed without his knowledge. In regard to Hadrian, I would say this discreetly (since there is no other place to mention it), only as a warning to those who despise their masters, that, after a very short time, he rotted away from a disease of the region.

(35) Taking Zananus with him, the old man went up into a ship[74] sailing for Sicily. While he was arranging to pay for his passage[75] by selling a codex of the Gospels which he had copied by hand when a boy—they were almost in the middle of the Adriatic—the shipmaster's[76] son was seized by a demon which began to shout and scream: 'Hilarion, servant of God, why are we not permitted to be safe[77] on the sea because of you? Give me time until I reach land, lest, cast out here, I fall headlong into the abyss.' The saint replied: 'If my God grants you permission to remain, remain. If, however, He casts you out, why do you bring ill will against me, a sinner and beggar?' Now, he said this lest the merchants and sailors who were in the ship report him when they reached land. Not long after, the boy was freed from the demon. His father and all who were present gave their word that they would tell his name to no one.[78]

---

74 Mark 5.18; 6.32,45; 8.10; Luke 8.22,37; John 6.17; Acts 20.13; 21.6; 27.2.
75 Jonas 1.3.
76 Acts 27.11.
77 Cf. Mark 1.24.
78 Cf. Matt. 12.16; Mark 3.12; 7.36; Luke 5.14.

(36) He disembarked at Pachynus, a promontory of Sicily, and offered the master of the ship the Gospels for his own passage and that of Zananus. The shipmaster was unwilling at first to accept it, especially when he noticed that, with the exception of the book and the clothes they had on, they had nothing more, and finally took oath that he would not accept it. The old man yielded[79] with confidence in the acknowledgment of his poverty and rejoiced the more because he possessed none of the goods of the world and was considered a beggar by the inhabitants of Pachynus.

(37) Hilarion realized that the merchants coming from the Orient might recognize and report him, so he fled twenty miles inland. There, in a small deserted field, he daily gathered a bundle of brushwood and, placing it on his disciple's back, sold it in a nearby village to buy a little bread for themselves and those who came to them by chance. Truly, as it is written, 'A city seated on a mountain cannot be hid.[80] A certain shield-bearer became possessed by a demon in the basilica of blessed Peter in Rome and the unclean spirits within him cried out: 'A few days ago Hilarion, the servant of Christ, landed in Sicily and, as no one knew him, he thinks he is unknown. I shall go and make him known.' Without delay, the shield-bearer and his servants went on board a ship that was ready in the harbor and sailed to Pachynus. Led by the demon, he found that hut of the old man and prostrated himself before his door. He was immediately cured. This beginning of miracles[81] in Sicily soon attracted a great multitude of the sick and of pious men. In fact, a prominent man was cured of dropsy[82] on the same day on which he had gone to him. Afterwards, when he offered Hilarion

---

79 Abbott: *assensus est,* not *accensus.*
80 Cf. Matt. 5.14.
81 Cf. John 2.11.
82 Cf. Luke 14.2.

boundless gifts, he heard the words of the Saviour to His disciples: 'freely have ye received, freely give.'[83]

(38) While these events were going on in Sicily, his disciple, Hesychius, was searching the world over for him. With confidence alone in the surety that wherever Hilarion was he could not remain hidden long, he paced the shores and penetrated the desert. After three years had passed, he chanced to hear at Methona from a certain Jew, a seller of trifling wares, that a prophet of the Christians had appeared in Sicily, working such signs and wonders[84] that he was thought to be one of the ancient saints. He inquired anxiously about his dress, his carriage, his speech, and, most of all, his age but could learn nothing. The Jew swore that only the man's reputation had come to his ears. Hesychius set out, therefore, for the Adriatic Sea and by fair voyage arrived at Pachynus, where, in a certain tiny village at the bend of the shore, he sought information on the old man. It did not take long to find out where he was and what he was doing. Nothing about him so amazed the villagers as the fact that, after performing so many signs and miracles, he would not accept even a piece of bread from anyone. To make a long story short, the holy man Hesychius threw himself at the master's knees and moistened his feet with his tears. Finally, the old man raised him up, and, after Hesychius had spent two or three days with him, he understood from Zananus that the old saint could no longer bear to dwell in those regions, but wanted to go to the barbarian countries where his name and his language would be unknown.

(39) Hesychius then led Hilarion to Epidaurus, a city of Dalmatia, but, after staying in a neighboring field for a few days, he could not remain hidden. A serpent of extraordinary

83 Matt. 10.8.
84 Acts 2.22; 5.12; 6.8; 7.36; 15.12.

size of the species the Gentiles call boa, because they are so huge that they are wont to swallow oxen, was devastating the province far and wide and was devouring not only cattle and sheep, but also the farmers and herdsmen, attracting them to itself by the sheer force of its breath. He ordered a pyre to be built and, offering a prayer to Christ, summoned the serpent. He commanded it to mount the heap of wood, and then set fire to it. With all the people looking on in horror and wonder, he burned the monstrous beast to ashes. After that event, becoming quite concerned with what he should do and where he should turn, he planned another flight. Traversing many solitary lands in his mind, he grieved because, though his tongue was silent, his miracles spoke and betrayed him.

(40) At the time of the earthquake which rocked the whole world after the death of Julian, the seas burst forth from their bounds as if God were threatening another deluge or all things were reverting to ancient chaos, and ships, driven out of their course, hung from the jagged peaks of mountains. When the Epidauritanians beheld the havoc of the storm, the raging floods, the masses of waves, and the mountain-high whirlpools that beat upon the shores, fearing a thing which they observed had occurred, that the city would be overturned from its very foundations, they hastened to Hilarion and, as if setting out for battle, placed him upon the shore. He marked the sand in three places with the sign of the Cross and stretched forth his arms against the flood. It is unbelievable to describe to what heights the swollen sea rose and stood before him, but, after raging and seething as if indignant at its barrier, it gradually began to subside. To this day, Epidaurus and the entire region speak of this miraculous event, and mothers instruct their children to pass down to posterity the account of the great wonder. True,

indeed, is the saying to the Apostles: 'if you shall have faith, . . . if you shall say to this mountain: Take up and cast thyself into the sea, it shall be done.'[85] Even to the letter it can be fulfilled if only one has the faith of the Apostles and such as the Lord commanded them to have. For, what does it matter whether the mountain descends into the sea or whether immense mountains of waves suddenly harden into rock before the feet of an old man, preserving everywhere else the properties of water?

(41) The whole city was in wonder over the quelling of the storm and the sea, and word of the stupendous miracle even reached Salona. The old man, knowing this, fled secretly by night in a light sailing boat, and after two days found a merchant ship and journeyed to Cyprus. Just as the boat was steering between the promontory of Malea and the Island of Cythera, some pirates, having left on shore their fleet which was controlled by poles instead of sailyards, made straight for them in two good-sized pirate vessels. The shipmen plied the oars on all sides; those on board, now thoroughly alarmed, wept, ran back and forth, prepared poles, and, as if one messenger were not enough, kept telling the old man excitedly that the pirates were coming. Hilarion watched the pirates intently from a distance, smiled, turned to his disciples, and said: " 'O thou of little faith, why didst thou fear?"[86] Are these men indeed more numerous than Pharoa's army? Nevertheless, at God's bidding, they were all drowned.'[87] While he was speaking, however the hostile craft bore upon them with foaming beaks only a stone's throw away. He stood firmly in the prow of the ship and stretched forth his hand against them as they came. 'It is sufficient to

85 Matt. 21.21.
86 Matt. 14.31.
87 Exod. 14.23-31.

have come this far,' he said. Oh, wonderful is faith! At once, the vessels rebounded, although the pirates continued to row them forward. They were astounded at the inexplicable frustration of their efforts and strained with all their power to reach the ship, but, more swiftly than they had come out, they were borne back to the shore.

(42) I am omitting the rest of Hilarion's miraculous works lest, in the narration of his signs and wonders, I seem to stretch out this book. I shall relate only this, that, while on a fair voyage through the Cyclades, he heard all around him the voices of unclean spirits echoing from the cities and villages and resounding along the shores. He entered Paphos, a city of Cyprus made famous by the songs of the poets. Frequently shaken by earthquakes, it now reveals its former splendor only in its ruins. Rejoicing that he could live peacefully and unknown for a few days, he took up his abode one mile from the city. Actually, however, not twenty full days had passed when, throughout the entire island, whoever had unclean spirits began to cry out that Hilarion had come, Hilarion, the servant of Christ, and that they ought all hasten to him. Salamis, Curium, Lapetha, and the rest of the cities took up the cry, and a great many asserted that they really knew Hilarion, that he was the servant of God, but did not know where he was. Within not much more than thirty days, almost two hundred came together to him, not only men but women, too. When he saw them, he grieved because they would not leave him alone. Then, angered to a degree of avenging himself, he scourged the devils with such persistence of prayer that some were freed immediately; others, after two or three days; all, within one week.

(43) Hilarion remained at Paphos for a period of two years, but, always thinking about flight, he sent Hesychius to Palestine to greet the brothers and look over the ashes of

his monastery, with instructions to return in the spring. When he returned, Hilarion wanted to sail back to Egypt, to those places called Bucolia, where there were no Christians, but only a fierce barbarian people. Hesychius, however, persuaded him to retire into a more remote part of that same island. After investigating the whole place, he found a spot twelve miles from the sea among lonely and rugged mountains,[88] a spot which could barely be climbed by crawling on hands and knees. The location, solitary and forbidding though it might be, was surrounded on all sides by trees and provided with water flowing from the summit of a hill. There was also an exceedingly pleasant garden with many fruit trees, but he never partook of the fruit. Nearby were the ruins of a very ancient temple from which (as he himself used to say and as his disciples bore witness) so innumerable were the voices of demons resounding day and night that you would believe them an army. Delighted with his new location, because it was evident that he had his adversaries close at hand, he lived there for five years. He was often visited by Hesychius during this last period of his life and his soul was refreshed because, on account of the roughness[89] and difficulty of the climb and the multitude (as it was generally said) of ghosts, it was extremely rare that anyone could ascend the mountain, or dared to try. On one particular day, however, when he went into his garden, he found a man lying before the gate, totally paralyzed.[90] He asked Hesychius who he was and how he came there. Hesychius explained that he was the procurator of the villa nearby, to whom the garden in which they were rightly belonged. Hilarion wept and, stretching out his hand to the man lying before him, said:

---

88 Cf. Sallust, *Catilina* 59.2.
89 Cf. Sallust, *Jugurtha* 17.2.
90 Cf. Matt. 9.2; Mark 2.3; Luke 5.18.

'I bid you in the name of our Lord Jesus Christ, to arise and walk.'[91] Miraculous speed! With the words scarcely spoken, the paralytic's legs regained their vigor and the man rose firmly to his feet. Later, when this miracle became known, the needs of a great many drove them to surmount the barriers of distance and impassability. The inhabitants of the farms in the country around were intent on one thing alone —that Hilarion in no way escape, for the rumor had been current that he could not long remain in the same place. This practice was not the result of any restlessness or childish caprice; he fled honor and the importunity of the public, desiring, only and always, silence and a humble, hidden life.

(44) In the eightieth year of his life, when Hesychius was away, Hilarion wrote with his own hand a brief letter which served the purpose of a will. He left to Hesychius—for Zananus, his minister, had died a few days before—his Bible, of course; his sackcloth tunic; his hood and cloak. Many religious persons from Paphus hastened to Hilarion, now a sick man, especially because they had heard him say that he was to journey to the Lord and to be liberated from the fetters of the body; among them, a certain holy woman, Constantia. He had saved her daughter and son-in-law from death by anointing them with oil. Now, all these people he earnestly entreated not to keep him even for a moment after his death, but to cover him at once with earth in that very garden as he was, in his tunic of haircloth, his hood, and coarse mantle.

(45) Only a little warmth was left in his breast nor did anything remain of a living man but his reason, yet, with his eyes open, he was speaking: 'Depart; why are you afraid? Depart, my soul; why do you hesitate? For seventy years you have served Christ and you fear death?' With these words, he breathed forth his spirit. They buried him immediately and

---

91 Cf. Matt. 9.5,6; Mark 2.9-11; Luke 5.23-25.

the city actually heard of his burial before the announcement of his death.

(46) As soon as the holy man Hesychius, who was then in Palestine, heard of Hilarion's death, he went to Cyprus to claim the body. In order, however, to allay the suspicions of the neighbors who were diligently guarding the place, he pretended that he merely wanted to live in the same garden. Then, after nearly ten months, with great danger of his life, he stole away the body and carried it to Maiuma, where all the monks and townspeople followed in procession as the body was buried in the ancient monastery, with his unimpaired tunic, hood and cloak, and his body whole and entire as if he were still alive, giving forth such delicate fragrance that one would think it anointed with sweet balm.

(47) At the conclusion of my story, it seems to me, I ought to say something about the devotion of that truly holy woman, Constantia. When the message was brought to her that the body of Hilarion was in Palestine, she immediately fell dead, thus attesting her deep love for the servant of God. It had become her custom to spend nightly vigils in the saint's sepulchre and converse with him as if he were there to aid her in her prayers. Even to this day you may find a wonderful and holy rivalry between the people of Palestine and the people of Cyprus, the former claiming to possess Hilarion's body; the latter, his spirit. In both places, great signs appear daily, but more numerous miracles occur in the garden at Cyprus, perhaps because that place was dearer to him.

LIFE OF MALCHUS

BY ST. JEROME

Translated by

SISTER MARIE LIGUORI EWALD, I.H.M. Ph.D.

Marygrove College

INTRODUCTION

THE LIFE OF MALCHUS was probably written by St. Jerome in his monastery in Bethlehem. His activities in Rome as secretary to Pope Damasus had aroused the jealousy and attacks of his enemies, forcing him into this seclusion. At the Pope's request, he had taken part in the Synod of 382 and had also accepted the important work of revising the text of the Bible. The marked success of his undertakings aroused further jealousy when it seemed for a while that he might even receive the highest honor of the Church and succeed Pope Damasus on his death in 384.[1] The cruel criticism, however, of his relations with the noble Roman women, whom he had ardently inspired with the ascetic ideal, made his position and life in Rome so unbearable that, like one of his ascetic heroes, he sought refuge in the monastery.[2]

During the years 386-392, Jerome seems to have given little time to correspondence. Most of his activity went into a profound study of Hebrew, the diligent reading of the Church writers, and the preparation of commentaries, revisions and translation of Scripture. With the *Life of Mal-*

---

1 Schanz, *op. cit.* IV 1.431; Jerome, *Ep.* 123.10; cf. J. Duff, 'Introduction,' *The Letters of St. Jerome* (Dublin 1942) 15-17; Leclercq, *DACL*, s.v. 'Jerome,' VII.2. 2252-2253.

2 Schanz, *op. cit.* IV 1.431; Duff, *op. cit.* 15-20; Leclercq, *DACL*, s.v: 'Jerome,' VII.2. 2254-2260.

chus, he broke his self-imposed literary silence and even
planned to write a more extensive history for which the
tiny biography was merely an exercise to rub away the rust
from his tongue.[3] 'He no longer thinks only of the *History
of His Times* which he announces in the preface of his
Chronicles; he plans now to describe the establishment and
the propagation of Christianity even to his own age,'[4] if
God will grant his life and his vituperators will cease to persecute him now that he is a fugitive and recluse.[5]

The *Life of Malchus,* written more than ten years later
than the *Life of Paul,* is closely related to it in subject matter
and treatment.[6] Both Paul and Malchus are driven into the
wastes of the desert to find refuge from persecution by members of their own family; the former, from his brother-in-law,
who for the sake of gold sought to betray him to the agents
of Decius and Valerian; the latter, from his parents, who employed all manner of wiles to induce him to renounce his
ideal of chastity. Both Paul and Malchus are recognized as
holy men of God even by wild animals who serve them. Having fought the good fight, both exemplify in their lives the
special protection merited to those who serve God faithfully
in holy purity. Like the *Life of Paul,* the *Life of Malchus*
'is a work of brilliant rhetoric destined to enchant the pious
imagination, to rouse hearts to enthusiasm for the ascetic life.'[7]
Both lives are original[8] writings of St. Jerome.

The *Life of Malchus* is an important source of the elastic
form of early monachism which in the course of time gradually became fixed. It is of special interest, too, for its revela-

3 Cavallera, *op. cit.* I 130.
4 *Ibid.* 131.
5 Life of Malchus 1.
6 Cavallera, *op. cit.* I 130.
7 *Ibid.*
8 Grützmacher, *op. cit.* II 86-88.

tion of the freedom of the first monks.[9] When Malchus determined to return to his home, he was not prevented from
doing so by his abbot, who, nevertheless, warned him that his
desire was a temptation from the Devil and urged him not
to look back, having put his hand to the plough.

The form of composition in the *Life of Malchus* is original[10]
in that the solitary tells his own life history. Jerome, an old
man now in his Bethlehem retreat, recalls the experiences
told him, many years before, by the saintly old Malchus
whom he met in Maronia, a hamlet of Syria under the
patronage of his friend and host, Evagrius. The glorious tale
of the monk's heroic preservation of chastity he vividly and
dramatically rehearses for the benefit and encouragement of
the chaste to whom he dedicates the work.

9 *Ibid.* 86.
10 Schanz, *op. cit.* IV 1.436.

THE LIFE OF MALCHUS, THE CAPTIVE MONK

HEY WHO INTEND to fight a naval battle, first—in the harbor and on a calm sea—steer the ship, ply the oars, prepare grappling irons and hooks, and train the soldiers at their deck stations to keep a firm footing on a swaying, slippery surface, so that in an actual battle they will not feel terror at what they have learned on manoeuvres. So, too, I who have kept silence for a long time (for he, indeed, to whom my speech is a torment has caused me to keep silence) wish to get in practice again in a small work[1] and remove a sort of rust from my tongue so that I may be able later to produce a more extensive history. For I have planned to write a history[2] (that is, if the Lord will grant me life and my vituperators[3] will cease to pursue me, at least now that I am a fugitive and recluse) from the advent of our Saviour down to our own age, that is, from apostolic times to the dregs[4] of our day, treating of how[5] and through whom the Church of Christ came to birth and maturity, how it grew under persecution, was crowned with martyrdoms, and, after it came into the hands of Christian emperors, how it became greater in power and

---

1 Cf. Florus 1. Introd. 3.
2 Cf. Sallust, *Catilina* 4.1-5.
3 *Ibid.* 3.3; 5.
4 Cf. Ps. 39.3.
5 Cf. Sallust, *Catilina* 5.9.

riches indeed, but meaner in virtue.[6] But this at another time;
for the present, let us explain what lies before us.

(2) Maronia, a rather small village, lies almost thirty miles
east of Antioch, in Syria. When I was a young man living
in Syria, this village, after being under the jurisdiction of
many previous lords or patrons, fell to the possession of
Bishop Evagrius, an intimate acquaintance of mine, whom
I mention by name here in order to indicate the source of
the information that I am about to relate. At that time, a
certain old man was living there, named Malchus, whom in
Latin we could call 'Rex.' He was a Syrian by nationality
and tongue and, as I thought, a native of Maronia. An old
woman was his companion, so very decrepit that she seemed
on the verge of death. Both were so very devout and so wore
away the threshold of the church that you would think them
another Zachary and Elizabeth[7] from the Gospel, except that
John was not with them. When I asked their neighbors about
them and wondered just what was the bond between them
—whether of wedlock, of blood, or of the spirit—they answered promptly and unanimously that they were a holy pair,
pleasing to God, and told some startling things about them.
Drawn by curiosity, I approached the man and inquired with
eager interest if there were any truth in what I had heard.
He related the following story.

(3) 'I, my son, was an only child and a tenant of a small
farm at Nisibis. When my parents were coercing me to marry,
because I was the last descendant of the family and their sole
heir, I told them that I preferred to be a monk. With what
threats my father assailed me, with what coaxing my mother
pursued me to betray my chastity, you can judge by the fact
that I fled both home and parents. Since I could not go to

6 Cf. Florus 1. Introd. 4-8.
7 Luke 1.5-6.

the Orient because of the proximity of Persia and the Roman
guard, I turned to the West, taking with me very few provisions, merely enough to keep me alive. To be brief, I finally
reached the desert of Chalcis, which lies between Immae and
Beroa, but more to the south. There, having found a community of monks, I placed myself under their guidance, earn-
ing my living by the toil of my hands[8] and curbing the lust
of the flesh with fasting. After many years, the thought occurred to me that I should return to my native land while
my mother was still alive (I had heard of my father's death),
to comfort her in her widowhood. After her death, I could
sell our few possessions, give part of the proceeds to the poor,
erect a monastery with another part, and (why should I
blush to confess my infidelity) reserve the rest to take care
of my own needs. My abbot protested that my desire to
return home was a temptation from the Devil and that under
a virtuous pretext lay concealed the snares of our ancient
enemy; in other words, the dog was returning to its vomit.[9]
Many monks, he said, had been deceived in this way, for
the Devil never comes without disguises. He set before me
many examples from Scripture and reminded me that in the
beginning the Devil tripped up Adam and Eve with the
hope[10] of godlikeness. When persuasion failed, he besought
me on his knees not to desert him, not to ruin myself, not to
look back, having put my hand to the plough.[11] Alas, miserable creature that I am, I overcame my admonisher in a
most evil victory, thinking that he was seeking not my advantage, but his own satisfaction. He escorted me from the
monastery as if he were attending a corpse in a funeral procession; bidding me a last farewell, he said: "I see, my son,

---

8 Abbott: *manu et labore,* not *manuum labore.*
9 Prov. 26.11.
10 Gen. 3.5.
11 Luke 9.62.

that you are marked by the branding of Satan; I do not seek the causes, nor do I accept the excuses. The sheep that leaves the sheepfold straightway exposes itself to the teeth of the wolf." '[12]

(4) 'Lying near the public highway from Beroa to Edessa, there is a desert through which nomad Saracens are always wandering[13] back and forth. For this reason, travelers along the way group together and, by mutual aid, decrease the danger of a surprise attack. There were in my company men, women, old men, young people, children, numbering in all about seventy. Suddenly, Ishmaelites, riding upon horses and camels descended upon us in a startling attack, with their long hair flying from under their headbands. They wore cloaks over their half-naked bodies, and broad boots. Quivers hung from their shoulders; their unstrung bows dangled at their sides; they carried long spears, for they had not come for battle but for plunder. We were seized, scattered, and carried off in different directions. A woman of the company and I, after my long absence an hereditary owner, too late regretting my decision to leave the monastery, fell by lot into the hands of the same master. We were led—actually, we were lifted up onto camels—through the vast desert, cling- ing to the beasts in constant fear of falling off. Our food was half-cooked[14] meat; our drink, the camels' milk.'

(5) 'At last, after crossing a great stream, we arrived in the heart of the desert, where, having been commanded to worship the mistress and her children according to the custom of that people, we bowed our heads. Here, practically a prisoner, I learned to go about naked, for the atmosphere and the climate admitted no covering but a loin cloth. I was

---

12 Cf. John 10.12.
13 Cf. Sallust, *Catilina* 6.1.
14 Cf. Florus 1.34.12.

assigned the task of pasturing the sheep and, in contrast to
the evils I might have been subjected to, I enjoyed the comfort of rarely seeing my master and fellow slaves. To myself,
I seemed to have something in common with holy Jacob;[15]
I recalled Moses,[16] too, for both of them had been at some
time shepherds in the desert. I lived on fresh cheese and milk;
I prayed continually; I sang the psalms that I had learned
in the monastery. In fact, I was delighted with my captivity
and I thanked God for His judgment, for the monk whom
I had nearly lost in my own country I had found again in
the desert.'

(6) 'Alas! nothing is ever safe from the Devil! How
multiple and unspeakable are his deceits![17] Envy and hatred
found me in my hiding place. My master, seeing his herd
increase, and finding in me nothing of fraud (for I obeyed
the Apostle's injunction that masters were to be served as
faithfully as God Himself[18]), and desiring to reward me in
order that he might the more insure my fidelity, offered me
in marriage the woman slave who had been taken captive
with me. When I refused and said that I was a Christian and
that it was not lawful[19] for me to have for wife one whose
husband was living (her husband had been captured with
us and carried off by another master), my implacable master
was seized with fury and, drawing his sword, started to attack me. If I had not made haste to throw my arm about
the woman, he would have shed my blood then and there!
All too soon for me, night came on, darker than usual. I led
my new bride into a ruined cave nearby and, with sorrow[20]

15 Cf. Gen. 30.31; 31.41.
16 Cf. Exod. 3.1.
17 Cf. Eph. 6.11-12.
18 Eph. 6.5-6; Col. 3.22-23; Titus 2.9-10.
19 Cf. Matt. 14.4.
20 Abbott: *tristitia pronubante,* not *pronubante nobis maestitia.*

as the sponsor of our union, each secretly abhorred the other.
Then, indeed, I realized the full force of my captivity and,
throwing myself down on the ground, began to lament and
sob for the monk I was on the point of losing, crying: "Is
it for this that I, wretched man, have been preserved? Have
my sins brought me to this fate that now with my hair
turning gray, I, a virgin, must become a husband? Of what
avail to have renounced parents,[21] country, property, for the
Lord, if I now do the very thing that I would not do when
I renounced them? It may perhaps be that I suffer this punishment because I longed to return to my own country.
What shall we do, my soul? Shall we perish or shall we
conquer? Shall we wait the hand of the Lord, or shall we
pierce ourselves with our own sword? Turn the blade against
yourself, my soul; your death is more to be feared than the
death of the body. Chastity preserved has its own martyrdom;
let the witness of Christ lie unburied in the desert. I shall
be both[22] my own persecutor and martyr." So I spoke and
drew my sword, gleaming even in the darkness, and turned
its point against myself. "Farewell, unhappy woman," I cried
to my companion. "I am yours to have as a martyr rather
than a husband." Then she threw herself at my feet, and
entreated: "I beseech you by Jesus Christ, and I beg you
in the agony of this hour, not to shed your blood; or, if you
are determined to die, turn the sword upon me first; it is
better for us thus to be united. Even if my husband should
return to me, I would preserve the chastity that captivity has
taught me and would rather die than lose it. Why should
you die for fear of marrying me? I should die if you wished
to. Take me, therefore, as a spouse in chastity and love the
bond of the soul rather than that of the body. Let our masters

---

21 Cf. Matt. 10.37.
22 Abbott: *et persecutor et martyr.*

believe you a husband; Christ will know the brother. We shall easily convince them of our marriage when they see us love in this way." I confess,' he said, 'that I was amazed, and, having admired the virtue of this woman, I loved her the more as my spouse. Never, however, did I look upon her nude body, never did I touch her flesh, fearing to lose in peace what I had preserved in conflict. Many days passed in wedlock of this kind. Our marriage rendered us more pleasing to our masters; there was no suspicion of flight. Sometimes I was absent for a whole month, all alone, the trusted shepherd of the flock.'

(7) 'After a long time, while I was sitting alone one day in the desert, seeing nothing but sky and earth, I let my thoughts wander back unconstrained. Among my many memories I recalled the companionship of the monks, and especially the expression on the face of the father who had instructed me, cared for me, and lost me. While I was meditating in this fashion, I noticed a colony of ants[23] zealously at work in a narrow path. You might see[24] [them carrying] loads bigger than their their bodies. Some were hauling the seeds of herbs by the forceps of their mouths; others were digging up the earth from small pits and building mounds with it to keep out the water from their storehouses. The busy workers of one group, mindful of the coming winter, were cutting up the seeds they had gathered, to prevent their granary from sprouting in the damp soil. Another group, in solemn mourning, were removing the bodies of the dead.[25] What seemed most wonderful was that, with so great a throng in motion, those coming out of the mounds and path never hindered the ones entering, but rather, if they met anyone

---

23 Cf. Virgil, *Aeneid* 4.402-407.
24 Abbott: *videres onera,* not *ferre onera.*
25 Cf. Virgil, *Georgics* 4.255-256.

staggering under his bundle or burden, they lent him the support of their shoulders. In brief[26]—that day offered me a noble spectable which reminded me of Solomon's sending us to learn wisdom from the ants, urging the sluggard[27] to profit by their example. I began to weary of my captivity and to yearn for the cells of the monastery and to desire the comfort of the solicitude of those ants in whose community all worked together and where, since nothing belonged to anyone, all possessed all things in common.'

(8) 'The woman met me as I was returning to my bed. My expression[28] could not dissemble the sadness of my soul. She asked me why I was so dispirited. She listened to my reasons, and I urged[29] her to escape with me. I pleaded with her for secrecy; she agreed; from that time on, in continual whispers, we wavered between hope and fear. There were in my herd two he-goats of unusual size. I killed them and made bags[30] from their hides; I prepared their flesh as food for the journey. In the early dusk, when our masters supposed that we had retired, we started out on our journey, taking with us the bags of skin and part of the meat. When we arrived at the river[31] (it was ten miles away), we inflated the skins and mounted them, entrusting[32] ourselves to the water. We rowed along slowly with our feet,[33] and the river carried us downstream and landed us on the opposite bank much farther down than where we had embarked, so that anyone pursuing us would lose our tracks. As some of our meat was lost in transit and part of it became water-soaked,

26 Cf. Cicero, *De oratore* 1.20.93; *Orator* 27.95.
27 Prov. 6.6; 30.25.
28 Abbott: *vultus potuit,* not *vultu . . . potui.*
29 Abbott: *hortor,* not *hortatur.*
30 Cf. Sallust, *Jugurtha* 91.1.
31 *Ibid.* 91.1-2.
32 *Ibid.* 90.1.
33 Cf. Florus 1.40.16.

we were able to salvage only a three-day supply of food. We drank as much water[34] as we could, preparing for the thirst ahead of us. We went at a run, always looking behind us, making greater progress during the night[35] than during the day because of the ambushes of nomad Saracens and the intense heat of the sun. Wretched man that I am, I tremble[36] with fear even as I tell what happened, and although I am now secure, my whole body shudders with the horror of the recollection.'

(9) 'On the third day of our flight, in the dim uncertain distance, we saw behind[37] us two riders mounted on camels, approaching rapidly. Our first thought, presaging evil, was that our master had come to kill us; the sun darkened on the joy of our escape. In terror because we realized that our tracks in the sand had betrayed us, we discovered to our right a cave that ran deep under ground. Although we were afraid of venomous animals (for snakes, serpents, and scorpions, and other deadly creatures of the sort are wont to seek such shady places to avoid the heat of the sun), we entered it and hastily took refuge in a small dark pit to the left in the entrance way, not daring to go farther lest, in trying to escape death, we should encounter death. We consoled ourselves with the reflection that if the Lord would help His wretched children, we had a place of safety; if, however, He rejected us as sinners, we had a sepulchre. You can imagine our state of mind, our terror, when right in front of the cave stood our master and a fellow slave! They had tracked us to our hiding place! Oh, how much more terrible is the expectation

---

34 Cf. Sallust, *Jugurtha* 91.2.
35 *Ibid.* 91.3.
36 Abbott: *Paveo miser etiam referens; etiam securus toto tamen corpore perhorresco.*
37 Abbott: *respicimus,* not *aspicimus.*

than the realization of death! I grow faint[38] and my tongue even now stammers in fear, and, as if I hear my master calling, I dare not utter a word! He sent his servant to drag us from hiding; he held the camels and with drawn sword awaited our coming. Meanwhile, the servant had pushed three or four cubits into the cave. From our covert we watched him pass us without discovering us (for it is the nature of our eyes to be blinded when one comes from the sunlight directly into the shade). His voice resounded throughout the cave: "Come forth, you gallows rogues, come to your death! What are you waiting for? Why do you delay? Come! the master calls."[39] He was still speaking when, all of a sudden, in the darkness, we saw a lioness rush upon him and drag him into her lair by the throat, strangled and covered with blood. Good Jesus! what was our terror then; what was our joy! As we looked on, we saw our enemy perish, unknown to the master. When he saw that the servant was slow about returning, he suspected that the two of us were resisting capture. No longer able to control his wrath, he came to the cave just as he was, holding his sword and bursting into a shout at the top of his lungs[40] at the stupidity of his slave, but, before he reached our hiding place, he was caught by the beast. Who could believe that, before our very eyes, a savage beast would fight in our behalf? Once that fear was removed, however, we realized that a similar destruction faced us, though the madness of the lion was less fearful[41] than the anger of man. Shaking with dread, and not daring even to move, we awaited the outcome of our highly dangerous situation, with only the comforting knowledge of our chastity as a wall of protection. Early in the morn-

---

38 Abbott: *conlabor,* not *cum labore.*
39 Abbott: *Dominus vocat. Adhuc loquebatur.*
40 Abbott: *clamore valido,* not *furore rabido.*
41 Abbott: *tutius,* not *potius.*

ing, the lioness, wary of snares and sensing that she had been seen, picked up her cub with her teeth and carried it away, yielding her refuge to us. We did not have enough courage to rush forth at once, but delayed for a long time, hesitating to move because we imagined what it would be to encounter her [outside the cave].'

(10) 'Having passed the day in this terror, toward evening we finally emerged from the cavern and saw the camels, which are called dromedaries because of their extraordinary speed, peacefully chewing cud. We mounted them and, revived by new provisions,[42] at last, on the tenth day of traveling through the desert, arrived at a Roman camp. Brought before the tribune, we explained to him all that had happened. He sent us to Sabinianus, the ruler of Mesopotamia, where we sold our camels. Because my old abbot had by this time fallen asleep in the Lord, I re-entered the monastery here at Maronia whither I had been conducted. My companion I gave to the care of the virgins, loving her, as a sister, but never trusting myself to her as to a sister.'

All these things the old man, Malchus, related to me when I was young. Now I, an old man, have told them to you. To the chaste, I set forth this story of chastity. You, in turn, pass this story on to posterity, so that all may know that in the midst of swords, and deserts, and beasts, chastity is never a captive, and that a man consecrated to Christ may die, but can never be conquered.

---

42 Abbott: *et nova sitarcia refocillati.*

LIFE OF ST. EPIPHANIUS
BY ENNODIUS

Translated by

SISTER GENEVIEVE MARIE COOK, R.S.M.

St. Xavier College for Women

INTRODUCTION

MAGNUS FELIX ENNODIUS, an outstanding literary figure—deservedly or not—of early sixth-century Italy, was born in 473 or 474, it is most generally believed, at Arles in southern Gaul. His childhood he passed with an aunt at Ticinum (modern Pavia) in northern Italy, whither he had come as an orphan. In 493, Epiphanius, then Bishop of Ticinum, admitted him to minor orders. Some eight years later, Ennodius passed to the see of Milan. To the years that he spent at Milan (501-513) belongs, with but one exception, his whole literary output. About 513, he left Milan and returned to Ticinum to become its bishop. During his episcopacy (513-521), Ennodius was a member of two unsuccessful embassies—one in 415, and the other in 517—dispatched by Pope Hormisdas to Emperor Anastasius at Constantinople in the hope of effecting a reconciliation between the Eastern and Western Churches. Shortly after his return from the second embassy, Ennodius died (521) and was buried at Ticinum.

The *Life of St. Epiphanius*, written between 501 and 504 and generally considered the best of Ennodius' works, is especially valuable historical source material for that chaotic period in Italian politics when Roman domination in the West was gradually giving way to barbarian supremacy. During the thirty years of his episcopacy (467-497), Bishop

301

Epiphanius acted successively as ambassador between the king-maker Ricimer and Emperor Anthemius, between Emperor Nepos and the dread Visigothic king, Euric, between the Ostrogothic king, Theodoric, and the Burgundian Gundobad. He saw his city Pavia overrun and ruthlessly sacked by one barbarian horde after another and his people carried off into captivity. His endeavors to maintain peace between warring leaders and to obtain relief and security for his afflicted flock fill the pages of the *Life*.

The *Life of St. Epiphanius*, moreover, in its affected phraseology, in its exaggeration, in its obscurity—now the result of extreme laconism, now of excessive verbosity—is of special interest as a concrete expression of the linguistic and stylistic characteristics of the Latin writers of the late fifth and the early sixth century.

The Latin text used as the basis for this translation is the critical text of Vogel made in 1885 for the *Monumenta Germaniae Historica*.

THE LIFE OF ST. EPIPHANIUS

TWOFOLD OBLIGATION constrains me to undertake this work, which I know will be free from neither labor nor adverse criticism, in view of the fact that it imposes upon me the treatment of a subject which, while it looks for a wealth of literary talent in the writer, places, at the same time, restrictions upon that talent. Even persons who are, as it seems, most prominent in worldly circles will be displeased both with him who through vain glory extols them with a too florid praise and with him who, lacking in eloquence, confines himself to an unadorned account of their deeds. For, in praise, as it is shameful to fashion fictions of which not even he who is their subject is aware, so also is it unjust and deplorable to pass over in silence what is truly worthy of commendation. We accord to the laudable deeds of our ancestors a credence and esteem proportionate to the ability of their narrator; what a writer of little literary ability undertakes to narrate is entirely lost to posterity or comes down in an attenuated form, while that eulogy which goes beyond the bounds of truth diminishes the glory of its subject to the degree that it has endeavored to augment it by falsehood. An eloquent but untruthful narration often deprives worthy deeds of due praise, whereas that narration which does not give merited glory to its subject is incomplete and beggarly.

I, therefore, about to narrate the life of blessed Epiphanius, Bishop of Ticinum, beg the Holy Spirit, as the witness and companion of his acts, to help me to leave an imperishable record, which will ever keep alive the memory of his virtues as an example for others. In this work, although the fixed precepts of the art of eloquence do not restrict me to the mere unadorned enumeration of meritorious deeds, I shall, however, find none of his labors so insignificant, so lowly, as to demand amplification by those ornaments of animated speech indispensable to the majority of writers. I shall, further-more, cite witnesses of recent combats and I shall display trophies adorned with the still-smoldering spoils stripped from the Devil. No one relates well-known events which have occurred almost under the eyes of his readers, without be-ing certain of their verity. And so, things of which they them-selves have been witnesses I shall review for my readers, whom, were my intention to transgress the truth in this nar-ration, I would avoid as conscious of my impertinence.

That remarkable Epiphanius, then, was by birth a native of the town of Ticinum. His father, Maurus, and his mother, Focaria, were both of freeborn ancestry, the latter being of the stock of the holy bishop and confessor, Mirocles. But, why do I recall the lineal prerogatives of those whose chief claim to family honors rests in their son? Under his predeces-sor, Bishop Crispinus, a man of greatest integrity, Epiphanius, when scarcely eight years old, began his service in the heavenly militia and as he had been previously indicated by a heaven-sent sign, entered upon the officer of ecclesiastical lector. When he was yet a suckling babe, many saw his cradle aglow with a celestial light, the harbinger and prefiguration of the keenness of intellect and beauty of soul that were to be his. After mastering in a brief time the art of writing in short-hand, he was enrolled among the exceptors, and even as a beginner he could take notes that needed no correction by masters in the art. Thus, his labors increasing with his advancing years, he by the grace of God attained his sixteenth year; though still a boy in years, he thought the thoughts of a mature man. There blossomed in him before all else that mother of good works, modesty. With such readiness did he minister to the bishop that, if he saw any task performed by another, he grieved because he had been deprived of rendering that service. He received the old with dignity, the young with courtesy, and even then he had the courage to correct the wicked. He was obedient to his superiors, submissive to his seniors enjoining upon him sacred duties, kindly and helpful to those of his own age and rank, and, with genuine charity, courteous and affable to those of lower status. He considered himself superior to none, although he outstripped all in the conscientious pursuit of perfection. He knew no desire for praise, though day by day laudable qualities increased in him. Each moment of the day he brought to completion works worthy of praise, yet he considered the fruit of his good works lost if men discovered what he in secret offered to God alone. In fine, mindful of the words of the Apostle, he refused approbation and adulation and was well content to have the testimony of his conscience as approval of his virtuous acts.[1]

Nor must I fail to touch at least lightly upon his comeliness, which was but a reflection of the beauty of his soul. His lips smiled even when his heart was heavy with sorrow and, whither-so-ever he turned his eyes, his glance proclaimed his serenity of soul. His brow had the beauty and brilliancy of wax which, exposed to the sun's rays, has drawn its color from the heavens. Nature had so perfectly moulded his nostrils as to defy emulation by the painter. He had well-rounded hands with tapering fingers, from which it was a

---

1 Cf. 2 Cor. 1.12.

joy—even for the stranger—to accept something. His stature was such as to prefigure in his person the eminent dignity that was to be his. Lest, perhaps, some malicious critic object that it is out of place to mention the physical attractiveness of so virtuous a man, [let him remember that] it has been commanded in that ancient source of the divine precepts that the bodies of priests be the object of diligent consideration and examination, so that there be in them no weakness or deformity, no member above or below what is proper in size, no deep-rooted blemish of the skin, no broken hand or foot, nor hump to render them unworthy to minister at the altar.[2] And when the teacher of the Gentiles and vessel of election proclaims that a man without defect should assume the office of the priesthood, we may believe that he refers to a body, as well as a soul, without blemish.[3] Willingly does He who orders that the infirm and the deformed be debarred from His sacrifices admit those who possess physical comeliness, especially those in whom beauty of soul surpasses a comeliness of body devoid of all artificiality.

Now that I have touched briefly on the points necessary to introduce in appearance him who is already known in deed, I shall proceed to those points which one may narrate with laudable boldness about God's servants. His manner of speech was well suited to instruction and to persuasion; even then he was masterful in intercession and most effective in correction, and, at the same time, when the occasion demanded, gentle and kindly in exhortation. His voice, though sonorous and seasoned with a certain virile elegance, was neither harsh and rustic nor weak and lacking in manly vigor. Whoever saw him then, although he had not as yet

2 Cf. Lev. 21.16-24.
3 Cf. Titus 1.7.

received any office of dignity, believed that he had already attained all the signal honors which were to follow.

Such he was when, having attained his eighteenth year, he was consecrated subdeacon and admitted, though a youth, to the ranks of the elders. Some were astounded, but they were strangers who gauged his character from the immaturity of his years; those, however, who knew him considered this dignity late in being conferred. But the venerable Bishop Crispinus, who knew no partiality, who was persistent and severe in correction, and who gave only well-merited approbation, while being kindly in thought toward his disciple Epiphanius, pierced him with the sternness of his glance and under the appearance of an austere brow nourished a secret affection for him. He took a father's delight in the becoming conduct of his foster son, watching his every action with joy and satisfaction. Epiphanius passed but two years in the rank of subdeacon; then his soul, too rich in grace to be confined within the bounds of mediocre honor, carried him aloft to higher office. His merits hurried on to the levitical dignity to which his prayers had never aspired; his life demanded what was stranger to his desires.

I should, however, relate in detail one task performed by Epiphanius during his subdeaconship, somewhat toward its close. Summias they call that region which is situated where the Po greedily gnaws upon the confining banks and, winding serpentlike, enriches one man with what it steals from another, making the loss of the one the gain of the other. Concerning the boundaries of this territory, a certain Burco was carrying on a contest, now ancient, with the clergy. The bishop, therefore, sent Epiphanius, though still a youth, to end this quarrel, already of long standing—just how long no one could say—because he considered the young cleric capable of hearing with patience and of refuting with

308 ENNODIUS

mature wisdom the arguments of his opponents. Then, contention, the mother of every crime, brought forth her usual fruit. For, in the course of his scandalous words, Burco so yielded to his own evil nature as to commit without fear an atrocious crime. With a cudgel, he so violently struck the holy man that a stream of blood straightway gushed forth. But Epiphanius, ever master of the situation, checked his anger; nor did he, though provoked, burn with the hope of revenge. Rather, with kindliest words, he addressed his stunned and terrified assailant. Thereupon, Capraria, the mother of Burco, ran up crying out that that ruthless deed had cost her, unhappy woman, her son. From her lamentations—such as at the death of a dear one put to flight all sane judgment—one would have thought that she were even then throwing herself upon the dead body of her son. She kissed the feet of the saintly youth, begging pardon for her son from him whom no violence had even impelled to resentment. But he bade her not to stir up hostility by her supplication, lest she keep him, through no fault of his, from the burdens the duty imposed upon him. Straightway, the whole city was in turmoil and every Christian heart filled with rage. They demanded that Burco be led to death; in that great gathering of people, no one was calm save him who had suffered the injury. The excellent bishop lamented his own infirmities and the suffering that they had occasioned his disciple. But the disciple himself rejoiced in his trials; in making satisfaction for Burco, now considered a common enemy, he neither sought glory by an ostentatious pardon nor transgressed the divine mandates by revenge.

Shortly afterwards, Epiphanius attained his twentieth year and was raised to the dignity of the diaconate. Because of his youth and inexperience, he entered upon this office with anxiety, he who even then was capable of discharging the

office of a Christian bishop. He to whom the whole city
turned its gaze as to the standard of salvation modestly
avoided the eyes of all. Meanwhile, Bishop Crispinus committed to Epiphanius the entire disposition of the episcopal
revenues assigned to the support of the clergy and church
buildings and to the maintenance of the poor, wishing to
know in advance what kind of a bishop he was preparing
to be his successor. And, although it rarely happens that
one is wholly free from envy toward those whom he even
slightly suspects of being in line to succeed him, the holy
father [Crispinus] considered as loss to himself any failure
to give due praise to his disciple. But the disciple, in his daily
advance in perfection, had surpassed even the desires of his
father asking much for him in prayer. For he was a father
who, filled with the seed of the divine word, had begotten
him, conceived through the Gospel.[4] What, then, shall I
say of the modesty of this youth? In him chastity had taken
up its abode and continence had fixed deep its roots. He
knew that he was man only through the endurance of labor
and fatigue; he knew that he had a body only when he recalled that he would die. And as he has told me himself,
as often as the sensual appetite allured him with its images
and reveries, he straightway had most zealous recourse to
holy vigils, prolonged fasts, and exceedingly long and fati-
guing periods of standing. And in conflicts between spirit and
flesh, the warrior right hand of his soul reduced his body to
such a state that aid had to be given it. And when the body
had been revived, he allowed it no rest. His rest and his
recreation were the reading of Sacred Scripture. What he
had read through once he repeated from memory. So that
his reading of Holy Scripture might not be a mere rapid running through the words, he portrayed in his acts the passage

4 Cf. 1 Cor. 4.15.

that he had read. If he had read a book of the Prophets, one saw him, having set aside the book, transformed from reader into prophet. If he had read the books of the ancient law,[5] he proceeded, a worthy emulator of Moses, just as if bands of Israelites were following him through the desert. Or if his Scriptural guide, tempering the severity of the Law, had revealed the sweetness of the Apostle's words and the love and tenderness of Christ's passion, speech sweeter than the honeycomb immediately flowed from his lips. In fine, his life made manifest the lessons he had learned from the Sacred Scriptures.

Epiphanius, meanwhile, so administered the ecclesiastical household that he neither exhausted by prodigality the substance entrusted to him nor by stinginess drew odium upon himself. He prepared himself even then in the art of mediation. Whenever his bishop sent him to secure help for the needy and oppressed, so successfully and skillfully did his plea exact the desired favor that many considered it to their advantage that the bishop himself had not come. Day by day, with each successful enterprise, the love and esteem of the people for him increased. Without desiring the death of the bishop, they were eager to see his deacon invested with the episcopal dignity. But Epiphanius himself had not the least suspicion of all this. For him, to render service deserving of commendation was sufficient advancement. When old age, weak and querulous in its infirmities, laid hold of the venerable Bishop Crispinus, the hands of his disciple fed him; the supporting arms of his disciple held him when he stood. To him, Epiphanius was foot, eye, and right hand; what he wished to be done he saw already finished before he had given the order, for good servants anticipate the desires of those to whom they render whole-hearted service. Such was

---

5 The Pentateuch.

Epiphanius at the completion of the eight years of the diaconate, which he had entered upon at the beginning of his
twentieth year. And, indeed, in those days the Church at
Ticinum was rich in good and worthy clerics. They were
saintly men whom he, perfect from the beginning, surpassed.
Sylvester, the archdeacon at that time, was a man well instructed in the ancient disciplines. There was the outstanding priest, Bonosus, celebrated for his sanctity as well as for
his descent, a Gaul by birth but a native of heaven. There
were others, many in number and outstanding in virtue, of
whom I make no mention, since he who is preferred only to
those of little worth merits faint praise.

Toward the end of his life, which he foresaw in spirit, the
holy Bishop Crispinus betook himself to the neighboring city
of Milan, where celebrated ancestors had produced a harvest,
as it were, of sincere and noble sons. And when these had
come together to see him, the man of God addressed them
as follows: 'See, my sons, old age now forces me to my
passing; now the earth reclaims this little particle, once
hers. To you I commend the city, to you I commend the
Church, to you I commend him, thanks to whose labor and
kindness, I, aged and weak, have lived as long as I have,
whose unwearying strength of body and virtue of soul have
supported me in my weakness, with whose feet I have walked,
with whose hands I have grasped, with whose eyes I have
seen and through whose lips I have given my directions. We
seemed two to those who saw us, but unity of heart made us
one.'

These words made a profound impression on the eminent
Rusticius, who, being excellently trained in every manner
of speech, began thus: 'We know, holy father, we know and
with deep admiration have observed that the worth of this
young cleric of yours is not to be reckoned from the im-

maturity of his years and that, for men of serious thought, his youth should not present an obstacle [to his elevation to the episcopal dignity]. For, maturity and integrity of character are doubly commendable in a man in whom a youthful body subserves the commands of a mature intellect. But, do thou live; live, and, as an example and model of good works, produce in him still greater fruits of holy living, if there be yet room for increase.' These words spoken, he was silent. Then the saintly bishop thanked Rusticius for the favor he had shown him in recognizing, as he did, the worth of his disciple, and, saying farewell, he departed and returned to Ticinum, hastening, as it were to his sepulchre. A few days later, stricken with jaundice, he exchanged the light of this world of ours for an eternal dwelling.

Straightway, all the prominent citizens agreed upon Epiphanius as the bishop's successor, and in the city a great crowd assembled. They snatched Epiphanius from the lamentation of the funeral and led him away to be consecrated. He mourned deeply for the death of his father, to whom the joyful multitude did not suffer him to render a due tribute of tears. He resisted in so far as he could, crying out that he was not worthy to tread in the footsteps of the Apostles. But the fact that, in that great crowd of people, he was alone in proclaiming his unworthiness served but to increase the love and esteem of all for him. But, what need for further details? Neighboring cities joined in the enthusiasm, and so great a throng assembled that one would think he were being consecrated bishop of the whole world. They led him to Milan, still resisting and promising great rewards for his release—he who would not have promised the least in order to attain the dignity. In the presence of all that vast crowd he was consecrated. The world took pride in the marvels of that holy consecration. The inhabitants of other cities rejoiced as if he who received the sacerdotal fillets were to be their own bishop. But gnawing envy consumed some who dwelt in the large cities because little Ticinum had merited to have so worthy a bishop while they had bishops whose sole claim to distinction was the ostentatious title of metropolitan.

The day of his consecration past, Epiphanius returned to Ticinum, and, calling together all his priests and deacons, he instructed and exhorted them as follows: 'Beloved brethren, although my youth and inexperience make me feel keenly the burden of the dignity of which you have deemed me worthy, I am not mindful that you have conferred upon me a very great honor, for which I should be grateful. My pleasure would have been rather to obey than to be obeyed, and although, in consequence of my office, I have discarded the role, I have not lost the spirit of him who serves. Be peaceful, be united; share with me my burden, for a burden that rests upon the shoulders of many is easily borne. In all humility I promise to preserve peace and harmany with you and to take offense at nothing save what offends God. Cherish modesty, the source of every virtuous act. And do not take it amiss that I, a youth, exhort you who are advanced in years and who are priests to preserve chastity and continence; for how one lives, not how long he has lived, reveals whether he is young or old.[6] Search into my inner life and reprimand what you find there unworthy of a bishop. Let no one fear to admonish me, a bishop of the church, if he find fault in me.' Then he was silent, and all arose and in unison, as if from long deliberation —but in reality on the inspiration of the moment—responded: 'Hail, most virtuous father; hail, singular bishop. Your unanimous election was a declaration of your goodness, but your own words are proof of a goodness that is unequaled.

---

6 Cf. Wisd. 4.8-9.

We constantly become more aware of your sanctity, and your conduct shows you to be even more worthy than public opinion has made you.' After these few words, each received his charge and departed.

Soon, the holy bishop drew up for himself laws by which to put a check on nature. First, he determined not to bathe, lest the public baths, haunts especially attractive to the rabble, might diminish his purity of heart and dissipate his inner strength. Then, he had resolved never to take lunch, but, lest the stricter fast of others bring dishonor to his resolve and make it appear as either a groundless boasting or a yielding to gluttony, he determined never to take dinner, so that thus he would take nourishment but once in the course of the day. He forced himself to be content with mean fare. Nothing in the dishes prepared for him was offensive to his sense of smell except what was seasoned with spices. His repast consisted of greens and vegetables—but of neither did he take sufficient. Mindful of the words of the Apostle, he took a 'little wine for his stomach's sake.'[7] He resolved that he would, in all seasons howsoever inclement, arrive at the church enough in advance of the others to point out the form of matins to the lectors and that, once he had approached the confines of the altar, nothing—however urgent—would draw him away before the completion of the office. To its very end, he determined to stand with feet so joined as with their moisture to mark out his place and make it visible even from a distance. He resolved that, in the defense and protection of the needy, he would consider himself personally responsible for any injury which his negligence had allowed anyone to inflict upon them. In time of tranquility, he prepared his body for the patient bearing of suffering in adversity. This rule of life—or system of discipline—he drew

7 1 Tim. 5.23.

up for himself, entered upon, persevered in, and fulfilled perfectly.

Rumor, which is generally somewhat laggard in spreading abroad the fame of good deeds, did not remain silent about Ticinum's bishop, but, proclaiming his saintliness to the whole world, soon brought knowledge of him to Ricimer, who at that time governed the state with an authority second only to that of the emperor, Anthemius. When the emperor was at Rome, envy, which sets at variance those who rule, and equality of power, which engenders discord, sowed the seeds of hostility between those two. So great was their anger and disagreement that they were making preparations for war. And not only did the cause of their enmity provide its own stimuli, but the supporters of each abetted the quarrel by their counsel. Italy tottered and threatened to collapse, while the prospect of the trials yet to come increased the burden of the woes it was then bearing. Meanwhile, the prominent citizens of Liguria gathered before the patrician Ricimer, then residing at Milan, and on bended knees and with bowed heads they begged that the two leaders live at peace with each other and that one of them take the first steps toward a reconciliation and thus put an end to the quarrel. What more shall I say? The tears of those many men appeased and deeply touched Ricimer, and he promised that he would do what he could toward restoring peace. 'But,' he said, 'who will assume the burden of this embassy? For whom can we reserve a task of such magnitude? Who is there who can bring to reason an irate Galatian, and him the emperor? For his wrath, knowing no moderation, ever renders all petition useless.' Then all in unison responded: 'Only give your assent to the peace; we have a man, recently raised to the episcopal see of Ticinum, whom even rabid beasts obey, who secures the favor he has come to seek even before he asks for it, whose countenance is the mirror of his life, whom every Roman Catholic would venerate, and the Greek Catholic certainly love were he to see him. If we consider the effectiveness of his words, the frenzied songs of a Thessalian wizard will never call forth dire serpents with the ease with which the intercession of Ticinum's bishop will extract the grant of a favor, even from those determined to refuse. When he begins to speak, his will determines the decision of his auditor. Given the opportunity to present his cause, he brings to naught any premeditated refusal of his request.' And the patrician Ricimer responded: 'Rumors have come to me concerning this renowned man whom you describe. While I marvel at his holiness, I marvel more at the fact that, according to report, he has only laudators and none of the detractors whom envy generally brings in abundance to one newly raised to a post of honor. Go, therefore, and ask the man of God to undertake the mission; add my petition to yours.' Leaving Ricimer, they straightway hastened to Ticinum and revealed their plight to Epiphanius. In tears they besought him to take upon himself this burden. And he, in order not to deprive his sons of the full benefit of his charity by allowing them to suffer the torment of long supplication, anticipated their request, addressing them thus: 'Although a task of such importance demands the mature judgment of a very experienced person and although one as inexperienced as I will totter under the weight, I shall not refuse to give this proof of affection which I owe to my country.' Being sparing of speech, he said these few words, and then proceeded to the patrician Ricimer, by whom he was no sooner seen than he was chosen to intercede with Anthemius.

Therefore, charged with the business of the embassy, he set out for Rome. Hurrying on to greater things, I pass over in silence the hardships that he endured on that journey and the virtues that he manifested. No sooner had he entered the gates of Rome than rumor, which had made him known even before his arrival, began to point him out; straightway, all eyes were turned to him and all hearts were filled with awe and wonder because his countenance, the mirror of his sanctity, inspired in them such reverence. Whoever of the potentates but embraced the bishop's knees recognized his own great sinfulness. A cry was raised to heaven.[8] No one reckoned him among mortals, in whom were manifest all the gifts of divine grace. They brought word to Anthemius that a bishop of Liguria had arrived on a mission, a man whom no one, howsoever eloquent, could adequately describe. To them the emperor responded: 'Cleverly does Ricimer contend with me even in his embassies; he sends men who can overcome by supplication those whom he provokes by injuries. However, bring the man of God to me. If it is at all possible, I shall grant his requests; if it is impossible, I shall ask him not to take offense at my refusal. But I doubt that Ricimer will obtain what he asks of me, for I know all too well how immoderate are his desires and how far beyond the limits of reason are the conditions he proposes. But let the bishop come at once and show to me that countenance whose praises I have long since heard.' All those employed in the imperial household then went forth to meet the bishop. 'Please, the emperor requests your presence,' the bishop heard them say.

And when the bishop, venerable and universally esteemed, had entered and had received the liberty to speak, the glory of his countenance cast into shadow the emperor's purple and gleaming gems—the insignia of fleeting power—drawing to itself the eyes of all, just as if the emperor himself were not there. Then, unsealing the portals of his lips, the bishop be-

8 Cf. Virgil, *Aeneid* 4.655; 11.878.

gan thus: 'Divine Providence has ordained that the governance of this powerful State be entrusted to you, who through
the teachings of the Catholic faith recognize God as the
author and lover of virtue; through His power, the arms
of peace break the fury of war; and concord, trampling on
the neck of pride, succeeds where strength fails. Thus, a
spirit of forgiveness, not of revenge, toward an enemy has
made David worthy of praise. So those who, in secular affairs, are excellent kings and masters have learned to be
godlike in granting indulgence to the suppliant. The ruler
whose charity sublimates his power possesses some likeness
to our heavenly King. Your Italy, relying on the truth of
what I have said—or, if you prefer, Ricimer relying on my
intercession—has sent me to you, convinced that a Roman
will grant as a gift to God the peace which even he, a barbarian, begs. To have conquered without bloodshed will be a
triumph which will bring special glory to the annals of your
reign. I know of no manner of war which will demand greater
courage than to contend against the irascibility of the fierce
Goth and to heap shame upon him by kindnesses. He who
until now considered it a disgrace to make supplication will
experience even greater shame if he obtain his request. Then,
too, you must consider that war will entail double losses for
you, since what both sides lose will be losses to your kingdom. On the other hand, whatever he holds intact you possess in common with him. Consider, also, that he who first
offers peace furthers his own best interests.'

At this point, the admirable bishop brought his speech to
a close. Then the emperor, looking up, saw that the eyes of
all were no longer upon him but were centered on that countenance, in admiration of which even he himself was absorbed.
Sighing deeply, he then began: 'O holy bishop, against Ricimer we have inexplicable cause for complaint; upon him we

have bestowed marked favors, all to no avail; we have even —not, I must confess, without dishonor to our sovereignty, to our blood—made him a member of our family, yielding, in our devotion to the state, to what would bring opprobrium upon ourself. Who of my predecessors has even, in order to assure peace and security to his people, included his daughter among the gifts that he will concede to the skin-clad Goth? In our concern for a stranger, we have spared not even our own daughter. But, let no one think that in this action we have been prompted by any fear for our own person; so great has been our care for the general welfare that we have known no fear for self. We know well that the emperor who has experienced no anxiety for the security of others sacrifices his claim to valor. But, in order to make clear to your reverence his intentions, we tell you that the more frequent and the greater the gifts we have bestowed upon Ricimer, the more frequent and the more violent his hostility toward us. What destructive wars he has prepared against the state! What hostility and violence he has stirred up against it among foreign peoples! Finally, where he could do us no injury, he planned ways and means of harming us. Shall we grant peace to this man? Shall we endure him who, while being of our household and wearing the garb of friendship, is an enemy whom neither the bonds of amity nor of kinship have held to his pace? It is an effective precaution against an enemy to have recognized him as such. To have sensed an enemy immediately is to have conquered him; hatreds when detected always lose the stimuli they possessed while hidden. But if, in this affair, your reverence come as both bondsman and mediator—you who by a supernatural power can uncover and correct wicked designs—I dare not refuse the peace which you, too, ask. But if his native cunning has deceived even you, let him, now wounded, begin the combat.

In any event, I entrust and commend to your hands myself and the welfare of the state, and through you I grant to Ricimer the favor which I had determined to refuse, even though he begged it prostrate before me. If, in the uncertainties of storm, we direct our ship of state in accordance with the orders of a skilled pilot, we very wisely look to our own advantage. For, who would dare to refuse you asking a favor which should have been granted even before you asked.' Thus the emperor spoke. And the venerable bishop said: 'Thanks be to God almighty who has given His peace to the heart of the emperor, through whom He has willed that His power be exercised among men after the manner of its exercise in heaven.'

When he had spoken these few words and had received from Anthemius an oath in confirmation of the peace, Bishop Epiphanius departed and hastened to return to Liguria, because the time of Christ's Resurrection was drawing nigh, which restores warmth and joy to bodies grown cold and lean with fasting and nourishes the faithful soul with the food of hope, while our Redeemer dying conquers death. He left Rome on the twentieth day before Easter and accomplished the journey with such rapidity that on the fourteenth day he entered Ticinum, unannounced and unexpected, and also unaccompanied by many of those who had set out with him but had been unable to bear the deprivations and fatigue of that journey. And the people, eagerly awaiting the return of their bishop, thronged about him. They saw him already home when they had not yet heard of his departure from Rome. The rejoicing of the happy city came to the ears of Ricimer; all were crying out together that peace had been made. The joy of the provinces was boundless. And as it is characteristic of men to be more grateful for what they have recovered than for what they have never lost, so doubly sweet to the Ligurians was the restoration of that peace of which they had already practically despaired. The Milanese, who had long awaited the bishop's return, summoned him to their city, but he, not wishing to seem by his presence to be seeking expressions of gratitude as his due, found excuse to decline their invitations.

And so, as time advanced, the accomplishment of each day's labor brought an increase of merit to Ticinum's bishop. He had a sister, younger than he in years but his equal in holiness, Honorata by name. It would take long to enumerate her virtues individually. However, to say that she was a worthy sister of such a man is sufficient praise. He consecrated her in the same year in which he returned from that diplomatic mission. Then, desiring even greater holiness in his sister, he entrusted her for instruction in the heavenly disciplines to a certain Luminosa, a woman of marvelous sanctity and exemplary life, of whose noble birth I should perhaps have had to make mention, had she not been more illustrious in her life than in her lineage. Such was she that he who was entrusting his sister to her guidance felt that he, too, could learn from her. Under Luminosa's direction, the bishop's sister blossomed and brought to maturity a rich spiritual life. Meanwhile, the venerable bishop advanced rapidly on the path of life he had traced out for himself. In his ever-constant distribution of alms, a kindly countenance and manner so increased the value of the alms that, had he offered to someone but a friendly word unaccompanied by any gift, that one would not feel that he was departing giftless. Even to have seen such a bishop was an inestimable privilege. Day by day, glorious victories increased his renown and filled almost the entire world with his praises.

Then, after the death of Ricimer and also of Anthemius, Olybrius succeeded to the throne, but died at the very beginning of his reign. Glycerius followed Olybrius, and, for the sake of brevity, I shall omit mention of the many measures he took to secure the safety and well-being of his people. In reverence for the saintly Bishop Epiphanius, he surpassed even his predecessor, for, in answer to the bishop's intercession, he pardoned an injury done to his own mother by some of his subjects. Nepos succeeded Glycerius. Between him and the Getic sons of Toulouse, whom King Euric governed with iron hand, dissension arose, since they, scorning the new emperor, incessantly encroached upon the boundaries of the Italian Empire. Nepos, on his part, by a more strenuous defense of the bounds set by God to his realm, strove to prevent these bold and destructive incursions from becoming habitual. Hence incentives to discord began to multiply on both sides, and since pride born of the desire for victory kept its hold on both, the cause of discord was prevailing.

The saintly Epiphanius had now reached the eighth year of his episcopate, when there suddenly entered the heart of Nepos a sincere desire to end the existing dissension and, with deadly distrust banished, to perserve by friendship with Euric what he could not protect with arms. He called a gathering of the leading men of Liguria, men of mature judgment, in consultation with whom he could devise a means of infusing new life into the languishing state and of restoring it to its earlier stability a task which until now had seemed hopeless. At the order of the emperor, all who had any solution to offer assembled to consider the question. The discussion turned to the organization of an embassy; straightway, the thoughts and eyes of all were directed to the saintly Epiphanius, and his election was as unanimous as if it issued from the lips and heart of a single man. What need of more? With joy the soldier of Christ embraced the opportunity of bearing this burden and hopefully anticipated its outcome; in view of the difficulty of the undertaking, he made inquiries in order to improve his method of procedure; then, with divine assistance, he undertook and brought to completion a negotiation almost impossible in its difficulty. The trials and vicissitudes of that journey I could not relate in detail, not even if channels watered by a hundred rivers of tongues were to pour words upon me.[9] For, from the time he left Ticinum until he reached his destination, he was ingenious in doubling for himself the fatigue of that journey. When from time to time, to rest the weary pack animals, they drew up to the inn at an appointed halting place, in addition to continuous recitation of the psalms and perseverance in reading —both of which he always did standing—he sought a recess enclosed by leafy trees whose interwoven branches afforded a kindly obscurity impervious to the sun's rays, where on nature's couch of green turf he prostrated himself in prayer and, pouring forth a flood of tears, made fertile the ground which, deprived of natural rains, was of itself sterile.

Weakened by such practices, he entered the city of Toulouse, in which King Euric was then residing. The news of his sanctity, having preceded him, had come to the ears of the Gauls, especially of the priests in that region, whom it filled with amazement and deep curiosity concerning the new arrivals. Leo, at that time the moderator and arbiter of the king's council, whose eloquence had already carried off more than once the prize in declamation, joyfully proclaimed to all the arrival of Bishop Epiphanius. At once, the king summoned the bishop to his presence, who, when he had come before the monarch, looked at him, greeted him, and addressed him thus: 'O awe-inspiring prince, although the fame of your might renders your name terrifying to the ears of many and although the swords with which you constantly

---

9 Virgil, *Aeneid* 6.625-627.

devastate neighboring lands cut down a harvest, as it were, of your enemies' sons, no blessing from above accompanies your cruel desire for war, nor, if you do what offends God, will the sword suffice to protect your domain. Remember that you, too, are subject to a Sovereign whose pleasure you must consider, who, when He was about to carry up to heaven the human nature that He had assumed, left, in that oft-repeated admonition, peace to His disciples as a great inheritance.[10] Of His precepts we must be the guardians, especially when we know that no man can be called strong whom anger has overcome. Then, it is also well for us to consider that he most effectively defends his own possessions who does not covet another's. Wherefore, Nepos, to whom Divine Providence has committed the governance of Italy, has commissioned me to bring about a restoration of mutual trust and a union in the bonds of charity of your adjoining realms. He does not fear battle, but he is eager above all for peace. You know, as well as we, how extensive was the domain of the former emperors; you know with what patient subjection the people of the regions lost to the empire have borne their new rulers. Let it suffice that he seeks, or at least is willing to be called friend, who ought to be called master.' Thus spoke the illustrious Epiphanius.

Then, Euric ceased to mumble in I know not what strange tongue, and the serenity of his countenance showed that the bishop's words had impressed him. And the marvellous speech of Epiphanius so charmed Leo, whom we have mentioned above, as to make him believe that with such words Ticinum's bishop could win any cause, even though, if one may say it, his demands be contrary to justice. They say, however, that the king answered as follows, through an interpreter: 'The cuirass scarcely ever leaves my breast, the shield of bronze,

10 Cf. John 14.27.

my hand, the protecting sword, my side; yet I have found
a man who with words can subdue me in all my armor. They
err who say that the Romans do not have shields, or better,
darts in their tongues, for they know both how to guard themselves from the words which we hurl against them and how
to drive deep into the heart those which they direct against
us. I shall, therefore, venerable father, do what you ask,
since you as ambassador carry more weight with me than
the power of him who sent you. Accept my pledge, then,
and promise in the name of Nepos that he will preserve intact this peace; for you, to have promised is to have taken
an oath.' Then, the truce concluded, the venerable bishop said
farewell and left the king's presence. Straightway, he received numerous requests to dine on the next day with the
king, but, since he had already heard that Euric's table was
polluted by the presence of his own priests,[11] he declined,
saying that it was not his custom to dine at the board of
another and that he planned to be on his way on the day
after the morrow. He hastened to act accordingly. And when
he set out from Toulouse, such a multitude followed him that
his departure seemed to leave the city almost deserted; so
great was the number of those whom he had bound to himself
by ties of sincere affection during that short time. And those
who could not accompany him but had to stay behind in
their native land lamented what they considered their captivity. On his way back to Ticinum, Bishop Epiphanius
visited the monastic centers along his way and on the inter-
jacent islands—the Stoechades, Leros, and that low-lying
rearer of lofty mountains,[12] Lerins. From each he plucked
certain blossoms of virtuous living, which, implanted within

---

11 They were Arians.
12 *Mons* (mountain) was frequently used by ecclesiastical writers to
   designate a bishop.

himself, might at the time of maturity produce a tree laden
with heavenly fruit. Meanwhile, the long-awaited return of
their bishop dispelled the darkness which had enveloped the
Italians and disclosed to them the sun once again shining
in a cloudless sky. Epiphanius entered Ticinum. He informed
Nepos of the success of the mission, but the multiplication of
his praises brought a corresponding increase in his humility.

While the servant of Christ our God was exercising himself in mortifications and labors such as these we have mentioned above, Satan, that ever-active perpetrator of evil,
multiplied the bishop's sorrows and sought means whereby
to afflict the holy man with sufferings. Secretly sowing the
seeds of discord, he raised up an army against the patrician
Orestes. He roused in wicked hearts the desire to revolt and
inspired in Odovacar the ambition to rule; in order to bring
ruin to Ticinum, he invited Orestes to that city with a promise of protection. The bishop remained there with his flock.
Within the city gathered vast hordes, inflamed with a mad
lust for plunder. Everywhere grief, everywhere fear, everywhere death, under many guises![13] One who formerly had
too freely disclosed his wealth to trusted friends, now seeking
to escape the penalty of that rashness, ran from place to place
in wild alarm. Some applied flame to edifices on the verge
of toppling over; others clamored for the death of a master
for whose safety they should have fought. Wholly aflame
with the frenzy of plunder, they rushed to the bishop's house,
suspecting that he whom they saw so generous in dispensing
alms had a hidden treasure. For shame! The rude barbarians
sought on earth treasures that he had transferred to heaven's
coffers. They even seized the bishop's holy sister and led her,
a captive, away from him. Captivity separated the members
of every prominent family; the glorious Luminasa suffered

13 Cf. Virgil, *Aeneid* 2.368-369.

a similar misfortune. Alas! They burned both churches; the whole city glowed, as if it were a funeral pyre. One heard the voices of all crying for their bishop. No one was mindful of his own peril while he was without assurance of the safety of that one in whom rested his own greatest security. That turbulent mob which clamored for the extermination of all showed, even in the midst of swords, such esteem for Ticinum's bishop that soon there were no captives to be seen. He rescued his saintly sister before the light of that sad day declined into evening, and his petition liberated many of the citizens before they experienced the sad lot of servitude, above all, mothers of families, for whom it would be even more terrible to remain long in that state. Finally, Ticinum, though still subject to barbarian vandalism, began to rise, supported by one strong pillar, and a hostile army was less effective in destroying the city than the person of one bishop was in restoring it. Moreover, after Orestes had been carried off and slain at Placentia, the impetus to plunder subsided.

Orestes was succeeded by Odovacar, who surpassed his predecessors in showing reverence and favor to Bishop Epiphanius. Meanwhile, so that God's house would no longer lie buried in ashes, the bishop set himself to the task of restoration, even before he had made any provision for securing the needed funds and materials, mindful of the apostolic admonition that for those who seek the kingdom of God there is ever at hand an inexhaustible wealth,[14] the fullness of which he shares whose generosity poverty does not restrict. For he was wont to say: 'It rarely happens that a man of generous heart has not enough to share with others, and scarcely, if ever, that a man of niggardly spirit has more than is sufficient for himself.' And, now, the work on the larger

---

14 Cf. Luke 12.31.

church had reached completion and the building had been consecrated, when, suddenly, the machinations of the wily Serpent caused the walls of the other church to collapse. For he wished to see if his multiple vexations could divert the bishop from his purpose. But the latter, in order not to yield to the wiles of the Evil One, straightway and without any show of perturbation, diligently and zealously set about the task of restoration. Then occurred a miracle which held the whole city in wonderment: when a heavy scaffolding with workmen upon it fell from the very vault of the larger church, not one of them received injury to limb or any other member. All were convinced that is was due to the bishop's prayers that the shattered vault sustained its own weight and did not come crashing down upon the workmen. Under the bishop's amazing direction, the restoration of the second church now reached completion, and he turned again to the larger church. Suddenly, before the people were even aware that work on the church had been begun, they saw it completely restored. Soon after Bishop Epiphanius had finished rebuilding the churches, divine grace manifested itself in him. In the course of that same year, a great multitude of demons began to cry out that, at Bishop Epiphanius' command, they were being forced with lashes and extreme tortures to leave the bodies they possessed. And he, having uttered a brief tearful prayer, by the power of his merits, drove them howling to the furthest confines of the earth. And, although he was constantly working miracles such as the above through God's grace, he did not presume to take any credit to himself for them. For those who take pride in their good works lose then their merit.

In the meantime, lest it seem that he had adorned the city only with church buildings, he set himself to the task of improving the conditions of the ruined inhabitants of the city.

Through a diplomatic mission sent to Odovacar, he obtained for his people a five-year exemption from the fiscal tax. In the distribution of these benefits, no one received less than he through whose intercession they had been secured. Meanwhile, the pent-up malice of Pelagius, the praetorian prefect at that time, burst forth, bringing ruin to the landowners of Liguria; by his excessive coemptions he doubled the tribute, placing two burdens on shoulders too exhausted to bear one. Soon, therefore, a multitude of the oppressed flocked to the holy man. He joyfully embraced this opportunity of helping them; he went quickly, asked and obtained for all the needed relief. But, why do I waste time in relating the manner and nature of his labors, for affection infers what cannot be expressed, and a restriction of the narrative checks him whose imagination may wonder too far abroad. Moreover, the holy bishop, although his laudable deeds were innumerable, desired little, if anything, to be said in their praise. Therefore, I leave to my hearers and readers to supply what I in my poverty of speech have omitted.

Persistent supplication had already required the sending of numerous envoys to the court of Odovacar when, by divine disposition, King Theodoric entered Italy with a great host of followers. When he had established himself at Milan, our noble bishop hastened to him. And when the excellent king had scrutinized our bishop with the eyes of his heart and when he weighed him, as was his custom, in the balance of his judgment, he found a weight of every virtue in him whose integrity he measured with the plumb-line of his mind. And thus the king described him to those present: 'Behold a man, the like of whom the whole Orient does not possess. To have seen him is a privilege; to live with him is security. While he lives, the city of Ticinum possesses a rampart which no siege machine can destroy nor missile from Balearic sling surmount. In the dangers of war, one can, if need be, safely entrust mother and family to his keeping and, relieved of concern for them, enter battle.'

Meanwhile, a desire to shift their allegiance burned in the hearts of the surrendered army, whose leader Tufa was already stigmatized by the disgrace of his earlier base desertion. He now conceived in his wicked heart the plan of rejoining with his army the faction that he had abandoned as lost. When King Theodoric, with royal foresight, had perceived Tufa's intention, he immediately gathered within the narrow limits of Ticinum that vast horde of his followers, whom the entire Orient could scarcely maintain. One saw the city teeming with family groups and the heads of great houses forced to take shelter in narrow huts. One saw immense buildings crowded to the point of starting from their very foundations, while not even the ground itself sufficed to receive that dense population. In these circumstances, the ever-zealous and charitable bishop, whose great heart was open to all, felt that the time was ripe to unfurl the sails of his bounty to the wind's favoring blast and to attain the part of glory by letting various peoples experience the benefits of his charity. During those trying days, when fear of imminent danger made even gentle hearts hostile and suspicious, he so dwelt with a shrewd people, susceptible to the least breath of suspicion, that, while remaining entirely loyal to them, he at the same time held their enemies bound to him by strong bonds of affection. He alone enjoyed peace with both of the warring kings, an achievement the like of which is not to be found in any of the ancient annals or writings, and which one relates with wonderment or reads with admiration. What the bishop received from the one he applied to the needs of the other, and the reverence which his person inspired and his gentleness so tempered the heart

of the giver that he felt no resentment when, through the
bishop, his enemy became his beneficiary. Bishop Epiphanius
was a man in regard to whose virtue even enemies agreed
and whose peace wars did not disturb. Daily, in his charity,
he fed the very despoilers, furnishing within the city the
necessities of life to those who had ceaselessly wasted and
pillaged his lands outside the walls. He met the needs of those
many thousands of individuals, at one and the same time
comforting them with words of encouragement, humbling
them with reprimands, and nourishing them with his gifts.
Children and wives seized in a hostile incursion by either
faction, although gold could not have redeemed them, were
straightway restored to their families at the price of the
bishop's prayer. So great was his reverence for the Bishop
of Ticinum, whom he knew he could enrich only by the release of captives, that King Theodoric restored to him the
Romans whom the license of war had made prisoners of his
men. I could not tell how many captive bands he restored
to their native soil, how many he protected from oppression.
And were I to recount the insults he bore from enemies, the
vexations under which he labored, the courage with which
he defied the violent attacks of the wicked—the tongue would
not suffice to relate these. Under such a cross, he passed five
years, revealing his hidden sorrows to God alone, whom he
begged to aid him in secret.

Then, after the departure of the Goths, the city of Ticinum
fell to the Rugians, men of excessive cruelty, whose unbridled
passions so goaded them to daily acts of violence that they
considered the day lost which, by some chance, they had
passed without the perpetration of a crime. But the holy
bishop so tempered them by the gentleness of his speech that
their cruel hearts became willing subjects to his authority
and learned to love—hearts which had ever been dedicated

to hate. And his kindness, implanting in their impious hearts the seeds of affection, previously an unknown thing among them, transformed their innate perversity. Who would believe without great astonishment that the Rugians, who scarcely deigned to render obedience to their own kings, loved and feared a bishop who was both a Catholic and a Roman? Yet, having lived with him two years, they wept when they left Ticinum to return to their kinsmen and homes.

When the state had emerged from that sad and destructive war, and when Theodoric had conquered—after whose victory no one saw an unsheathed sword—then the bishop immediately turned his attention to the restoration of his city and with prudent deliberation considered how he could fill it as soon as possible with worthy inhabitants. Although, thanks to his prayers, no tempest of those turbulent times had brought complete desolation to the city, he felt that, after the ruin of all the cities of Liguria, Ticinum should not rest so selfishly satisfied in the possession of only its native inhabitants. And so, like a diligent cultivator, he began to gather certain flowers of the citizenry of neighboring cities and to bring to his own gardens good plants, as it were, from which he would gather fruit in season.

Meanwhile, the excellent King Theodoric suddenly decided to allow the rights and priviliges of Roman citizenship only to those who had proved their loyalty by joining his faction. Those who for any reason had not supported his cause he ordered to be deprived of the right of giving testimony and of receiving or disposing of property by will. This law, when put into effect, trampled on the rights of many and placed all Italy under a deplorable suspension of justice. Again the people had recourse to him whose healing hand had been accustomed to bring relief to public wounds and whose kindness had often allayed the intensity of their griefs. And when

Bishop Epiphanius said that he did not feel able to bear so heavy a burden alone, they asked Laurence, Bishop of Milan, to assist him. And so the two set out from their respective cities, reached Ravenna at the same time, and were received will all courtesy and respect. And when the king gave them the liberty to present their cause, blessed Laurence thought that Epiphanius should be the one to speak, whose feet the laborious trail of many a mission had wearied, and whom, hurrying on errands such as this, the dust of the camp had more than once befouled. And so, Epiphanius thus began: 'O ever-victorious king, were I to pass in review the innumerable successes by which divine favor has promoted your prosperity, you would see that you, sparing in vows, have received from our God greater favors than you asked. It will suffice to mention only one—but the greatest—of these favors, namely, that we now plead the cause of your subjects before you as master on the spot where your adversary was wont to rejoice in the possession of this throne. You have much for which you are indebted to Christ, our Redeemer; He has given to you those for whom we now intercede. We must take care not to offend the giver of a gift by not cherishing what he has given us. I have long refrained from what I shall now presume to say. I wish to recount one by one all the triumphs that have been yours with God's help—those I know from hearsay and those I have seen. You know the promises that you made when you were hard pressed by the dense battle lines of the enemy and when the shrill blast of the enemy's trumpet sounded round about the walls of narrow Ticinum. You know what you promised when, assisted by no other ally than an invisible power from on high, you were able to resist your adversaries, superior to you in numbers and in arms. The enemy, estimating the strength of your armies only by what he saw, dared to attack you, but all

his machines of war availed nothing against the strength of
your auxiliaries. How often has the very weather contributed to your success; if you recall, serene skies have fought
for you and, in answer to your prayer, dark skies have released their torrents. How often have your adversaries been
slain by the poniards of their colleagues? How often has one
unwittingly conquered for you while striving for the advantage of the enemy? For these divine favors let your charity
make return. Not to scorn the tears of suppliants is to make
a whole burnt offering. Consider the monarchs you have succeeded—what sort were they? If, as we know, their wickedness led to their expulsion, then you who have followed them
should learn from their fall. The failures of those who have
gone before teach those who come after; the downfall of
a predecessor is a warning to his successor. He does not contend without a model who looks back to see what brought
the expulsion of his predecessor. Your Liguria, therefore, prostrate with us, entreats that as you extend to the innocent
the benefits of your laws so, likewise, you absolve the guilty.
Before our God, it is but scant mercy to exempt from punishment only the guiltless. To forgive wrongs is divine; to avenge
them, human.' Then he was silent.

And then the most renowned of kings began, and, as he
spoke, fearful anticipation of his decision contracted the
hearts of those who heard him: 'Although, O venerable bishop, I entertain toward you an esteem proportionate to your
merits and although your kindnesses to me in times of distress have been many—the fruit of which you ought to enjoy now that peace has been restored—yet the restrictions
placed upon one who rules leave nowhere an opening for the
mercy which you advocate. Moreover, in the dangers to a
rising power, the need of severe measures tends to crush all
gentleness and compassion of heart. The testimony of Scrip-

ture supports my assertion. We read that a sovereign sinned who spared an enemy appointed by heaven to be slain; upon him leniency brought the penalty which his severity should have inflected upon another.[15] He who refuses to take vengeance, himself becomes its victim; he who, having an enemy in his power, pardons him, either makes light of or despises the weight of God's judgment. Rightly do they suffer punishment who have done wrong. He who pardons present faults transmits them to posterity. As for what you say concerning the patience of our Redeemer—mercy and grace embrace those whom the severity of the law forms. Never has a doctor restored a sick man to perfect health without first cutting away the putrid members and drawing out the filth hidden deep within. He who lets the guilty go unpunished urges the innocent to commit crimes. But, since mere mortals cannot resist your prayers, to which heaven gives assent, we extend pardon to all. Guilt shall bring death to no one, since you can obtain from our God that wicked hearts abandon their perverse ways. Some few, however, whom we know to have been instigators of dissension, we shall not permit to remain where they now dwell, so that, should rebellion arise by chance, it will not find abettors at hand in them whose impunity may become the source of wars.' Thereupon, the excellent king sent for the distinguished Urbicus, who, in managing the general affairs of the palace, had surpassed Cicero in eloquence and Cato in equity, and ordered him to draw up a decree of general amnesty. He, in his exceeding liberality, concisely and clearly drew up a decree which pardoned even those offenses generally understood to be reserved for punishment.

In the meantime, the excellent King Theodoric called aside the venerable Epiphanius and addressed him thus: 'O

15 Cf 1 Kings 15.3,8-9, 28.18.

glorious bishop, learn the extent of our esteem from our
choice of you as the one bishop among the many within the
circuit of our realm equal to the difficult mission which we
are imposing upon you. Nor does our esteem measure up to
your merits. And rightly have we chosen you who, like the
moon, surpassing in brilliance all lesser lights, casts them into
obscurity. Who seeks a night lamp when the sun shines bright?
Who, the aid of a candle, when a very fire of faith burns
with undiminishing flames? In fine, I must send to Gundobad a man whom he will rejoice to receive and will willingly heed. You see every region of Italy deprived of its
native inhabitants. It grieves me that once-productive plains
bring forth but thorns and wild plants and that Liguria, that
mother of a human harvest, whose progency of husbandmen
was wont to be so numerous, now childless and sterile, presents to our gaze but clods of barren earth. The land, where-
ever I look back upon its once-rich vineyards, chides me
while uncombed by the plow, it grows sad. Oh, grief! Not
even a drop of wine moistens the lips of those whom antiquity called Oenotrians, from the abundance of the vine.
Although this sad state of Liguria is the work of the cruel
Burgundian, we, too, share in the guilt if we take no steps
to remedy the situation. Shall we fail to help our ruined
country while we keep gold stored up in our coffers? What
difference whether we bend the will of an enemy by money
or by the sword? To have offered to an enemy what his
heart desires is to have conquered him; to have kept it hidden is to bring defeat upon oneself. With Christ's help, therefore, accept the burden of this mission. From it, may we both
receive in heaven the promised rewards. For us to conquer
our assailants through your hands without bloodshed will
be a new title to glory. Their king, Gundobad, is very eager
to see you whom he has long revered. Believe me, the sight

of you will be the ransom price of the Italian captives. If you go to those parts as redeemer, I shall consider the redemption accomplished and my wish fulfilled. With what great admiration will he to whom we are sending you be filled! But, why do I delay to give the fields the laborers they beg? I promise you that Liguria will live again. I promise that your transalpine pilgrimage will mean the return of happiness and fecundity to the soil. From the gold that we have at hand, you may take what you deem necessary for the redemption of the captives.'

And Epiphanius, light of bishops, answered the king: 'Were it possible to express in words the great joy with which you have filled my heart, O venerable ruler, I should pour forth my gratitude in the spontaneous and continuous speech that your charity deserves. But tears, grief's daughters, to which excessive joy now gives birth, break in upon and check my words. Know, then, that, when I return thanks to the best of kings, my feeling of gratitude will far exceed its expression. Shall I recall first your justice, or your skill in warfare, or, what is greater than either of these, your clemency, a virtue in which you have surpassed all previous emperors? You have grounds for complaint against the leaders of our people, since you are redeeming those whom they very often permitted to be taken captive or even themselves reduced to servitude. Scripture gives us an example of singular praise when it extols David to the very skies because, having his enemy Saul in his power, he spared him, cutting off but the hem of his robe as evidence of both the opportunity that was his and of his loyalty.[16] Good God, how munificently will You reward the deed of this man who now negotiates for the liberation of so many oppressed souls, You who have exalted David for sparing the life of a single man! Hasten,

16 Cf. 1 Kings 24.4-13.

therefore, to bring to completion what you have begun and with happy heart make your oblation; ready as I am, spur me on so that no tardiness of mine may delay you in the offering of so acceptable a sacrifice. Christ, in so far as we can conjecture the outcome of the good work you have undertaken, will permit you to offer this holocaust through my hands. But I beg you in your clemency to permit me to have, as companion on this journey, Victor, Bishop of Turin, in whom is the perfection of every virtue. Accompanied by him and trusting in God, I promise you that our petitions will meet with no refusal.'

When the eminent king, having heard these words, had given his assent, the reverend bishop said farewell and departed. Straightway, the sum to be dispensed in the redemption of the captives was determined and given to Epiphanius, who then set out in all haste for Ticinum. Dull wintry March still held the rivers fettered in icy bonds while the snow-laden ridges of the Alps threatened destruction to any who dared to cross. But the warmth of faith overcomes the deadly cold and ice-covered passes. He whose steps God makes firm never loses his footing on the ice. And so, with all provisions made for the journey, he set out. Everything that one would expect to restrain him served but to spur him on; he begrudged even the little delay occasioned in taking nourishment. And when the way, fraught with perils, terrified his companions, he alone, attended by an unfaltering hope of eternal life, knew no fear in the midst of dangers. Meanwhile, rumor, his ever-diligent precusor on the journey, went before him, giving to the Gauls so full an account of his virtues and miracles that they were as awe-struck as they would have been at the appearance of a divine being from on high. In eagerness to see Bishop Epiphanius, persons of all ages and sexes, even those who dwelt long distances from the road he was following, hurried to meet him. Whatever each had of value he presented to the bishop, and he who had no gift of worth to offer purchased one from another. Everywhere, he was received as in his native land with an outpouring of generosity. The travelers sat down to tables heaped high with unbought viands and enjoyed without expense foods which the inhabitants could secure only by purchase. To the needy whom he came upon, Bishop Epiphanius gave whatever he had received. Whether at home or abroad, he fed the poor; nothing that had been given to him could he be constrained to withhold from the needy.

Traveling in this manner, Epiphanius entered Lyons in a miraculously short time. Rusticius, who, even while holding secular magistracies, had displayed the qualities of a bishop and while wearing the garb of the forum had conducted himself as a pilot of the Church, was then bishop of that city. Filled with great spiritual joy, Rusticius hastened across the Rhone to meet Epiphanius, and, when he had inquired as to the purpose of his journey, forewarned him of the craftiness of King Gundobad. And, so that the cleverness of the king find him not wanting in objections or replies, Bishop Epiphanius strengthened himself for the combat by preliminary contests within the recesses of his own heart. When Gundobad, the king of that region, learned that the Bishop of Ticinum had arrived, he said to his attendants: 'Go and see this man whom in merit and in countenance I have ever associated with the martyr Laurence. Ask him when he desires to see us and set the audience in accordance with his pleasure.' Soon, all the Christians in the king's service gathered to see the bishop. They were amazed to discover that the glorious report of many-tongued rumor fell so far short of giving due praise to Epiphanius—that rumor, which in the case of others was ever ready with a store of praises far exceeding just measure, could not with words equal the bishop's glory. On the day set for his audience with the king, Epiphanius entered and greeted Gundobad. Each was happy to see the other. Then Epiphanius asked Victor if he wished to open the business of the mission, but Victor in his great humility declined, leaving the presentation of their cause entirely to Epiphanius.

Thereupon, our bishop, Italy's glory, addressed the monarch as follows: 'Ineffable love for you, O most upright sovereign, has compelled me by this journey to take up arms against nature and to brave the perils of ice-crusted mountains, whose waters, stiffened into ice, threaten disaster. In unseasonable months, I have traversed the snow-clad passes; I have trodden where the force of the cold held my feet bound in their tracks. Finally, I have not feared death in order to bring to you an opportunity to attain the reward of eternal life. I shall one day bear witness in heaven between two excellent monarchs whether you in your clemency grant what Theodoric in his mercy asks. Divide in equal parts the recompense which the Lord has promised, and both of you will experience an increase while neither will suffer loss. Strive, O unconquered princes, to surpass each other in conforming to the divine precepts. In such a contest, both victor and vanquished receive the palm. Follow my counsel and you will both be superior, both equal. He desires to redeem the captives; do you, without ransom, return them to their native soil. Believe me, in this transaction, no one will receive more abundantly than he who receives nothing. If you consent to release without ransom those whom even to release at a price would be laudable, you will deprive Theodoric of his part of the reward and transfer it to your account. If you return the gold which he offers, what a loss of the promised reward will it bring to him! If you

accept it, what poverty will it bring to you! The money, if
scorned, will enrich your armies; if accepted, will impoverish
them. Heed the prayers of the suppliant Italians and forbear
to grant the prayers of those who trust in you. Hear Italy,
which has never been separated from you, which reposes
great confidence in your clemency, and which, if it had a
voice, would say: "Do you remember how often for my sake
you have presented an iron-clad breast to the enemy, how
often you have fought for me by seeing that wars carry none
of my sons captive into other parts?" You yourself have
cared for those whom you now hold in servitude. That courage of yours, it seems to me, has offered a treacherous kindness if it has reduced to captivity those to whom it was
guardian and protector. What fettered captive would not
pour forth more copious tears for his sad lot, were it his liber-
ator who was reducing him to such a state? Who, when he
heard the clangor of your arms, would flee from you who
had been for him a secure refuge in times of danger? When
they dragged the noble matron, hands bound behind her
back, off to captivity, she promised herself that in you she
would have an avenger. The virgin believed that she would
displease you were she to violate her purity by yielding to
the will of the debaucher. In fine, they are captives whom
no one ever overtook in flight. These tireless sons of the soil,
men accustomed to ply the heavy mattock and to live in unfeigned simplicity on the produce of their land—these, although iron collars encircle their necks and tight fetters bind
their hands, cry out in their own defense nothing other than:
"We know you, we know you well; are you not our Burgundians? See that you do not excuse before the pious king
what you now do and conceal these outrages after the manner of city folk. How often have these hands which you dare
to bind paid tribute to our common master? We know that

he has not ordered you to do what you are doing." This con-
viction was a comfort to them in their misery; yet these and
like responses, prompted by trust in your integrity, being
considered too haughty for captives, brought death to those
who uttered them. Restore, then, to their fatherland those
who still survive; restore them to their families; restore them
to your glory. Do you, its former master, love that province
which even its new master cherishes. Send the captives back
to their homes, even though it be to the dominion of another;
even there they will know that they are yours. For we feel
little gratitude for the power of one to whose mercy we owe
nothing. Free that Liguria, which you know so well, from
briers, and fill it once again with cultivated fields. Once
Liguria recognizes it own features, it will know how much
it owes to your favor. It has ever been your custom to be
indulgent to the suppliant, severe to the proud. In either
case—in the former by moderation, in the latter by the sword
—your strength and courage will bring victory. Be moved by
our tears and those of our people. So may a legitimate heir
succeed you to this realm of yours, and may you live again
in the hope of a grown son who will rule the Burgundians.
Although you are making this gift to God, you should also
consider that the benefit of the gift which you offer does
not fall to strangers. For the king of Italy is now joined to
you by the very ties of kinship. Let the liberation of the
captives be your son's wedding gift to his spouse, a gift in
which Christ also may share.' When he had concluded thus,
Epiphanius arose, beckoning Victor to follow, and the two,
weeping, prostrated themselves before the king. And all who
were present wept, too.

Then the excellent king, a facile and eloquent orator, answered point by point as follows: 'You, as an advocate of
peace, know not the rights of war, and in bringing about

concord you eviscerate terms decided by the sword. What you consider wrong is law for those at war. Enmities know not, O bright star of Christianity, the restraint which you advocate. No one employs in battle the moderation which you, O excellent mediator, so beautifully extol. The law of those at war allows everything that would at other times be illicit. In times of peace, one might perhaps adopt measures such as you have suggested, but, in war, he who does not injure an enemy aids him. An enemy, the roots of whose power are successively cut off, gradually loses the bulk of his realm. What you consider an injury done by me to the king of those parts was but retribution. Mocked by the pretense of an alliance, I have done nothing more than take the ordinary precaution of recognizing open enemies. But, may heaven approve the peace now established between us and grant its long duration. Those lands will find me constant in friendship, whose destructive fury they have experienced in war. Now, holy men, depart to your residence, freed from anxiety. When I have considered by what means I can best promote the welfare of my soul and of my realm, I shall announce what concession I see fit to make.' At these words, the bishops withdrew.

Gundobad then summoned Laconius, to whom he always confided his words and his deeds with absolute security, and whose prestige was increased by illustrious ancestors, who not only held the curule magistracies but were conspicious for honesty in them. The king held conference with him as often as he contemplated some charitable or pious act, and, since the noble of character do not company with the base nor the virtuous with the vicious, Laconius, when consulted by the king, urged him to double the good he planned to do. 'Go, Laconius,' he said, 'unfurl the sails of your good desires. We willingly have heard the blessed Epiphanius, and tears, the soul's mirror, testified that his words moved you when he spoke before us. Go and with generous heart draw up the document which will sever the bonds of that cruel pact. With our consent, release without ransom all those Italians whom fear of servitude has made captives of our Burgundians, those whom hunger, destitution, and fear of danger have brought hither, and, finally, those whom their own king has given over or assigned to us by agreement. But, for the few whom our soldiers seized from their own adversaries in the heat of battle, as it were—for these let them receive some little payment, lest they conceive a repugnance for the hazards of battles, whose hardships they have borne without receiving the spoils.

In accordance with the order of the venerable king, Laconius promptly drew up a concise statement of the terms of the pardon and brought the document to the excellent bishop, who took it eagerly and embraced affectionately the bearer of so precious a gift. When word of the pardon had spread abroad, so great a multitude of liberated suddenly appeared in the city that one would think that the Gallic countryside had been deserted by its inhabitants. I speak of what I myself saw, for, at the order of the bishop, I brought to the fortresses the notices of release. On that one day, four hundred departed from Lyons alone to return to Italy. We know that the same thing also happened in all the cities of Savoy and of the other provinces. By prayer alone, that blessed bishop ransomed more than six thousand souls and restored them to their homeland. I could not learn the exact number of those redeemed by gold, for, even of those whose release was set at a price, many regained their freedom by flight. Thus, there was open to all the captives a sufficient opportunity of regaining their liberty and returning home. And, when the bishop had poured out the money given him by Theodoric, Syagria, the treasury of the Church in those regions, straightway provided for the needs of the redeemed. Her life is worthy of a detailed account, but it suffices to know her from her works, since they transcend all that words can say. Avitus of Vienne, most illustrious of the bishops of Gaul, in whom learning dwelt as in a splendid mansion, also contributed. What more? It was due in chief part to their gold that the youth of Liguria were no longer carried off to serve the Gauls. Nor did the great-souled Epiphanius confine himself to one locality within that region, lest, perhaps, that cruel master might not release those held in captivity in distant parts. He was at Geneva, where King Gundobad's brother Godigisclus, had his court; after consultation with his brother, Godigisclus made himself a companion in the good work. But, to be brief—so vast was the multitude of liberated returning to their homes that the roads seemed to swarm with them as they marched along praising God and the blessed Epiphanius, through whose intercession and labors they had been saved. And our saintly bishop came along with them so that, in this most beautiful of spectacles, his eyes might enjoy to the full the reward of his victory. There, one saw a freed people being led in a heavenly triumphal procession and the earth bathed, not in the blood of sacrificial victims, but with the tears of exultant men, when their leader, mounting the chariot of Elias, was carried aloft to heaven by his merit. Ticinum's bishop led back to their native land such a multitude of captives as never graced the triumphal march of Pella's prince, Alexander, whom vain praise has called the conqueror of the world. Lo, then did we see the hearts of warriors subdued by sanctity, and a king who feared not to face the hostile lance submissive to the prayers of a bishop. How much sharper was the blade of the tongue than that of the sword, learn, reader, from this: words van-

quished him whom swords protected. When, in the third
month, the bishop was returning to Ticinum with such a
trophy, he came to Tarantasia (this was the name of a town
situated in the neighborhood of the Alps). Here, a certain
woman, who suffered grievous vexation from an unclean
spirit, upon receiving the bishop's blessing, straightway departed freed from the affliction. And then Bishop Epiphanius
appeared all unexpectedly before his flock.

Now, returned to Ticinum, the bishop wearied himself
with concern for those to whom God had granted liberty
through his intercession, fearing lest they suffer from the loss
of their possessions. And he was especially concerned about
those of high station, whom, now restored to their homes,
an even harder lot awaited, were they to continue to bear
the want and sufferings of exile, having lost by their redemption even the comfort which pity brings. He did not wish
to present himself immediately to the invincible Theodoric,
lest he seem by his presence to be demanding a return for his
labor. For, a man who, after he has fulfilled the commands
of a ruler, reports in person what he has accomplished is,
as it were, claiming recompense as his due. Eager to avoid
any such conduct, the bishop wrote to the king, entrusting
to a letter the details of his mission to Gaul, thereby bringing upon himself neither the accusation of contempt by making no report, nor of vainglory by hastening to tell the king
what he had done. How much more, O admirable bishop,
your absence effected, how much more your humility, when
comprehended, demanded, let those say whom you transformed from exiles into wealthy men. At once, the worthy
bishop obtained from the pious king all that his letter requested for his needy flock. The king responded generously
to the bishop's appeal, who he knew would consider as

ample compensation for his labor whatever the redeemed and the poor received through his intercession.

Then, when by a concession of the worthy king all who had been redeemed had received just compensation, the admirable bishop thought that his many trials and labors had reached their end. But, two years had not yet passed when he was driven from the haven of his anticipated repose like a ship which the blast of a tempest drives with swelling sail from port. For, the Ligurians could scarcely support the heavy burden of tribute now placed upon their weak and drooping shoulders. Again to you, O consoler of the afflicted, they had recourse. They told you that you had restored them in vain to their fatherland, were you to fail to assist them now, endangered on their native soil. Their persistent supplication prevailed, and again you took upon yourself the cause of the oppressed and straightway prepared yourself for renewed labors. To intercede for us with the king, you hastened to Ravenna, whither you would not go after your successful mission to Gaul, lest anyone there might praise your work. Threatening skies and perilous tempests you overcame, as if you were still young and fortified by strength of limb. Your health, though feeble, never deterred you in your work for souls. Cold, rain, the Po, hunger, danger, thunder, roofless shelters, unsafe havens on flooded river banks—all these were delights to your virtue and stimuli to your progress. But the sight of you saddened the excellent king, much as he desired to see you. Even before you spoke, your very presence there disclosed our need, and the dangers that you had faced bore witness to the tears and prayers that had constrained you to undertake that journey.

And the bishop approached the king and began thus: 'Venerable king, hear with your accustomed tranquility the

petitions of your subjects. Experience has fashioned me to
beg life's necessities; you, to grant them. It is your custom,
O unconquered leader, to be merciful. By not refusing petitions of the moment you have ever fostered hope in those of
the morrow. Confidence in your unfailing beneficence has
opened the way for further supplication on our part. Give
to the Ligurians. What you give you will receive back multiplied, for present generosity is future gain. A good ruler
seeks renown in virtuous deeds and administers his realm with
a view to its passing to members of his own famly. Weak
masters delight in what they receive; strong masters in what
they leave to others after them. The few seeds that we commit to the earth we reap multiplied; we triple our interest
without reproach. Where the landowners are prosperous,
there the emperor is good. Grant to the Ligurians immunity
from taxation for the present year. Those who now petition
you, you yourself have brought back from foreign lands. Let
your Clemency ask those here present how abundant has
been the produce of our fields during this year. No one lies
to him who has in his service those who may prove the words
false.' Then the king responded: 'Although we bend beneath
the burden of heavy expenses and of gifts which we must
make to legates in order to maintain peace, nevertheless your
great merit reverently prevents any rejection of your request
on our part. What you enjoin must be done; what you advise
is to our own advantage. What you take from us we consider
added to our gains. Nor will you have taken anything to
which you are not entitled, for your claims upon us are many.
Therefore, we remit two-thirds of the tax imposed for the
present year; the other third we shall exact. Thus, neither
will the Romans bear a heavier burden of taxation because of
a deficiency in our treasury nor will your supplication fail
to bring the anticipated joy to your people.' Thereupon, the

distinguished bishop thanked the king, said farewell, and departed.

Alas, grief and lamentation! The zealous bishop hurried to all, eager, as it were, to render a last service, to pay a last visit. And, although from his abode great throngs of Christians poured forth, he himself went to each in his home. No suspicion of his approaching death, which the Holy Spirit had revealed to the bishop himself, entered the dull human minds of those who saw him. On a snowy day, such as generally drives men to seek the shelter of their homes, he set out from Ravenna and passed quickly through all the cities of Aemilia, hastening, as it were, to his sepulchre. To all the bishops on the way he was courteous and kindly, outstripping even himself, so to say, so as to leave after him an example for imitation. When, however, he entered Parma, a city on the same road, congealed fluid flowed into his vital organs (an ailment which the doctors call catarrh) and, penetrating into the innermost parts, vent its fury upon the whole body. My discourse, why do you fear? Why do you tremble as if nearing ship-wrecking rocks? Whether you wish it or not, now that you have told his life—although briefly—you must recount his death. You can escape it by no prolongation of your account, by no extension of his praises. Like a sailing vessel, you may flee the Scyllaean dogs and gaping jaws of Charybdis, which with threatening roar portend destruction, but you do not leave untold the tragedy of his death. Therefore, seemingly alert and well, he approached the now unfortunate city of Ticinum. Although he had entered the city amid universal exultation for his return, he soon changed its joy to tears. On that very day he made known he was ill; on the next, that he was worse. His condition, becoming more serious from day to day, was aggravated by the ministrations of unskilled doctors. The people stood about whispering and dazed, in the loss of this one man fearfully anticipating the ruin of the province and of the world. The seventh day brought unbelievable disaster, unspeakable tragedy, inexpressible sorrow. When the holy bishop, whose motto had ever been, 'For me to live is Christ and to die is gain,'[17] saw that, casting aside the burden of his body, he was hastening to the pure light of heaven, with happy heart and serene countenance, he said over and over again those verses of David: 'Lord, I will sing forever, I will show forth Thy truth with my mouth to generation and generation;'[18] and also: 'Into Thy hands, O Lord, I commend my spirit.'[19] And, secure in the perfect accomplishment of his work, he added: "My heart hath rejoiced in the Lord and my horn is exalted in my God.'[20] Thus his soul, resounding with hymns and canticles even in death, returned to its heavenly home. He died in his fifty-eighth year, having passed thirty years of his life in the episcopal office, as you, reader, find here described, although briefly.

I must not pass over in silence this fact—that, up to the third day, when with the greatest veneration they laid away his holy remains, all saw his countenance aglow with a radiance and beauty which confirmed the sanctity of his life and proclaimed that the predestined glory had even then taken possession of the glorious vessel in which had reposed the treasure of the great King. The tears, the lamentations of that day, I shall pass over in silence so that I, writing after years have passed, may not open the wound anew. Every mother who came there cried out that he had freed her son; every wife, her husband; every sister, her brother; every un-

17 Phil. 1.21.
18 Ps. 88.2.
19 Ps. 30.6; Luke 23.46.
20 1 Kings 2.1.

married man, himself. Finally, in that great multitude, in
that great concourse—I may without fear say—of the whole
world, there was not one who did not owe something to his
kindness.

But I ask that we now temper our grief and smooth our
brow drawn in sorrow. He whose death we on earth mourn
possesses heaven with God. And I who would bring consolation to you—what shall I do when sobs interrupt my
words, tears flood my cheeks, and every word that I speak
becomes a groan. I know full well that a tearful consoler
brings little comfort to him who weeps. Rendered worthy of
the task by affection rather than by learning, I have devoted
these few pages to the holy father and learned teacher; like
the wayfarer who, having a long journey ahead, does not
stop to greet all whom he meets on the way,[21] I have gathered
together but some few flowerets from the garden of his life.
Do thou, who hast great power with our Redeemer, obtain that I, with heart free from care and defilement, may
render thee due praise. Henceforth, desert not me who trusts
in thee after God, and beg for me, whom thou hast invested
with the titles of religion, a share in the divine reward promised to those who have dedicated themselves to God's service.

---

21 Cf. Luke 10.4.

A SERMON ON THE
LIFE OF ST. HONORATUS
BY ST. HILARY

Translated by

ROY J. DEFERRARI, Ph.D.

The Catholic University of America

INTRODUCTION

MONG THE MOST influential of the early monastic institutions in the West was that of the Island of Lerins, founded in the early part of the fifth century. A veritable stream of bishops and saints who by their holiness and learning did much to strengthen the Church in Gaul and other parts of western Europe went forth from this island monastery. Accordingly, we may rightly consider its founder, St. Honoratus, a person of genuine importance in the history of the Church. Accordingly, also, the sermon on the Life of St. Honoratus by Hilary of Arles, the chief source for the life of St. Honoratus, is an important contribution to Christian biography.

Hilary of Arles was born in the early years of the fifth century somewhere in Gaul, but the exact date and place are unknown. Conjecture indicates the year as 401 and the place as northern Gaul. His family was prominent in the life of the region, and this fact, together with a gifted mind and a good education, foretold much worldly success for Hilary. But, when still a young man, he abandoned all these prospects and embraced the monastic life, having been won over to it by the pleading of his kinsman Honoratus, founder of the hermitage at Lerins. When Honoratus was summoned to the archbishopric of Arles in 426 or 427, he took his protege, Hilary, with him. But Hilary preferred to return to his mon-

astic home and did so shortly after his arrival at Arles, only
to be recalled two years later to Honoratus' deathbed. When,
after the archbishop's death, he tried to return to Lerins, the
people seized him and proclaimed him Honoratus' successor.

Arles at this time was an important city. From it the Via
Aureliana led to Rome; to it the Via Domitiana led from
Spain. It was the commercial rival of its neighbor, Marseilles, and the center of transalpine Roman politics. Emperor
Honorius designated it in 418 as the meeting place of the
seven provinces of Gaul. Ecclesiastically, Arles ranked as a
metropolitan see.

Sometime after Hilary's death, an admirer, not yet indenti-
fied, wrote a *Life of St. Hilary of Arles* (*PL* 50.1219-1246),
a poor imitation of Hilary's own *Life of St. Honoratus*. Out
of a mass of rhetorical bombast we get a picture of a man
very strong in character, strict with himself, and not afraid to
be strict with others when he judged it his duty. Consistent
with this impression are the biographer's references to Hilary's
love of poverty and the manual labor which he undertook to
provide for the poor.

The sermon on the Life of St. Honoratus was given by
Hilary on the anniversary of Honoratus' death, as the opening
sentences tell. Thus, it must be placed on January 18 (XVII
Kal. Februarii, as the MSS. read), between 430 and 432.
The former date is set by the fact that Honoratus died in
429, as we learn from a letter of St. Prosper; the latter date
by the fact that Leontius, Bishop of Fréjus, who died in
432, seems from the mention of him in section 15 of the
Life, to be still alive at the time of the delivery of the sermon.
The most natural date for the preaching of such a panegyric
is on the first anniversary of the subject's death. This, accordingly, would be in all probability 430.

It has been said that Hilary's *Life of St. Honoratus* was

greatly influenced by Sulpicius Severus' *Life of Blessed Martin*. It is true that the *Life of Martin* was very popular in Hilary's day and was undoubtedly known to him, especially since its subject was the hero of a cause so dear to Hilary's heart, monasticism. Thus, in all probability, the popularity of the *Life of Martin* was a stimulus to Hilary to do like honor to his own monastic champion. But Sulpicius' work is chiefly an account of St. Martin's miracles and was written to be read, while Hilary's is a sermon, mainly devoted to the praise of Honoratus' virtues. As a matter of fact, except for one instance, Hilary deliberately avoids the mention of miracles. Thus, the two *Lives* differ both in content and in form. Furthermore, there were already in existence not only models but definite rhetorical principles for the literary type which Hilary wished to follow. Hilary very naturally studied these precepts and was influenced by them.

In general, we may say that the *Life of Honoratus* belongs to epideictic oratory, also called encomiastic oratory or panegyric. Its structural model, accordingly, is the rhetorical schemata for the encomium of a person. We may say also that Hilary definitely shows the characteristic mark of the Christian Latin sermon: parallelism of sentence and clause structure. He is also definitely a Gaul and writes in the Gallic tradition, described by the ancients as certain richness (*ubertas*), fullness (*copia*), and abundance (*abundantia*), together with a straining after emotional effects. But Hilary manged on the whole to avoid the excesses into which this style fell: bombastic elegance, extravagant underplay, and sound effects. Hilary's genuine admiration and gratitude toward his hero are not entirely disguised by his rhetoric, but rather seem to be the influence which keeps it within relatively moderate bounds and gives his style a certain firmness and sincerity. In short, Hilary was deeply immersed in the rhetorical tradition of his day, but by no means completely submerged by it.

The text used as the basis of this translation is that of Migne, *Patrologia Latina,* Vol. 50, which is essentially that of Pietro Ballerini. The Douay-Reims Bible has been used for quotations from both the Old and the New Testament, changes being made whenever St. Hilary's quotations differ from the readings of St. Jerome's Vulgate.

CONTENTS

THE LIFE OF ST. HONORATUS

Preface

YOU ARE WELL AWARE, dearly beloved, that this day which has been hallowed by the public grief of the faithful, as long as the Lord grants me the passing days of this life, will always come around laden with anguish yet full of grandeur. For on this day that virtuous and priestly bishop of this Church, of blessed memory, Honoratus by name, laid aside his mortal life. Whatever I add as a fitting tribute of praise will undoubtedly be considered out of place. For, if I say: He has journeyed to the stars—why even while he lived on earth he was numbered among the most brilliant stars of God. Shall I add: He is standing at the side of Christ? But, when in his life did he not stand at His side? His entire life fulfilled that word of Elias: 'The Lord liveth, before whom I stand this day.'[1] Shall I say: He left the things of earth, when, as the Apostle says, his conversation always was in heaven.[2] Similarly, therefore, whatever my soul feels, whatever occurs to it to say about such a man, cannot be a tribute befitting his personal worth. Joy and grief are in conflict in

---

1 Cf. 3 Kings 18.15.
2 Cf. Phil. 3.20.

my heart. It is a delight to recall such a man; to be deprived
of his presence is a deep sorrow.

(2) Therefore, a twofold motive urges me on. On the one
hand, the charm of his praises draws me on to this discourse;
on the other, our mutual loss draws me aside to overwhelm-
ing grief. And so, be indulgent when these two affections
distract my attention, if the organ of speech, as it were, refuses proper obedience to two masters. Whatever my memory
suggests along the lines of praise, grief entirely assumes, reck-
oning it among its losses. Moreover, even if I had calmness
of mind at my command, and though my tongue obeyed my
thoughts with fitting service, could his praises be sung more
fully by my words than they remain fixed in our very senses?
There is no one, I think, who does not feel the charm of
this great man more fully than could be expressed by the
most splendid eloquence of any orator. Since, however, as
Scripture says, the memory of the just is always with praise,[3]
and men of illustrious merit can be recalled with some profit, I shall mention, as the opportunity presents itself, a few
thoughts from among those which your own loving hearts
entertain concerning him. Your senses, too, will give assistance to my poor attempt; and whatever is difficult for my
words to say your hearts will speak out of the fullness of
their deepest thoughts.

(3) It is written: 'wisdom is made known in death';[4]
that is to say: the life of the wise man is praised at the end
of his life. Wherefore, we read also in another place: 'do
not praise a man during his lifetime.' And again: 'praise not
any man before death';[5] now suppose someone says: praise a
man after death; for in the praise of the living there is a possible occasion of vain exultation for the object of the lauda-

---

3 Cf. Prov. 10.7.
4 Cf. Prov. 1.20.
5 Eccli. 11.30.

tion, and a note of flattery is attached to the one bestowing
it. In many ways, however, it is useful to praise the dead:
in the first place, because, while he is absent who might be
gratified by our praise, it is necessary that the whole glory be
referred to the bestower of grace; secondly, because only admiration for his virtue remains when the suspicion of flattery
is removed. Therefore, praise of the dead which is proclaimed
in the holy congregation of the faithful is full of edification
and utterly free from ostentation. Furthermore, the merits
of the object of our praise increase in this, that many profit by it. Nor shall I fear that perhaps I shall be thought to
speak too favorably of someone dear to me because, aside
from the fact that nothing really worthy of his virtues can be
said, there is no one who does not consider, feel, and actually
believe him to be his own. Not relying, however, on confidence in my ability or powers of eloquence, I am undertaking to treat the life of so great a man. And even if an
author of recognized ability were to handle this life, not only
would his eloquence fail to adorn it, but, overcome by the
greatness of his subject, he would give up the attempt. Your
love urges me on, your affection gives me confidence to speak
a few words about him. This sermon will be animated, we
believe, by the merits of our subject, although delivered by
mediocre talent. What the mere words imply will be embel-
lished by the reality, and, since your love for him overflows, he
will continue to live in the dwelling of your hearts.

Chapter 1

(4) It is the well-known practice of all students of oratory
to praise first the country and origin of those whose life they
have undertaken to eulogize, so that what is lacking in their
virtues may seem to have gone before in the glory of their

fathers. But we are all one in Christ; and the height of nobility is to be numbered among the sons of God, nor can the
glory of earthly origin confer any honor on us save through
its being contemned. No one among the inhabitants of heaven
is more glorious than he who rejected his ancestral lineage
and chose to be distinguished solely by Christ as his father.
I pass over, therefore, his ancestral distinctions and worldly
honors, and—a thing that the world considers most desirable and almost supreme—the advance of his noble family
to the consulate, an honor disdained with even greater nobility of soul, and the fact that he did not take pride in the
empty honors of his kin, who through love of truth had already ceased to desire his own honors.

(5) My sermon rather hastens on to this aspect of his
life: the faith with which, in the years of his youth, by his
own free choice he desired baptism; the mature wisdom
which he showed in fearing death, though in good health;
how he clearly discerned that without baptism he would be
without life; how he thirsted and yearned for the renewal
of his life; how sweet was infancy to him; how modest his
boyhood; how serious his youth; how he surpassed all, even
of every age, in grace and virtue, and was always found older
than himself, so that you would think truly that he had been
trained in some heavenly school. He was instructed without
any urging on the part of his family. With God's help, he
persevered in his desire of baptism without being importuned
by men; and, what is greater than all this, while his baptismal
splendor was still fresh and unmarred, with no one to urge
him, he embraced the monastic life. With no one to urge him,
I have said. But what of the fact that his native district stood
in his way, that his father opposed him, that all his kin with-
stood him? For his charm had penetrated the hearts of all,
and, when Christ took him unto Himself, the world in all

his associates clung eagerly to him. Some were attached to him because of his charm; others were bound fast by the pleasure of his companionship; others were held by admiration for his worldly skill in the various exercises of youth. All the accomplishments of his former life were so many chains holding him back from entrance into the monastic life. All feared that, as it were, the common glory of their family was being snatched away. Indeed, what attire did not receive him as its own? What garments did he not sometime adorn? Consequently, at one and the same time his native district, his friends, his parents, all felt that the shining jewel, as it were, and common glory of all was being snatched from them. For they did not believe that all these qualities were to be changed and transformed into something better, as we have so seen, but that they were, so to speak, to perish. And hence it was that his father, because he had observed that he acted energetically in everything he undertook, held him off from baptism as long as he could, fearing—what actually took place—that he would be totally carried away by love for religion. Yet, his yearning and love for Christ prevailed, and, as a youth shaking off his father's delays, he faithfully approached baptism. For, while still a catechumen, thus had he trained himself in the first stages of instruction in the faith, spurning wantonness out of reverence for the baptism he was one day to receive, honoring clerics as fathers, sometimes helping the poor out of his boyish wealth. All that a boy at his age might possess, and, besides, love, all the more because of the novelty of possessing, he gave away prodigally in his compassion, even then, in little things, planning the contempt of all things, and the giving away of all his possessions.

(6) Thus, his catechumen's faith, made strong by these and similar practises, hurried him on to baptism. Hence,

his father, with the foresight and anxiety engendered by
earthly love, now began to tempt him with various pleasures,
to allure him with the pursuits of youth, to entangle him in
diverse worldly vanities, and to grow young again, as it were,
for companionship with his youthful son. He began to occupy
him with hunting and all sorts of games and to arm himself
with all the sweetness of this world in order to conquer a
man of that age. Nor was it unreasonable for his worldly
father to fear that the son was being snatched from him, the
son whom, among all other most excellent young men, he
loved as entirely his own.

(7) But, in the midst of all this, the young man's greatest
care was the preservation of his baptism. As a youth he
scorned the things that delighted his aged father, ever exhorting himself thus: 'This life is pleasant, but deceitful. How
different are the precepts that are proclaimed in the church,
and the exhortations that have been dinned into my ears;
there, modesty and continence and a quiet life and decency
are taught; here, unbridled excess is fostered. There, piety
reigns; here, the training of the body. There, Christ invites
to the eternal kingdom; here, the Devil tempts to the temporal.
Everything that is in the world is vanity and the concupiscence
of the eyes, and the world passes with its concupiscence.[1]
But he who does the will of God abides forever, as God
abides forever. Let us therefore hasten to break away from
these snares, while we are still not held. Bonds long tied are
difficult to loosen. It is easier to tear up the tender shoot
than to cut down the hardy tree. Save thy soul in the mountain lest, perchance, evil thoughts seize thee.[2] The poison of
pleasure spreads quickly; Christ must preserve the liberty

1 Cf. 1 John 2.16-17.
2 Cf. Gen. 19.17-19.

we have gained by His grace. Let others admire gold and silver; let the metal master its masters as I see it does. Let others own estates and slaves, yet not without the captivity of their own hearts. Let others take their delight in honors, and ignore the honor of the divine image within them. For me it is enough not to be the slave of vice; salvation is my joy; my spouse is wisdom; virtue is my delight; Christ is my treasure, who will recompense me for these transitory joys with better things, who will grant me even in this life to find pleasure and glory in zeal for religious life and in the midst of these to become worthy of the kingdom of heaven.'

(8) These thoughts of his produced no long delay, but the spark, fed by such tinder, straightway burst into the flame of conversion [to monastic ideals]. He took up the yoke of the Lord's service and laid it upon his shoulders, shaking off the yoke of liberty, realizing that the license of youth is the worst type of captivity. His luxuriant hair was reduced to short locks. The splendor of his garments was transformed into brightness of soul. A stiff cloak covered the glory of his white shoulders. Joy was changed into tranquility. Vigor of limb was turned into vigor of soul, strength of body became strength of spirit. The handsome countenance grew pale from fasting, and, once so full of animation, became full of dignity. In short, he was so suddenly completely changed into another man from what he had been that his father grieved as a parent would grieve who had been bereft of his son. And, truly, the mortification of his body was complete, but his life was spirit. Hence, the persecution of his parents was revived in full force. And then, when he was hastening to become the son of God the Father, for the first and only time did he refuse to yield to his father, for now at last charity had been put in order within him, as Solomon bade. For the Prophet, inspired by the voice of God, says: 'Set charity in order in

me.'[3] He set it in order completely and under the guidance of charity he aimed first at the love of God, and then that of the neighbor. As a result, his aged father felt himself rejected by the youth's desire of the monastic life. He objected, he resisted, he threatened. But none of these things shook the body's reliance on God.

Chapter 2

(9) The Lord stood by His novice as a consoler, and He did not neglect to raise up one of his brothers as a companion for him. The elder brother followed the younger, attracted by his example to monastic life, and, during the brief time he remained in this life, walked with him both in comradeship and in virtue. Hence arose between them a pleasing rivalry in striving for their ideal: whose heart should be more easily bent to piety, and whose food should be the harder; whose words should be softer, whose garments the ruder; who should speak less and pray more; who should linger less in bed and longer at reading; who should be less moved by injury and more by compassion; who should give more promptly that of which he had deprived himself; who would more willingly offer a guest his goat's-hair covering and his accustomed pillow of stone; who, before giving alms to a traveler, would more promptly embrace him with tears, and honor Christ with love before feasting the stranger with a banquet; on whose lips there should be less of the world and more of Christ; who on those heights of virtue should seem to himself the lesser, and feel greater remorse the greater grew his merit. Their life at that time was, as it were, a lay episcopacy. I should deceive you, if it is not true that many bishops, by

3 Cant. 2.4.

the welcome they received from them, learned how to extend a welcome. For, those who were not frightened away by the rigor of their ideal departed with their soul enjoying more of humanity than their body had of refreshment. Thus, together they were an ornament to the whole region and—how, this still remains in the memory of many—the bodies of some and the souls of others were cared for by them, and, accordingly as each one was in need of clothing or doctrine or money, they were clothed, nourished, and fitted out. No one came there wearied by the toil of his pilgrimage who did not feel that he had come to his own native region and his own paternal estate. No one left to go on farther who did not feel that he was stepping forth a second time from his own home, who did not seem again to be leaving his own fellow citizens and his own kin.

(10) In the meantime, the love of all for them was growing, multiplying, being spread abroad, and their fame was being carried into distant regions everywhere, and presently the whole land strove to show them deference and love and honor. They were not permitted to attain to obscurity and poverty; the more their life became hidden, the more their fame shone forth, and one began to propose the other for praise and put him in the way of honor and to refer their common virtue to but one of themselves. But, while each sought to be hidden in the shadow of the other, both were illumined, as it were, by reflected light. Moreover, how great was their dignity, how worthy of advanced age their maturity, how rare their visits with women, even their next of kin, and, in the midst of so many virtues, how prompt their flight from all vanity! How pleasant their words of comfort, how solicitous their care for the salvation of those who had given themselves over to their teaching! They led an angelic life on earth, in much patience, in watching, in fastings, in chastity, in

knowledge, in long-suffering, in sweetness, in the Holy Spirit, in charity unfeigned, in the word of truth, in the power of God.[1] In the meantime, their glory made them tremble, and they began to fear that the odor of their good life, spread far and wide, though they referred it to the glory of God, was nonetheless bringing upon them the danger of vanity. They felt that they had received their reward in their own lifetime, and, despising all human intercourse and favor, they began to burn with a love of solitude.

(11) Therefore, they determined upon a plan, and, having endured, as it were, a persecution of their honor, they sought to journey to foreign lands. Again their native land rose up; again their kin opposed. They feared, but now for sounder reasons, that they were being deprived of their light. Good Jesus, what a struggle of faith and love was this! What strivings, then, of advice and prayers and tears! Who did not claim for himself the office of kinship, or whose tears did not vie with the tears of their father? For the whole land felt that in these youths it was losing its fathers. And truly, their old age was venerable not because of years but because of graces; was marked not by withered limbs, but by the beauty of their way of life. Oh, how wise a dispensation of Thy providence, Lord, who suffered not Thy lamps, bright with the fire of faith, to stand fixed in one place, but bore them along to illumine many places inspiring them with the desire of departing and fleeing from glory which was to multiply everywhere by the very increase of virtue through having undertaken the pilgrimage. They had indeed long been disrupting and making inroads upon their substance by their works of mercy, but it was still large, and they admitted auctioneers from near and far on equal terms to their property. So far as their gains were concerned, they showed no regard for

---

1 Cf. 2 Cor. 6.4.

their relatives at least, quite as if they were selling property not their own. The possessions which had been at the service of the poor from the time they had possessed them were now divided for distribution among the poor. Their country received this outpouring of mercy and repaid it with an outpouring of tears.

(12) They departed from their land and their home and their kindred, and by like example showed themselves true sons of Abraham. But, lest anyone should think they had begun their undertaking rashly in a spirit of youthful daring, they took with them an old man of complete and consummate gravity, whom they always called their father in Christ, St. Caprasius, who had dwelt up to now on the islands, leading an angelic life. Although until today you have not heard his name, dearly beloved, and as yet know nothing of his life, Christ numbers him among His friends. This man they took to themselves as moderators in the Lord and protector of their youthful years, though many a youth already had chosen them as his protector. And so they sought hiding in travel and fled from the fame of their virtue. But wherever they went, there, regardless of the desires, their fame grew up anew. Happy lands, blessed havens, illumined by the pilgrim thirsting for his heavenly home! Other men seek the shores of the East, or whatever other lands there be that are full of holiness, in search of good example; these aroused every place they entered by their own good example. They scattered their substance everywhere, and, wherever they came, the good odor of Christ was stirred up.

(13) Even then, this man in whose memory we take joy today, was almost taken from our city by the Church at Marseilles, so strong were the urgings of its bishop and so great his joy in such a colleague. But, what might his fervor not have conquered by the earnestness of his tears and the

persuasive sweetness of his words? Quickly, therefore, warned
by this new peril, they crossed the seas and sought shores to
which that Roman speech which was so strong in them was
a foreign tongue. It would be tedious to relate the profit each
place derived from them, the salutary results they produced
in the churches without any help from the clergy, how many
teachers they silently taught.

(14) Let it be enough to recall that in their yearning for
Christ they fearlessly braved the billowy deep, and seeking
the desolate and barren shores of Achaia, in spite of their
delicate and comfortable upbringing, battled against the
mighty vicissitudes of wind and wave. How hard, how intolerable that struggle was to their tender age was proved
by the death there of that blessed man in Christ, Honoratus'
brother Venantius, and by the illness to which he and his
companions fell prey. What, in that funeral, Methone believed it had carried to burial or gained possession of was indicated by the crowded processions of people singing psalms.
On every side, Hebrew, Greek, Latin were rejoicing; even the
Jew who rejects Christ showed admiration for the faithful
servant of Christ. The fervent choirs beat upon the very
stars, and, so we believe, the angelic choirs sang in concord
with the human voices as Christ came to meet His faithful
servant. 'Well done, Venantius, good and faithful servant.'
And when you hear these words: 'Enter into the joy of thy
Lord,'[2] remember us whom the joys of the world still assail.
It was the end of the struggles between flesh and spirit; it
was the beginning of eternal life and glory.

---

2 Matt. 25.21.

Chapter 3

(15) From this point onward, Christ began to lead your Honoratus back to you, and with hidden hand to restore his servant's health by his return. And now, whatever he touched, passing by, he made illustrious. Italy rejoiced in the blessing of his coming. Tuscany revered him and embraced him with honor, and through its priests contrived most persuasive delays. Furthermore, the providence of God, looking to our welfare, broke all these bonds, and as a yearning for solitude had called him forth from his native land, so Christ called him to a solitude near this city. And so he sought out an island, lying not far beneath the Alpine peaks, uninhabited because of its excessive desolation, unapproachable because of the fear of poisonous beasts. Besides the opportunity afforded for solitude, he was pleased with the nearness and bound by the charity of that holy and blessed man in Christ, Bishop Leontius, although many tried to withhold him from this new venture. For the surrounding inhabitants related the terrors of that wilderness and strove with the ambition of faith to hold him in their own districts. But he, impatient of life among men, and eager to be cut off from the world even by the interposition of the sea, carried these words of Scripture in his heart and on his lips, uttering them now to himself, now to his friends: 'Thou shalt walk upon the asp and the basilisk, and thou shalt trample under food the lion and the dragon';[1] and the promise made by Christ to His disciples in the Gospels: 'Behold, I have given you power to tread upon serpents and scorpions.'[2] Therefore, he entered the island without fear, and by his composure dissipated the fear of his companions. This horrors of the wilderness fled; the horde

1 Ps. 90.13.
2 Luke 10.19.

of serpents gave way. But, what darkness did not flee before
that light? What poison did not give way before that remedy?
This I consider truly unheard of and assuredly to be counted
among his miracles and favors, that the encounters with serpents in that desolate land, which were so frequent, as we
have seen, being stirred up especially by the agitation of the
sea, were never a source of danger to anyone or even the
cause of fear.

(16) But, why delay longer on this point? Through
Christ's co-operation, so to speak, all the obstacles that had
formerly caused fear were overcome; your Honoratus pitched
there, as it were, the camp of God, and the place which had
long driven men away from lingering therein became renowned for angelic observance. The hiding place was illumined, while its light was being hidden. The darkness of
this formerly unknown wilderness yielded to the brightness of
this voluntary exile. What, then, was wrought by his coming;
what, by this purification? Wherever Honoratus went, there
inevitably must honor be. Here, for the first time, he assumed the bonds of the clerical state which he had long
shunned. Here, he who had fled them was clothed with the
priestly insignia, and the honor sought him out who had refused to seek out the honor. He showed himself there a priest
most worthy not only of twofold, but of manifold, distinction
of title. No bishop ever assumed so much to himself as to
reckon himself the associate of this priest. Yet, in his priesthood, he kept his monastic humility as undiminished as in
his monastic life he had possessed the perfection of priestly
merit fully.

(17) By his industry a church was built there sufficient for
the elect of the Church of God; shelters arose, fit dwellings
for the monks; waters, denied from the beginning of time,
flowed in abundance, reproducing in their one appearance

two miracles of the Old Testament.[3] For, when they burst
forth from the rock, they were sweet water flowing amid the
bitterness of the sea. And now every land began eagerly to send
there seekers after God. Whoever yearned for Christ sought
Honoratus, and whoever sought Honoratus found Christ
fully. For Christ reigned there supreme and dwelt in the
heart of Honoratus as in a lofty citadel and a shining temple.
There abode chastity, which is sanctity, fidelity, wisdom, and
strength; there shone forth justice and truth. And so, as it
were, with arms spread wide he sent forth his invitation to
come to his embrace, that is, to the love of Christ; and all
flocked eagerly to him from all sides. For, what land, what
nation, is there still which does not have its citizens in his
monastery? What barbarous manners did he not tame? How
often did he, as it were, turn savage beasts into gentle doves?
How harsh, at times, the lives that he filled with the sweetness of Christ? Men whose perverseness had once been a
source of pain to themselves afterwards gained a charm that
was pleasing to all; then, when once they had tasted the sweetness of virtue, they could not but hate more and more what
they had been. For, being brought into this new light, as it
were, they began to detest that ancient prison of long-en-
trenched error. Many a plague of souls was driven out by his
exhortations. Bitterness, harshness, and fierce anger gave
way to the freedom of spirit brought by Christ, and they rejoiced in rest after a long and heavy slavery under the
Pharaos. It was an amazing and marvelous change, not of
men into beasts, wrought by the cup of Circe, as the saying
goes, but of beasts into men, by the word of Christ, that
sweetest of cups proffered by the hand of Honoratus. What
shapes did he not mold with his eager insistence, or what

---

3 Cf. Exod. 15.22-25; 17.1-7; Num. 20.8-11.

stones were not turned into sons of Abraham,[4] where was a
workshop of the virtues so effective in refining the souls of
men that, if he could not move a man to his salvation by
his lively exhortations, he would constrain God by his prayers.
He looked on everyone's sufferings as his own, and lamented
them as his own; he considered the successes and labors of
all as his own; knowing how to rejoice with those that rejoiced, and weep with those that wept, he transferred both
the vices and the virtues of all into the store of his own merits.
For, as virtue incites to virtue, so compassion spent upon the
wretched bears fruit. For it will reap a greater harvest from
each one than each one reaps for himself. For the salvation
of each confers upon him a single glory. Ready, quick, tireless, he pressed on persistently, according to his insight into
the nature and character of each. One he would approach
in secret, the other openly; this one with severity, the other
with soft words; and in order to work a change in one who
was to be corrected, he often changed the very appearance of
the correction. Hence it was that we could not easily find
anyone who was so much loved or so much feared, for these
two feelings toward him were so deeply implanted in each
of his followers that love of him brought a dread of trans-
gression, and fear brought love of discipline.

Chapter 4

(18) It is incredible how great a care it was to him that
no one should be afflicted by sadness or be oppressed by
worldly thoughts; how easily he saw into the cause of each
one's troubles, as though he bore within his own mind the

---

4 Cf. Matt. 3.9.

mind of every individual. Again, with what provident affection he saw to it that no one should be oppressed by too great toil, and that no one should grow slothful from too must rest! He meted out, so to speak, with affectionate care the sleep of each of the brothers. While he always roused the strong of body from idleness, he forced the fervent of spirit to rest. He knew, by the inspiration of God, I believe, everyone's strength, everyone's disposition, everyone's stomach, being truly made the servant of all for Jesus Christ. It is marvelous how one man performed so many offices at one time, troubled especially as he was by such varied infirmities. He joined the strongest and those who were most vigorous because of their still recent entry into this life on an equal footing in their fasts and watches, although he was of unequal strength. He visited the infirm, himself more infirm; he provided refreshment for both soul and body, and, lest he should fail in any degree in his provisions for anyone, he ever reverted to these thoughts: this man is cold; this man is worried; the work is hard for that man; this food does not agree with this man; that man has been injured by another; it was a grave injury that this one inflicted, and no less grave the injury that other felt; there is need of strong urging, that the offense may attain forgiveness, and that this man may reckon the affronts done him as trivial or as nothing; that this man, moreover, may sigh for having inflicted the most serious injuries. This was his constant effort, his constant aim, to make Christ's yoke easier for all, to turn away any suggestions made by the Devil, to scatter the clouds of sin and bring back the bright sky of grace, to implant by love the love of Christ and neighbor, to cherish the hearts of all as if they were his own breast, to renew joy, and ever to burn unto a yearning for Christ as if in the first day of his monastic life.

(19) Hence it was that that whole congregation, eager for

divine service and gathered together at his name from different parts of the earth, varied as were its customs and languages, was united in love for him. All called him master and father, deeming that in him country, kin, and all things together had been returned to them. As he had shared their sufferings, all had learned to count his distress as their own, so that not without reason did that blessed man in Christ, the priest Salvianus, one of his beloved disciples, say in his writings that, just as the sun changed the face of the sky according as it was abscured or shone bright, so that congregation, thirsting for heaven and devoted to heavenly pursuits, derived cloudiness or brightness of soul from him, as it were their own peculiar sun in Christ, and were afflicted when he was afflicted, and revived when he grew strong again. Hence the grace of the Holy Spirit was diffused throughout his monastery, and remains there still by his prayers, strengthened by the example and the lesson of so great a teacher, revealed in varied charismatic gifts, in humility and meekness, in charity unfeigned, and in the one glory of the head in the diversity of the members.

(20) Great was the care that he had amid all this for strangers and guests. For who ever could pass him by at any time? What man, despising his own advantage, did not directly interrupt his ship's course, however prosperous, and ignore the winds, however favorable, because of his desire to see this great man? Or, if it was not permitted him to reach the island, he counted the blessing of a favorable voyage violent and a most severe storm. There was no one who did not come there with haste; no one felt his stay there long; no one set sail thence but with a sense of security, as the holy man bestowed his love and gifts and prayers and sent forth men whom he had just then met for the first time, as though they had long been his own disciples. Amid the desola-

tion of this wilderness, he provided comfort by his very appearance, receiving all with such great joy and love, as if he
had been awaiting them. Moreover, he had riches equal to
the munificence of his heart, administered with equal fidelity.
For, as he had so joyfully listened to the words: 'Sell all thy
goods and give to the poor and come follow Me,'[1] all who
had any vow in the spirit of mercy joyfully placed what was
promised into his hands to be distributed, feeling secure in
committing their all to him whose example they had followed
in leaving all things. Hence, the throngs that rushed to him
from many far distant regions. And truly, unlike a thirfty
and timid steward, it was his wont, with regard to the daily
growing congregation that had been entrusted in his care,
to distribute some things, but to reserve more. But, why should
he not have done daily with others' riches what he had once
done with his own? That is, he reserved nothing for himself
and nothing for his disciples beyond each day's needs for
food and clothing.

(21) The riches at his disposal were sometimes exhausted,
but never his faith. For, on one occasion, when his money
box that was ever ready for works of mercy held but one
gold coin of the many thousands it had once contained, he
calmly gave that very coin to a poor man passing by, though
he himself was in need of many things, and to myself and
others who were standing by he said: 'I am sure that someone is even now approaching who will contribute, if our generosity has nothing to distribute.' Scarcely had the space of
three or four hours passed, as the day advanced, when forth-
with there came one who proved the truth of his words. O
blessed munificence, to which faith gave service; O blessed
faith, which munificence never caused to falter! And truly,
he had no thought of dispensing with his own hand alone

---

1 Matt. 19.21.

all that his faith had supplied. He had many trusted men in many places, through whose hands he regularly distributed what was brought to him. Thus, by the favor of one dispenser, there were many dispensers, and his faith flowed forth as from a kind of common source upon many givers and many receivers. The straits of no one came to him which had to extend beyond him or did not find their end in him.

(22) On this account, though he was zealously leading a hidden life, as he thought, or certainly as he hoped, letters came to him from all sides. These he answered, and how full his answers were and how varied in the expression of his new affection, how dignified, how pleasant, how sweet! His blessed rival in virtue, that light shining bright unto the world and still brighter unto Christ, Eucherius, who dwelt on the island next to him, having received a letter from him in his desert, written on tablets smeared with wax, as is the custom, said: 'You have given back to the wax its honey.' Who then but deemed himself and his house and his letter case blessed, when he had been enriched by the great benediction of a small favor from his lips? And assuredly, there was so much good sense, so much sweetness in his letters, that they deserved to be kept, not in letter cases, or caskets, but in the treasure chest of one's heart. Hence it is that many carry them about inscribed on their memories and produce them most readily as a testimony of his love. Finally, who ever had so many friends bound to him by favors done in their presence as he had friends unknown to him who loved him and longed to see him?

Chapter 5

(23) Meantime, while I recall his great services to all, I pass over the infinite care he spent on me. For, certainly, his care brought me salvation in Christ, no less than his love left honor and love among you. For, because of me, a thing that redounds to his merit and my judgment, he did not disdain to approach the native land which he had contemned, nor did he shrik the toil of so long a journey, especially grievous as it was to him because of the many infirmities that had so long afflicted him; and even in those years, when I was too close a friend of the world and obstinate toward God, as an honest seducer he turned me with his gentle hand to the love of Christ. It would be tedious to introduce here the impetuosity of character he showed in his exhortations, for, as he had been able, even before he took up this vocation, to apply to himself the sharpest spurs to enter the monastic life, so in his exhortations he poured himself out in copious streams from the fountains of wisdom of which he had long drunk. But, when his words of piety made little impression on my ears, he turned to his accustomed refuge of prayer, and his loving cries, repulsed by my hardness, struck upon and entered the most holy ears of God even unto mercy. And truly, though I struggled, and, given over to my worldly and very dangerous way of life, sometimes bound my obstinacy with an oath, with a prophetic spirit, so to speak, he had even earlier made a prediction, saying: 'This which you will not give me, God will give.' O how long he strove to soften my hard heart with a storm of tears! With what holy kisses and embraces he struggled with me for my salvation! But for the time being, as he said, I won a disastrous victory. Then the right hand of God took me up, to torment me and tame me, for he had handed me over to God in his prayer.

What floods then swept over my heart! What storms of diverse and conflicting desires were stirred up! How often did willingness and unwillingness succeed each other in my mind! But, why should I say more? While he was absent, Christ did His work within me; in two days, by his prayers and the mercy of God, my obstinacy was conquered. For my thoughts had put sleep to flight, and, while the good Lord was calling me, the whole world with all its pleasures stood close at hand. As though holding deliberations with a friend, my mind pondered what course it was advisable to take, which to abandon. Thanks be to Thee, good Jesus, thanks to Thee, who, moved by the holy entreaties of Thy servant Honoratus, broke my bonds and cast upon me the bonds of Thy love; if I continue to be held in them, the bonds of sin will never regain their strength. And so, I who had left him in pride came to him conquered, and, dropping all resistance, I approached him as a new suppliant. Thus, thus does the saint's prayer bring back those that flee him; thus does it subdue the stubborn; thus does it capture the rebellious.

(24) With what tears did he then water my barrenness; with what holy weeping did he bring me, too, to tears! With such humility and kindness, as if he were being received by me, did he receive me! Immediately, any cause for delay was removed. Then for the first time did he recognize that native land which he had long felt he must avoid. He led me out with him, his booty; he was joyful, triumphant, exultant. Yet, though I was already eager for the life of solitude after his example, he hastened to bring me within the confines of the desert. He nourished me first with milk, and afterwards with food. He also gave me to drink of that flowing fountain of heavenly wisdom which was within him. And would that the narrow confines of my spirit had received as much as he strove to infuse! He would then indeed have

prepared me for you and rendered me worthy of your desires, and all unconsciously have raised up a suitable successor to himself. But how generously did he turn upon me, if I may say so without pride, that overflowing charity of his for all, and how much lighter did he make the light yoke of Christ by his kindness! How often did he call me his mind, how often his soul, how often his tongue! How impatient he was of my absence, how eager he always was for the sight of my great unworthiness! What shall I say of all this, save to recall the word of the Prophet, that the Lord has made return to him for me?[1]

Chapter 6

(25) Meantime, dearly beloved, touching briefly on all these things rather than relating them, I have unfolded facts about your solicitous pastor which were known to others rather than to you. In this church, of course, we saw his priesthood augmented in name, a priesthood which had long before reached the height of perfection through his holy life and deeds. But how was it, I ask, that a man so unknown, dwelling so far off, was sought out? Who implanted in your breasts that esteem for one not in your midst and never before seen? Who stirred up the desire that he be born to you, while they be left fatherless upon whom he had been bestowed by the Lord in the desert? Certainly, He who dispenseth all things, He who both conceded him to his native land as long as it seemed fitting, and led him about over land and sea to the profit of those who beheld the great graces of His servant.

(26) Finally, from that brief period during which he lived

---

1 Cf. Ps. 115.12.

in your midst, you may easily judge what I have exaggerated in my narration of life, and what I have understated. For you have seen, dearly beloved, that watchful care of his, that zeal for discipline, those tears of devotion, and that constant and unbroken serenity of soul to which his unchanging countenance bore witness. You have heard, too, his lips speak in a fashion worthy of his life, lips on which there was fitting purity of heart and beauty of speech. You have seen the breadth of his charity, which was so great in him that it was not without reason that the same saint, whose words I but just now quoted, said of him that it seemed in his opinion, if charity itself had to be portrayed, the painting ought to be made after the model of Honoratus' countenance in preference to all others. Who, then, ever felt that he had seen enough of him? Who did not feel that he had taken the place of all loved ones? Who so united charm with severity? Who ever proposed discipline so tempered with such pleasantness? Whom did he correct without bringing joy to the one corrected? When did his joy ever savor in the slightest of wantonness? When did his sadness fail to bring salutary effects? When was a groan of his heard, save it proceeded from grief at another's sin? Who but found him greater than when he had last seen him? Though he was always at the summit of virtue, he always found the means with which to increase it.

(27) Moreover, what tortured soul did not spurn its grief under his exhortations? What savage character failed to renounce its madness? What arrogant spirit was there who did not himself detest his own pride more than all others? What libertine did not come to hate his licentious ways? But, what need is there to say more? Being made all things to all men, as the Apostle says,[1] he was the universal remedy for all.

---

1 1 Cor. 9.22.

There was scarcely any agreeable quality that he did not possess in himself so fully as to be thought to be cultivating it specially and to possess it, as it were, uniquely. There was no rank of life in which he was not held in such esteem as to seem especially adapted to it.

(28) Finally, as soon as he accepted the government of this church at Arles, his first care was harmony and his main effort to unite in mutual love the community that was divided by hot disputes over the choice of a bishop. Like a tested charioteer of Israel,[2] he knew well that it was not an easy thing to rule over quarreling men. Moreover, he strove to rule by love rather than to dominate by fear, so that voluntary rather than forced correction might add this distinction also to his subjects, that they might not seem driven to their duty. And so, having speedily expelled discord, he made room for charity, which is the mother of all the virtues. Therefore, Christ's Church flourished under him, just as his monastery before had flourished. It increased in grace, it decreased in wealth. For, with the entrance of discipline, he excluded the mammon of iniquity from his house as from the house of the Lord, and what had been long heaped up and lying idle he finally put to worthy uses: he spent the treasures of those long dead, and those who had offered them again received refreshment through their offerings. He kept in reserve only so much as was sufficient for his ministry. But, if need had demanded, he would not have spared, as I think, what was required for his ministry. He assumed as his care petitions made at a difficult time.

---

2 Cf. 4 Kings 2.12.

Chapter 7

(29) Even at the very end he did not cease to work. From his bed he enriched many with the ministry of his word. But how long could his bed retain this man, who had long formed the habit of overcoming weaknesses that were nigh unto death? He delivered his last sermon in the church on the Feast of the Epiphany, though his sufferings now made it difficult; when faith struggled with infirmity, never knowing how to give in to bodily suffering rather than to fervor of spirit, he gratified your desires beyond his strength. For it was not an illness coming upon him from outside, not a sudden burning fever that devoured him; rather, the long protracted weakness, incurred long ago by the excessive rigor of his ideal, and growing still more serious because he hardly assented to any relaxation, wore him down little by little, and on the eighth or ninth day after the aforementioned feast carried him off. Yet, hardly for four days did he deny his presence to us who were engaged in the offices of charity, fearing, undoubtedly, that the nearness of his passing would sadden his followers. In the midst of the severest suffering, he was never severe to anyone. To no one, as so often happens, did his illness bring any horror. And thus, in truth, that temple of the Holy Spirit rested in peace.

(30) For the rest, it is incredible how he preserved the vigor of his pure soul unimpaired up to the very end. And first, he always consoled his followers most abundantly, and he feared nothing more than that they would be overcome by long-drawn-out despair, knowing that the last moments are almost easier to bear than continued uncertainty. With pleasant words he continually dried the tears of the by-standers; yet, the more he dried them, the more he provoked them. Hence, he deemed our pain greater than his own. Not

easily has anyone been of so brave a heart in the midst of every kind of hardship and circumstances difficult to endure and has not at some time either wished for death or feared it. He who never shrank from a life in the service of Christ amid every kind of severity did not have to pass to a new life through the common gate of that new life. For that last destiny of men had not come upon him unexpectedly, but as something long meditated upon. And so, in the very sight of the end, as though he were going away, as though he were saying farewell, that he might leave nothing undone, that everything might be put as fully in order as he had planned, he began to question each of us and to exhort us to remind him if anything had slipped his memory. Meanwhile, he was confirming everything with his signature, and urging us, who sought to spare his fatigue, to do everything that had to be done; but he urged, as ever, with kindly authority.

(31) Moreover, on a certain occasion, when I was struggling to repress the tempest of my grief and check my flowing tears, he said: 'Why do you weep at the inevitable destiny of the human race? Should my passing, then, find you unprepared, when it has not found me unprepared?' To these words of his I answered as best I could in words that were broken by sobs that I was not now grieving for my own destitution, since I trusted that the protection of his prayers would never be lacking to me, and indeed was confident that after his passing it would be still stronger, but, rather, the bitter grief that afflicted me was solely because of his pain and the difficult struggle of his last hours. But he said: 'And what do I, the least of all, endure in comparison to those very bitter sufferings which very many of the saints endured in their final hours?' And having named some of them, he added what I think he had read somewhere: 'Great men suffer much, and are born to be models to teach others to suffer.'

(32) But when the high public officials began to flock
to him, the prefect and ex-prefects, though the chill of death
was already upon him, how fervid were the instructions he
uttered, taking his own death as a pointed beginning to his
exhortation. And it was clearly fitting that as he had always
given an example in life, so he should call upon his death
as an example. 'You see,' he said, 'how perishable is this
hospice in which we dwell. To whatever heights we ascend
in life, from these we are dragged down by death. From this
destiny no one is redeemed by honors, no one by riches. It is
common to just and unjust, to the powerful and the lowly.
We owe great gratitude to Christ, who by His own death and
resurrection has given life to our death by the hope of resurrection, offering us eternal life, dispelling the honor of eternal
death. So live, therefore, that you may not fear the end of
life, and await this which we call death as a sort of change
of dwelling. Death is not a penalty, if it does not lead to
punishment. Hard, indeed, is the separation of body and soul;
but much harder will be the union of body and soul in the
flames of hell, unless all through life the soul, recognizing
its nobility, has declared war on the body and battled bodily
vices, and, having kept itself apart by a happy divorce from
the impurities of the flesh, keeps both substances unstained
unto eternal peace, and unto their blessed union there where
the saints will rejoice in glory and will be joyful in their
beds,[1] that is, in their bodies as in a dwelling, when they will
recognize these comrade members, which they had dedicated
to justice, as their accustomed habitation. Strive after this,
therefore. This inheritance your Honoratus leaves you; with
his last breath he invites you into the inheritance of the
heavenly kingdom. Let no man be held too greatly by the
love of this world. It is best that you despise voluntarily what

1 Ps. 149.5.

you see you will be deprived of by necessity. Let no one abandon himself to riches; let no one be the slave of money; let no one be corrupted by the vain display of wealth. It is a crime for any man to turn the price of salvation into an occasion for damnation and to become a captive of that whereby he can be redeemed.' He taught us more meanwhile by his countenance, more by his eyes, more by the leaping of his spirit heavenward. It is true that the words of my narration are unequal to his glowing words, but no less were the words of his exhortation unequal to his spirit. And so, having poured forth that exhortation and prayer with unaccustomed emotion, he bestowed the unusual gift of his blessing.

(33) As the service of his limbs failed him, an ever-fresh beauty of soul continued to grow in him. And so, having put everything in order—for few details in his affairs remained incomplete—he ran over in his mind all his beloved disciples, and all whom his weakness did not prevent him from mentioning by name he enriched by sending them a salutation through those who stood by. But in my ear he whispered: 'Offer this excuse for that holy man so-and-so, that what he wished could not be done.' What great and admirable keenness of mind, to have taken care, in the midst of the grievous distress of death, that there be no one whose sorrow he did not wipe away, in so far as he could, that he should leave nothing at least unexcused. And what, I ask, of the fact that, though he was leaving amid truly strange surroundings, to no one of all the disciples whom his love had attracted to this city did he commend a return or any community, to none did he appoint a fixed place of abode; as though he truly foresaw that there would be no dispersion of his disciples except of those who had already, during his lifetime, departed because of narrowness of soul. And truly we

know that scarcely anyone left our community save one whom he himself had warned us would leave it, and who had found either his native land more precious than Honoratus' presence or the discipline too severe. Meanwhile, a heavy sleep fell upon him, and, although frightened for a time, we called him. But he said: 'It is strange, when my weariness is so oppressive after the long sleeplessness that has gone before, that my sleep should seem oppressive to you.' And when, being anxious about everything, we said that he was sitting too long in these last moments, he replied with a pleasant jest, as was his wont, and with his accustomed serenity of soul, that he suffered us to be troublesome in this office of solicitude. So his life came to an end almost before its sweetness.

(34) He then fell into his last sleep, and passed away while sleeping the repose of death, with none of the struggle that so often attends last moments. He felt none of the hard delays of death. Angel choirs took up his soul, holy, noble, pure, untouched by any worldly taint. Meanwhile, the sleep of many was disturbed by various visions, all according to the same form: namely, that the saints came to meet this saint. And actually, at the very same moment of midnight, crowds filled the church to attend upon his holy body, so that it can only be thought that they were aroused by angelic messengers. The lifeless body was left still animated with spirit, and full of beauty, for the face that had been so pleasing to all kept all its comeliness of feature intact. You yourselves know these things well, and the reflections of your hearts describe them to you far more fully than my sermon can do.

(35) There was no one who did not seem to have suffered a great loss, if he failed to view his body, if he did not, as one's reverence or love moved him, impress a kiss upon his face or some part of his body, or upon the bier on which that holy body was laid out in funeral dress by the great zeal

of the faithful, that holy body which was almost stripped by their still greater zeal, when it was being moved to the tomb. For faith did not spare the coverings which were sanctified by that which they covered, but considered it equivalent to a most precious reward to have snatched away some thread of his garments. Your love struggled to express itself at his funeral rites. You refreshed my sojourn among you while it was still unknown to you. You caused me to rejoice, so great was the outpouring of your hearts' love upon him. For, who kept to his home on that day? Whom did the dwellings of this city not send forth to this cathedral as if overwhelmed by their own peculiar sorrow? It was deemed a greater favor to have put one's hand to the bier or to have laid it upon his shoulder. Not with glory to yourselves have you looked upon his glory, for the reverence you showed his earthly remains was the piety of faith, and it was as much a joy to have possessed so great a man as it was serious to have lost him. The grace of his tomb gives us no small assurance, for we are truly confident of his patronage in heaven whose remains we have buried here. We saw spices and incense carried then before his bier, but God received sweeter fragrance from your souls in your great love for so great a shepherd. The glory of God leaped to the fore in its glory, and amid the dissonant choirs of varied tongues was the harmony of love.

Chapter 8

(36) The good Lord who, in stimulating your wills to the election of my humble self, granted that I should not be far distant from the holy man's tomb, will also grant this to your prayers, that I shall depart not far from his ways, but shall hasten, without any questioning or discussion of the

facts, to do whatever I shall learn that he has done. For, as I see it, it was for you that even at that time God begot me through him. It was for you that he prepared me, however unworthy. It was for you that he unwittingly sought me out at the cost of so much toil. It was for you that he trained me in some way or other with such ready solicitude and care, searching for the vein of faith in me as though it were the channel of his own blood. It was for you that, by the letters he so industriously wrote and the visit he so zealously made, he busied himself with the task of bringing me back from the island to which I had betaken myself when through my love of solitude I left him at the beginning of his episcopate, perhaps with foreknowledge—I do not dare to say unwittingly —so that he might place his country near his tomb in your love. But, what shall we do, since his untimely death has given me to you, a man not yet prepared for his task? It is not our part to censure the secret judgment of the eternal King in anything, however lightly; you would not easily have felt how great a good you had lost, if your good had been restored to you in full.

(37) Great and illustrious is your glory, Honoratus! Your merits needed not to be proved by signs, for your very life among men, full of virtues and exalted by unusual admiration, furnished, as it were, a continual sign. We who stood close to you knew that many divine favors had been granted you; but you made little account of these, and it was a greater joy to you that Christ was recording your merits and virtues than that men should mark your marvelous works. Yet, what can be a greater sign of virtue than to flee signs and hide one's virtues? And truly, your prayer was so familiar, so to speak, to the ears of Christ that I think you gained the grace by your most earnest petitions that signs should not proclaim your virtue. Peace also has its martyrs, for you

were a continual witness of Christ as long as you lingered in this body. This also must we marvel at: that your youthful strength, weakened by the constant rigors of abstinence, and brought, though without loss of its beauty, to that emaciated condition which we saw, was assuredly consumed by a daily cross. Yet you always clung to that cross without any discernable excess, always avoiding any exaggeration or any desire of glory that bordered on excess. Never on your lips was there anything but peace, purity, piety, charity. Never in your heart anything but the source of all these, Christ, who conferred upon you, and through you upon many, the fruits of charity, joy, peace, patience, kindness, benignity, faith, modesty, continence, fruits that grew to overflowing abundance unto the salvation and joy of many, so that not without reason you could sing to Him: 'They that fear thee shall see me and shall be glad.'[1] To Him you always ascribed all that was good in your life, constantly repeating to yourself and to your disciples: 'For what have you that you have not received? Or if you have received, why do you glory as if you had not received?[2] But the more you denied it, so much the more was the good in your life yours.

(38) In you was the common solace of all who sought the Lord. Some glory in the successes of this life; you, on the contrary, urged us to rejoice in God, whispering in words of sweet melody that re-echoed with your love: 'Let the heart of them rejoice that seek the Lord.'[3] No delight was sweeter to you than that which you found in prayers and psalms. Christ had so taken possession of your inmost being that, sometimes, for I speak from experience, though your limbs were bound in placid sleep, your tongue, performing

1 Ps. 119.74.
2 1 Cor. 4.7.
3 Ps. 104.3.

its accustomed task, even in slumber called out His name.
Often, while asleep, you poured forth words of wise exhortation; often, prayers full of love. While your body was taking
its rest in the bed, your soul was resting in Christ. And indeed, we experienced these things, according as each of us
was present. But you, always the one best of all, how readily
and how often did you relate your dreams, which were not
foreboding nor vexed by any anxiety for the future, but were
stirred up by the restless desires of your soul! For, clearly, with
the Lord, as I believe, playing upon your desires now and
again and stimulating them, you went through the martyrdom
which you always bore in your thoughts, as though a persecution had been raised up against your faith. And truly,
I think, no one denies that you lacked the executioner, for
martyrdom, not the desire. For, in your most candid homilies
you daily were a witness of your faith in Father, Son, and
Holy Spirit. Not easily could one discourse on the Trinity
of the Godhead as openly and lucidly as when you distinguished the Persons in It and uniting them in the eternity
and majesty of Its glory.

(39) Remember us, therefore, friend of God; remember
us constantly, standing undefiled before God, singing that
new canticle and following the Lamb wherever He goes. You
are His attendant, you are our patron, the acceptable interpreter of our prayers and our strong advocate; bring to
Him the petitions that your foster-flock pours forth at your
tomb; obtain the grace that all of us, priest and people alike,
by united efforts may merit in some degree to hold to that
which you commanded and taught us, through our Lord
Jesus Christ, who has taken you into His glory, and lives and
reigns with His Father and with the Holy Spirit, God, through
all the ages. Amen.

INDEX

INDEX

397

398   INDEX

Assyrians, 162
Athanasius, St., Bishop of Alexandria, x, xi, 33, 116, 118, 234; *De incarnatione verbi,* 199 n.; *Life of St. Anthony,* 127-216
Augustine, St., viii, xii; *Confessions,* xii-xiv, 27, 69, 74, 99, 130; *Speculum,* 108
Aurelius, Bishop, 65
Auxentius, 36
Avitus, of Vienne, 34

Babylon, 268
Bactrian camel, 262
Baisane, deacon, 268
Balakios, an officer, 209, 210
Ballerini, P., 358
Bardenhewer, O., 220 n., 221 n., 222 n., 242 n.
Basilica, Ambrosian, 41, 52, 59-61, 63; Portian, 40, 43; of the Apostles, 52, 53
Bassianus, St., Bishop of Church of Lodi, 61
Beatitudes, 130
Beelzebub, 42
Beroa, 289, 290
Bethlehem, 242, 283, 285
Betilium, town, 268
biography, Christian, vii-xiv
Bologna, 49, 51; Church at, 61
Boniface, Count, 110
Bonosus, priest, 311
Bruchium, near Alexandria, 271
Bucolia, 278
Burco, 307, 308
Burgundians, 341, 342, 344
Busuris, in Tripoli, 187
Butler, E. C., 129 n., 131, 136 n.

Cades, desert of, 263
Caecilianus, 9
Caesarea, city in Mauretania, 89
Calama, Church at, 86, 87
Campbell, J. M. 127 n., 131
Candida, 35
Capraria, mother of Burco, 308
Caprasius, St., 371
Carthage, 24, 65, 75, 80, 87-89
Carthusians, in the West, 129
Castus, deacon, 59, 61
Cato, 335
Cavallera, F., 220-223 n., 241 n., 284 n.
Cayre, F., 128 n., 131
Cellier, R., 134 n.
Celsus, martyr, 53
Centuriators (Magdeburg), 128
Chalcis, desert of, 221, 222, 289
charity, 116
Charybdis, gaping jaws of, 319
chastity, 116
Christ, the Judge, 15; philosopher of, 37
Chronos, 201
Church, Catholic, 37, 41, 42; benefit and ministrations of, 118; in Gaul, 355; ministers of, 119; 207;
Cicero, 226 n., 227 n., 230 n., 245 n., 254 n., 294 n., 335
Circe, 375
Circumcellions, 84, 86
Cirta, 110
Cleopatra, 228
Coelestius, 27
Coma, birthplace of St. Anthony, 127 n.